D1205458

TESTS OF CHARACTER

TESTS OF CHARACTER

EPIC FLIGHTS BY LEGENDARY TEST PILOTS

DONALD MIDDLETON

Airlife
England

DEDICATION

This book is dedicated to all test pilots and their crews. They have served their companies, Services, and countries well and with immense skill and courage for minimal reward save the one which is most precious to them – the respect of their peers. They *are* special people in spite of their modest protestations to the contrary. It has been this author's especial privilege to meet them and hear their stories.

Copyright © 1995 by the Executors of the late Don Middleton

First published in the UK in 1995
by Airlife Publishing Ltd

British Library Cataloguing in Publication Data
A catalogue record for this book
is available from the British Library

ISBN 1 85310 481 7

All rights reserved. No part of this book may be reproduced or
transmitted in any form or by any means, electronic or mechanical
including photocopying, recording or by any information storage
and retrieval system, without permission from the Publisher in writing.

Printed by Butler & Tanner Ltd., Frome and London

Airlife Publishing Ltd.

101 Longden Road, Shrewsbury SY3 9EB, England

Contents

Introduction		7
Chapter 1	The Inter-War Years – I	11
Chapter 2	The Inter-War Years – II	19
Chapter 3	The Inter-War Years – III. Engine test flying	29
Chapter 4	The Second World War – I	43
Chapter 5	The Second World War – II	53
Chapter 6	The Second World War – III	65
Chapter 7	The Second World War – IV	77
Chapter 8	Post-War Developments	85
Chapter 9	The Dangers of the Transonic Years	101
Chapter 10	The Transonic Years – II	111
Chapter 11	Transonic and Subsonic Experiences	123
Chapter 12	Post-War Transonic and Supersonic Achievements	139
Chapter 13	Post-War Transonic and Supersonic Achievements – II	151
Chapter 14	The Development of Vertical Take-off and Landing Aircraft	167
Chapter 15	The 'V' Bombers	189
	Epilogue	217
	Bibliography	219
	Index	221

Test Pilots and Others Consulted

†George P. Aird; Geoffrey C.T. Alington; Mrs Helen Alington; John W. Allam OBE, FRAeS; Godfrey L. Auty AFRAeS; S/Ldr Peter P. Baker AFC; W/Cdr Roland P. Beamont CBE, DSO*, DFC*, DL, FRAeS; †Hank Beard (USA); A.W. 'Bill' Bedford OBE, AFC, FRAeS; E.W. 'Jock' Bonar GC; †Roger Brooks; Tom W. Brooke-Smith CEng, FRAeS, MIPR; A/Cdre C.B. Brown CB, AFC, AE; Capt Eric M. Brown CBE, MBE, DSC, AFC, MA, FRAeS, RN Rtd; G.R. 'Jock' Bryce OBE; A/Cdre David L. Bywater MRAeS, MBIM; Ron E. Clear CEng, FRAeS; A/Cdre Arthur E. Clouston CBE, DSO, DFC, AFC*; Gp/Capt John Cunningham CBE, DSO**, DFC*, DL, FRAeS; Maj. James L.B.H. Cordes FRSA, MRAeS; N. Michael Daunt OBE; David P. Davies OBE, DSC, FRAeS; S/Ldr Neville F. Duke DSO, OBE, DFC**, AFC, FRSA, AFRAeS, Czech MC; J. David Eagles AFC, FRAeS; W.H. 'Bill' Else; †Prof. J. Ernsting CB, OBE, BSc, PhD, MB, BS, FRCP, FFDM, FRAeS; John F. Farley OBE, AFC, CEng MRAeS; Dr John Fozard OBE, FEng, FRS; †S/Ldr Eric Franklin DFC, AFRAeS; Harry Fraser-Mitchell CEng, FRAeS, MIMechE; Capt Ron E. Gillman DFC, DFM; A.E. 'Ben' Gunn OBE, MRAeS; Ronald W. Harker OBE; S/Ldr Jock Harvey AFC, MRAeS; W/Cdr Ralph E. Havercroft AFC; S/Ldr Hedley G. Hazelden DFC*, AFRAeS; W/Cdr Jack M. Henderson OBE, AFC*, AFRAeS; Alex H. Henshaw MBE; S/Ldr A. James Heyworth DFC* AFRAeS; Charles T.D. Hosegood AFRAeS; †Wm T. Immenschuh (USA); †Charles F. Kreiner (USA); W/Cdr Charles G.B. McClure AFC, DL, MA, AFRAeS; S/Ldr David J. Masters DFC, AFRAeS; †Lt-Gen. Thomas H. Miller (USMC); S/Ldr Frank Murphy DFC, AFRAeS; Philip 'Spud' Murphy; Capt James H. Orrell OBE; Harald J. Penrose OBE, CEng, FRAeS, MRINA; Ranald Porteous FRAeS, MIEx, MInst M; Jeffrey K. Quill OBE, AFC, FRAeS; Capt H.C. 'Cliff' Rogers OBE, DFC*, CEng, FRAeS; Sir Archibald Russell CBE, FRS, CEng, FIAeS, Hon FRAeS; †Capt J.E.D. Scott; Gp/Capt David C. Scouller AFC, MRAeS; Duncan M.S. Simpson OBE, CEng, FRAeS; †John W.C. Squier; †Jock Still; †Barrie J. Tonkinson; E. Brian Trubshaw CBE, OBE, MVO, FRAeS; L. Peter Twiss OBE, DSC*; A/Cdre Allen Wheeler CBE, MA(Cantab), FRAeS, Dutch DFC; Gp/Capt H.J. 'Willie' Wilson CBE, AFC**, MRAeS; Gp/Capt S. 'Sammy' Wroath CBE, AFC* MRAeS.

* Bar to decoration.

† Not interviewed personally

The author acknowledges with gratitude the support and help given by the following in the production of this book:

All the test pilots recorded in the list of those consulted, in particular, those involved in the Concorde, Harrier and Victor programmes for their assistance in preparing and checking the text; Ken Ellis, Editor of *FlyPast and Air Enthusiast* and Richard T. Riding, Editor of *Aeroplane Monthly* for permission to use text which has already appeared in their journals, for the loan of photographs and for their considerable assistance and encouragement in writing this book; Dr Richard T. Hallion and Dr James O. Young, Historians to the US Air Force. Dick Hallion checked the detail on US supersonic flights and gave permission for the use of material in his books *Test Pilots* and *On the Frontier* of which he kindly sent a copy. Dr Young supplied most of the photographs of US research aircraft; Dr L.J. Hart-Smith and Donald N. Hanson of Douglas Aircraft Company for loan of photographs; Harry Fraser-Mitchell of the Handley Page Association for the loan of photographs. Thanks are also due to Godfrey Lee for permission to quote from his article in *Aerospace* and to Roger Brooke for his advice; Mike Evans and David Birch of the Rolls-Royce Heritage Trust have also given valuable assistance in providing data and photographs; Howard Berry and Dave Charlton of BAe Airbus Ltd Bristol for photographs of Concorde and Bristol aircraft.

Introduction

Public awareness of the test pilot has undergone several changes in the nine decades since two of the earliest ones, the Wright brothers, flew at Kitty Hawk in 1903. In the early years of this century he was seen as a leather clad superman with cap on backwards, large goggles and a devil-may-care nonchalance. The inter-war years still saw him as a bit of a dare-devil but now wearing smart white flying clothes and a leather helmet, often a dashing figure prompting a rash of extravagant and unconvincing films such as *Test Pilot*.

The earliest practitioners of the art were, of course, the pioneers who were designers, builders, engine fitters and then had to teach themselves to fly their machines. In many cases they were the ones whose names were on the letterheadings of the great aircraft builders, A.V. Roe, de Havilland, Handley Page, Short Brothers, Sopwith, Blackburn, Fairey, Fokker, Boeing, Douglas and Curtiss to name but a few of them. Other pioneers such as Otto Lilienthal and Cody were killed in their aircraft but left behind them data of inestimable value to those who followed them.

The years preceding World War One saw many new flying machines in the air, handicapped by the weight of the primitive engines available to their builders. The conversion of them to play a role in warfare and the pressures imposed by the exigences of war advanced aeronautical technology at a rapid pace. The training of pilots and the testing of their aircraft coming off the production lines at a rapid rate were both inadequate and fatal crashes were a regular occurrence in the field of battle.

One of the prime movers in improvement of standards of construction and flying was the Royal Aircraft Factory at Farnborough. Its talented and dynamic Superintendent, Mervyn O'Gorman, laid the foundations for a scientific approach to test flying by prescribing certain factors in aircraft design which required work to achieve the optimum performance. He recruited a first class team of scientists and pilots to undertake the work and instrumentation was devised to check the design parameters of aircraft and conformity with the final specification before delivery to the Royal Flying Corps and the Royal Navy Air Service.

One of the major worries of most pilots was the outcome of a spin which was looked upon as an almost fatal aberration. Parachutes were not, of course, issued in those days. In 1916 the RFC took delivery of the FE8, a new fighter designed at the Factory and flight tested by the chief test pilot Major Frank Goodden. A number of pilots were soon killed in spinning accidents. Goodden resolved to prove that the RE8 was not dangerous so he climbed to 3,500ft (1,067m), throttled back and let the nose drop, the aircraft began to spin and the angle of descent steepened. He switched off the engine, centralised the control column to initiate a nose dive from which he was able to recover easily. He repeated the manoeuvre several times spinning in both directions, recovering without difficulty in each case.

The training problem was overcome when Capt. R.R. Smith-Barry took command of a

de Havilland DH1, a characteristic airframe design of the early years of the First World War.
(de Havilland Aircraft Co. Ltd.)

Handley Page Heyford.
(Handley Page Ltd.)

training squadron at Gosport in 1917 and devised a new system of pilot training which became the basis of flying training in Air Forces throughout the world and led to the establishment of the famous RAF Central Flying School. From this school came Wing Examining Officers who checked out pilots at squadrons and, of course, became the nucleus of the long line of first-class test pilots which has made a massive contribution to the success of British aircraft.

The post-war period saw the proliferation of freelance test pilots; the RAF, as the RFC had become, had a glut of aircraft so the factories were short of work, so short that the employment of a full-time test pilot was out of the question. Prominent among them were Capt. Norman Macmillan, Harry Hawker, Frank Courtney and Fred Raynham. Macmillan was one of the first to concentrate upon the vital function of engine flight testing.

One company which recruited a full time test pilot was the Westland Aircraft Company who recruited Capt. A.S. Keep when he was demobilised from the RFC at the end of 1918. He had an interesting experience soon after his arrival at Yeovil when he flew for the first time an ugly abomination built to meet a naval requirement. This was the Walrus, based upon a DH9A airframe. He took with him one Harry Dalwood, the foreman of the erecting shop, as ballast. The flight was uneventful until Keep closed the throttle on his approach to land. The nose dropped ominously so he opened up again. Clearly he could not land at full throttle and the aircraft was nose heavy to a dangerous degree. Keep instructed the nervous Dalwood to climb out of the cockpit and work his way along the top of the fuselage towards the rudder until the pilot was satisfied with the trim. A safe landing was made. Mr Dalwood was known as a man of sober habits with a lined face – hardly surprising after such a flight.

This book is intended to inform the reader of the immense contribution made by test pilots and their crews in developing military and civil aircraft which meet the aspirations of their designers, builders and users.

It cannot do justice to all the pilots who had given their all – in all too many cases, their lives, in pursuit of these objectives. In the last four decades technology has moved so far and so fast that the development of a new design using just one or two prototypes is quite out of the question. The introduction of the 'Weapon System' concept towards the end of World War Two now involves teams of test pilots who specialise upon one particular aspect of the aeroplane; in a military aircraft it may be handling, avionics, engines, navigation systems or armament. Books could be written about each of these subjects, particularly about the development of blind landing in which the Royal Aircraft Establishment at Bedford played a major part. Unfortunately space precludes such accounts in this book. The pilots have been assisted in their task by the designers of simulators and test rigs which have eliminated some of the unknown factors associated with any new aeroplane. The problems which have bedevilled the Saab Gripen and other prototypes in recent years underline that even with four channel back-up, fly-by-wire systems still contain some nasty surprises.

The greater certainty associated with new designs and the fact that there are now so few new ones means that the public image of the test pilot is no longer associated with drama – not that drama is unknown in the business. The last major test programme on a military aircraft in UK was the Handley Page Victor – the magnificent TSR 2 was not completed, the Government of the day deciding to scrap it once W/Cdr Roland Beamont had proved its potential merit. So the last chapter concerns the work done with the Victor to turn it into what many pilots consider to be the finest V bomber of the three. As this introduction is being written, the last flight of a Victor has just been made when a K2 tanker flew from RAF Marham to RAF Shawbury for museum storage; one of the passengers was John Allam, the last deputy chief test pilot of Handley Page.

Major J.L.B.H. Cordes in his 'Salon d'Aviation' holding the control column of Fred Raynham's Handley Page 31 fighter. 1983.
(Don Middleton)

'Bee' Beamont flying the prototype of TSR 2 in 1964. After a number of problems with engine vibration and other elements of this most complex aeroplane the first part of the test programme was completed by the twentieth flight. By the fourteenth it had flown at Mach 1 plus. The nav/attack systems including inertial navigation, Doppler radar to measure accurately speed and drift and sideways-looking and terrain-following radar was 80% fully developed by the date of cancellation by Government decree, a decision which cost the British aircraft industry severe redundancies and the loss of many able designers and engineers to the west coast of the USA, to say nothing of the loss of confidence overseas.
(British Aerospace, Warton)

CHAPTER 1

The Inter-War Years - I

The photograph opposite provides a link between the experience of Fred Raynham flying the Handley Page 31 and one of the prominent test pilots of the inter-war years, Major James Cordes, who flew with Handley Page from 1928 to 1941 – from 1933 he was chief test pilot. Jimmy is seen holding the control column which Raynham found to be detached from the elevator push rod as he made his landing approach. This historic relic now graces the author's filing cabinet.

Cordes learned to fly in the RFC during World War One and joined HP in 1928 when the famous Handley Page slot high lift device was under development. He tested some memorable aeroplanes including the Heyford, the last biplane heavy bomber to serve with the RAF. This unusual looking machine, with the upper wing connected to the top of the fuselage to give an almost unobstructed field of fire to the upper gunners, gave him little trouble during the development flying phase in 1930/31 but, as seems inevitable with military aircraft, the Ministry insisted upon load increases. When the all-up weight rose from 12,000 lb (5443 kg) to 14,760 lb (6695 kg) there was unsufficient rudder power to hold the aircraft straight in single-engine flight and a further increase to 15,270 lb (6,926 kg) required fairly substantial modifications, including a rudder area increase of 25 per cent. Problems also arose on the ground with unreliable hydraulic brakes which had to be changed to a pneumatic system. Martlesham Heath received the prototype after Cordes had pronounced himself satisfied with it. A few criticisms were made and dealt with. The machine was being demonstrated by Cordes to RAF top brass at RAF Upper Heyford on 10 June 1932 prior to appearing at the Hendon Air Show at the end of the month. Murphy's law was apparent when an outer end of the centre section front spar collapsed through fatigue leading to failure of the starboard undercarriage. The damage was repaired on site by an HP repair party and the Heyford appeared in the New Types Park at Hendon.

After the RAF Show the one and only prototype was flown to North Coates in Lincolnshire to compete in bombing trials against its chief competitor for the RAF order, the more exotic-looking Fairey Hendon monoplane bomber. The Hendon was designed to carry a larger bomb load than its competitor, the Heyford, so the RAF crew of the Heyford decided to load it to the same weight as the Hendon. As it took off it was seen to be in trouble; it completed a slow circuit, sank into the sand dunes and was destroyed be fire. Fortunately the crew escaped. In spite of this inauspicious start, the Air Ministry ordered the type which went into service in 1933. One hundred and twenty-four were built and the Heyford remained in service until 1941. It had the distinction, in July 1935, of being the first aeroplane to be detected by radar, or radio-location as it was known at the time. Robert Watson Watt established a beam from a transmitter at the BBC Daventry station in Northamptonshire. The Heyford was flown along the beam and when it was 8 miles (12.9 km) from the transmitter a signal was observed on a cathode ray oscilloscope proving that the aircraft had reflected the beam. From this modest achievement grew the war-winning radio-location systems and, ultimately, radar.

Harald Penrose is probably unique among test pilots in spending the whole of his working life with one company, Westland Aircraft Ltd. Becoming interested in flying at the age of six when he rose four feet into the air riding a Cody kite, he studied aeronautical engineering after World War One and joined Handley Page in 1924, moving to Westland as a draughtsman in 1925. Subsequently he was made manager of their civil aircraft department and joined the Reserve of Air Force Officers for flying training at Filton under the renowned Bristol chief test pilot, Capt. Cyril Uwins.

After thirty-six hours of *ab initio* training he returned to Westland and was soon permitted to take their Widgeon light aeroplane to air displays. It was in this machine that he had his first near disaster when, at the top of a loop at low level, the ailerons ceased to function. By cautious use of the rudder he managed to return to the aerodrome and, on landing safely, discovered that the wing-folding rear hinges had failed and both wings had swept back several degrees until the rear spar ends jammed on the centre section. He began his career testing Westland aircraft and, in 1931, at the age of 27 he was appointed chief test Pilot after his chief, Louis Paget had been seriously injured in a Widgeon crash. Paget's assistant pilot had recently left so Harald's debut in this exacting role involved the Mk IV swept wing Pterodactyl tail-less aircraft, a revolutionary design resulting from Capt. G.T.R. Hill's quest for controllability at the stall. In the absence of an orthodox tailplane, control in pitch was achieved by pivoted wing tips acting in unison and working as ailerons when operated differentially. So Hal Penrose was thrown in at the deep end with, as he put it 'A few soothing words from Hill about the straightforwardness of the controls'. As he later wrote:

> 'For a hundred yards we bucked, lurched and yawed, the controllers being totally ineffectual at low speeds until a sudden surface roughness bounced her airborne, almost stalled, then she touched, only to be thrown into the air again, my instinctive control movements momentarily building up an increasing longitudinal oscillation combined with yawing and lateral lurching that was almost beyond control. If this was Pterodactyl flying it seemed beyond me!'

Nevertheless he quickly became accustomed to its peculiar ways, including the risk of a wing-tip stall on take-off which, on one occasion, caused the machine to turn through a right angle a few feet from the ground and then continue to fly on this unpremeditated course. The later Mk V, in 1934, was an all-metal two-seat fighter powered by a 600 h.p. Rolls-Royce Goshawk evaporatively cooled engine with a propensity to overheat at the least provocation. The gunner's position at the rear of the nacelle gave an unprecedented field of fire whilst a top speed of 190 mph (305.9 km/hr) compared well with the 182 mph (293 km/hr) of the Hawker Demon two-seat fighter in service with the RAF.

The initial trials seemed ominous as the complete port wing assembly of this sesquiplane collapsed due to an unforeseen off-set loading in a strut connecting the top rear spar to the outriggers carrying the lower wing-tip balancing wheels. After rectification the test programme proceeded smoothly at the lower end of the speed range but at high speed the notorious bugbear of aero-elasticity reared its ugly head. Operation of the wing-tip controllers caused the wing to twist, nullifying the effect of the control surfaces and necessitating stiffening the wings.

On what was intended to be the delivery flight to Farnborough a bump on the grass airfield bounced the pivoted bicycle undercarriage high enough to hit and turn off the cock

Westland-Hill Pterodactyl Mk V with Harald Penrose at the controls. (Aeroplane Monthly)

controlling the coolant flow to the radiator. In seconds the red warning lights indicated that the notoriously hot Goshawk was in dire trouble. The engine seized solid at low altitude over Yeovil town. Penrose overcame a potentially catastrophic situation by making a 180° turn and just managed to reach the airfield.

This near disaster coincided with the retirement of the founding Managing Director, Robert Bruce, because of his disapproval of the appointment of his young assistant, W.E.W. 'Teddy' Petter, to the Board at the insistence of his father, Sir Ernest Petter, the Company's Chairman. Following Bruce's widely regretted departure, Teddy was made Technical Director, whereupon Capt. Hill also resigned. A difficult if brilliant man, Petter abandoned this highly innovative and promising design. One senses the presence of the 'not invented here' syndrome at Yeovil at that time for the Pterodactyl never flew again but was dismantled and delivered to the RAE at Farnborough.

In America, in the 1930s, the terminal velocity vertical dive became a fundamental part of the test flying procedure for military aircraft; it was a procedure which killed many pilots who over-stressed the machine in pulling out. The fighters, or pursuit aircraft as the Americans called them, were generally powered by radial engines, the drag of which restricted the terminal velocity to a reasonable figure from which, in most cases, a pilot could pull out safely if he was careful in the imposition of G forces. When, later in the decade, such clean and powerful aircraft as the Lockheed P–38 Lightning appeared it was out of the question to retain the TV dive in the test programme. As the diving aircraft approached speeds as low as Mach 0.7–8 compressibility effects would begin to affect control and stability as local airflow over the airframe approached Mach 1.

Douglas Dauntless dive bomber. (Flypast)

Connoisseurs of American war films will have seen the Douglas Dauntless which was very effective in the battles of Midway and the Coral Sea. A striking feature of it was the large flap with holes across the surface. This originated from a Northrop design for the US Navy, the XBT–1 dive-bomber, which had large dive brakes to reduce the diving speed to increase accuracy of aim. The test pilot, the famous Vance Breese, would often take, as his observer, the equally famous designer, Ed Heinmann, who was later responsible for many Douglas aircraft. As the dive brakes were deployed a serious tail flutter developed. It was decided that a home-movie camera should be taken up to photograph the flutter when it occurred. Many dives were undertaken, each fraught with considerable danger when pulling out at up to 9 G. It was found that the tips of the tailplane were moving through an arc of about 2 ft (0.6 m). At this point it was decided to try cutting holes in the flap, a modification which completely solved the problem.

Grumman had difficulties with one of their pursuit aircraft, the F3F. All the Grumman biplane pursuits were bluff radial-engined aircraft, made distinctly tubby by retracting the undercarriage upwards into the fuselage just aft of the engine. The XF3F–1 was a highly developed version of an earlier design, the F2F, dating from 1933 and being a remarkably good and manoeuvrable machine. In March 1935 it had flown a number of test sorties in the hands of James Collins; also involved were Naval test pilots. In the programme was a series of test dives with a 9 G pull out at the end of each. On the tenth dive from 18,000 ft (5,486 m) he achieved terminal velocity at 8,000 ft (2438 m) at which point the aircraft was seen to pull out very sharply and disintegrate, shedding wings and engine. The loading was proved by the instruments on board to have reached 11 to 15 G, far beyond the defined limits of the structure. The pilot was, of course, unable to get out and was killed in the crash.

A second prototype was flown by a Grumman test pilot who, during a programme of ten spins in a clockwise direction found the machine in a flat spin from which recovery was impossible so he baled out. Because it was felt that directional instability may have been the cause of this accident the third aircraft had a small fin added under the tail. This was entirely satisfactory. It was at this time that the National Advisory Committee for Aeronautics (NACA) Laboratory at Langley Field had put into operation a spinning research tunnel. This was a vertical tunnel with air being blown vertically so that a small test model, built to follow the aerodynamic and mass characteristics of the original aircraft, could be injected into the tunnel airflow so that its performance was seen to indicate the spin of the actual aeroplane. It proved to be a valuable research aid and, unquestionably, saved the lives of many test pilots and also prevented the loss of valuable prototypes.

Even as late as 1939 the terminal velocity dive test was used in the specific case of the Curtiss Hawk 75 low wing monoplane fighter already in production for the USAAF. The French Armée de L'Air showed keen interest in the type; indeed, five Groups were equipped with them in 1939/40 and put up a remarkable performance against the Luftwaffe over France in May 1940. Although outnumbered and of inferior performance to the German aircraft they shot down 311 enemy machines, a total larger than their own field strength at the fall of France. The rest of the order for the 75A, as the export version was known, was taken over by the RAF and named Mohawk. In spite of the awkwardness of its throttle control – the French opened the throttle by pulling it back – they gave good service in Burma.

The Spanish Civil War had provided an opportunity for combat testing of a number of aircraft, primarily of German origin; the Heinkel He 111 bomber, for example, was shown to be able to escape from the average fighter in service at that time. The French, recognising this fact, included in their purchasing specification for new fighters the ability to dive at 500 mph (805 km/hr) for at least a mile (1.6 km) to give them a chance of catching these fast bombers. Having ordered a trial batch of the 75A they sent a special mission to the Curtiss plant at Buffalo, New York with instrumentation to be fitted to a production aircraft.

Curtiss test pilot Lloyd Child was selected for the test. He climbed to 22,000 ft (6,706 m) in slightly hazy weather deciding to use a greenhouse off which the sunlight was reflected, as his aiming point through his ring and bead gunsight. He trimmed the aircraft nose heavy and set the propeller blades to coarse pitch; rolling inverted, he began his dive with all his senses tuned to the highest degree of awareness to detect a malfunction before it became serious and, perhaps, too late to rectify. He was well aware that at that speed and attitude the likelihood of survival in the event of structural failure was virtually nil. He soon saw the ASI reading the excess of 500 mph (805 km/hr). At 5,000 ft (1524m) he slowly eased back on the control column, recording 7 G as he did so. At 2,000 ft (610 m) he was speeding along in level flight. When the data recordings were examined they indicated that at 9,000 ft (2743 m) the speed of 600 mph (966 km/hr) had been reached. This was a marvellous result for the publicity department who made full use of it but no aeronautical engineer or pilot could possibly accept that the tubby radial-engined P–75A could reach M 0.813.

In 1943 S/Ldrs Martindale and Tobin, of RAE, carried out extremely dangerous diving trials in a Spitfire XI to determine the limiting Mach Number of the design. A figure of M 0.90, around 615 mph (990 km/hr), was recorded. It seemed certain, therefore, that the Hawk was much slower, the high figure probably due to position error of the pitot head.

It is interesting to recall the experience of Gp Capt. 'Sammy' Wroath, one of Britain's most experienced test pilots who, in 1943, was selected, in the rank of Wing Commander to open the famous Empire Test Pilots School which set, and continues to set, the highest possible standards in the profession. 'Sammy' told the author of his detachment in 1944 to the British Joint Services Commission (BJSC) in Washington. He was promoted Group Captain and was the chief test pilot to the BJSC. In this role he flew many American aircraft including the famous Republic P–47 Thunderbolt, nicknamed 'Jug' – short for Juggernaut. He flew it at Wright Field where he was based and found it to be in trouble with compressibility problems. Due to its weight, in the case of the P–47D, 19,400 lb (8,800 kg) it was very fast in the dive. It proved to have a limiting Mach No. of 0.67; above this speed the controls became very heavy with a strong 'tuck-in' tendency which needed a stick force of over 200 lb (90.8 kg) to initiate recovery even after 'riding the ship' down to 10,000 ft (3,048 m). Several P–47s lost their tails in pulling out. In spite of this potential hazard the 'Jug' was popular with its pilots and gave outstanding service in the war; 15,660 were built.

'Tucking under' in the dive was also experienced with an earlier fighter, the elegant Lockheed P–38 Lightning. This interceptor fighter with its two supercharged Allison engines at the front of two long tail booms was highly manoeuvrable and was first shown as the XP–38 in January 1939. Its debut was distinctly inauspicious, the aircraft running into a ditch during the first taxying test. Two weeks after the first flight the pilot undershot whilst attempting to land at Mitchell Field and wrote it off. A record breaking flight across America created a sensation and the type went into large scale production. In 1941 one of the YP–38, pre-production aircraft, was flown to check out a new elevator control system which was believed to be capable of solving a problem encountered by a USAAF pilot several months before. In a high speed dive the pilot experienced heavy buffeting and a tendency to 'tuck-in' with the tail vibrating alarmingly. He throttled back and pulled out safely with prudent use of the elevator trim wheel. The pilot attributed it to flutter but the Lockheed aerodynamics department was not convinced that this was the full explanation. It was believed that, at high speed the airflow was being seriously disturbed.

The new control system was to be tested by Lockheed pilot, Ralph Virden, in a series of high speed dives from 15,000 ft (4,572 m); during one of these, Lockheed pilots and executives, including 'Kelly' Johnson, the designer, were horrified to hear an unearthly scream and see the aircraft disintegrate in the air, the tail breaking away as the rest of the machine hurtled, inverted into a housing estate, killing Virden. This was the second accident attributable to compressibility effects; in July 1937 a Messerschmitt Bf 109 prototype failed to pull out of a TV dive, killing the pilot Dr Jodlbauer.

In the transonic flight régime when the aeroplane may be flying at say, Mach 0.75, there will be certain airflow streams which have been accelerated to a much higher Mach No. due to aerodynamic characteristics of parts of the airframe; indeed, some of these flows may become supersonic. The relationship between the subsonic and supersonic flow can cause heavy turbulence and the generation of shock waves and movement of the Centre of Pressure resulting in serious instability and loss of control which, in turn, as happened to the Lightning, can overstress the structure far beyond its normal limits. During the Second World War pilots had to learn to avoid the dangers of transonic flight, difficult enough in combat but likely to be fatal if they were not alert to the problem, which will be discussed in detail in a later chapter.

It was not only fighter aircraft that caused grief in American aviation in the 1930s. One of the saddest and a totally unnecessary disaster befell the new Boeing 299, which was developed into the immortal B–17 Flying Fortress. It was designed to meet a 1934 USAAC requirement for a multi-engined bomber to carry 2,000 lb (908 kg) of bombs over 1,020 miles (1,640 km) at 200 mph (322 km/hr). The new design exceeded these requirements by a handsome margin and an order was placed. On 28 July 1935 Les Tower, the Boeing chief

Lockheed XP–38 Lightning prototype before its first flight on 27 January 1939. It was 100 mph (161 km/hr) faster than any other U.S. fighter.
(Ken Ellis Collection)

Boeing 299 prototype.
(Aeroplane Monthly)

test pilot, took off for a satisfactory first flight. During the next month it was delivered by Tower to Wright Field for service trials. From Seattle the distance was 2,000 miles (3,218 km) which Tower covered at an average speed of 233 mph (375 km/hr) – a remarkable performance for this time, and one which caused very favourable comment among the Army test pilots, two of whom were to fly it on 30 October with Les Tower as test observer and a test crew. As the handsome new bomber left the runway its climb angle increased alarmingly; observers quickly realised that the 299 was in dire trouble; at a very steep angle it suddenly stalled, dropped a wing and hurtled to the ground where it burst into flames. Heroic rescue attempts recovered the pilot and Tower but neither survived for more than a few hours. The reason for the crash, and indeed, many, many more before and since, was that the aeroplane took off with the elevator locks in position.

Fortunately its early promise convinced the authorities and, of course, Boeing that development must go ahead. The Pratt & Whitney Hornet engines of the 299 were replaced with the more powerful Wright Cyclones, later to be fitted with the new General Electric turbo-superchargers driven by the engine exhaust gases. This version, known as the Y1B-17A would achieve 311 mph (500 km/hr) at 25,000 ft (7,620 m) in March 1939 and led to the definitive Flying Fortress, the B–17B. Although of high performance the name 'Fortress' could hardly be justified. Its armament was of manually operated guns and, as the RAF proved with the few B–17Cs which it operated over Germany in 1941, it was no match for German fighters of the calibre of the Bf 109. The Americans learned fast from this débâcle and quickly made major improvements to the armament to convert it into a very formidable day bomber when flown in close formation.

A.J. 'Bill' Pegg, after five years as test pilot at the Aircraft and Armament Experimental Establishment (A&AEE) at Martlesham Heath in Suffolk, being faced with the unwelcome prospect of a return to General Duties, decided to accept an invitation from Capt. Cyril Uwins, the chief test pilot of the Bristol Aeroplane Company, to join his team. This resulted from a visit by Uwins to A&AEE to see the new Bristol Bombay troop transport under test in 1935. The project pilot for it was Bill Pegg, he managed to organize a situation in which Uwins was closely involved in the tests which Pegg was carrying out. As he hoped, Uwins invited him to join Bristol where, of course, he ultimately became chief test pilot.

CHAPTER 2

The Inter-War Years - II

Even highly skilled test pilots can make mistakes, as was proven at Martlesham in 1933 when the highly innovative Airspeed Courier single-engined low-wing monoplane was under test. This aircraft had been designed by Hessell Tiltman and Nevil Shute Norway to the order of Sir Alan Cobham, a founder director of Airspeed, to carry out work which led to his remarkably successful in-flight refuelling company, now the FR Group. This handsome all wood aeroplane, which was the first British aircraft to go into series production with a retractable undercarriage, had a top speed of 163 mph (262 km/hr); with the undercarriage lowered the top speed fell by 37 mph (60 km/hr).

Realising that pilots would, perhaps, be sceptical about this new-fangled idea and doubt its reliability, Airspeed prepared a special rig mounted upon a lorry which was sent to Martlesham to demonstrate the undercarriage retraction mechanism. Doubts about it were largely allayed by this device. The pilots were told that various safety features made the undercarriage 'fool-proof'; nothing was said about it being 'damn fool-proof'. One of the devices was a Klaxon horn which was activated when the throttle was closed with the wheels up, a useful feature which was fitted to many subsequent aircraft. One afternoon onlookers saw the Courier approaching to land with the undercarriage still retracted. It was too late to fire red flares so it subsided on its belly with little damage other than to the propeller and under-fairings. It had been designed with the retracted wheels protruding below the wing to protect it from damage in the event of such a landing. There were nasty remarks to the Airspeed demonstrator such as 'Perhaps it only works on a lorry!' The undercarriage was blameless; the pilot, being required to do a series of tests at altitude which involved closing the throttle, became irritated by the distraction of the horn blowing every time the throttle was closed so, sensibly, he had it disconnected.

Sir Alan himself had a similar experience at Portsmouth where the Company was based. To his considerable irritation and embarrassment he landed with the wheels up, but, following the principle that a virtue can often be made out of necessity, he immediately called a technical press conference at the aerodrome to see the result of a very important test to prove the value of the protruding wheels in protecting the underside from damage in the event of a belly landing!

Spinning still continued to haunt aircraft designers and pilots. In 1931 RAE at Farnborough had commissioned the world's first spinning tunnel; one of the first models to be tested in it was of the Vickers Jockey, a pugnacious little low-wing monoplane with a Bristol Mercury radial engine. First flown in 1930 it had problems with buffeting and inadequate torsional stability of the rear fuselage. A Townend ring cowling made little difference and the one modification which could have solved the problem, a streamlined fillet between wing root and fuselage, had not been thought of at that time. From results in the spin test tunnel the Jockey was virtually re-designed with a changed fuselage taper, a new rudder and a longer tailplane. An RAF pilot was detailed to check the effect of the modifications upon the spinning characteristics. He climbed to 10,000 ft (3048 m) and initiated a spin; the nose lifted and the aircraft entered the disastrous flat spin which the tunnel tests had shown to be unlikely. Recovery was impossible so the pilot baled out at 5,000 ft (1,524 m). Dismayed by the evident disparity between scale and actual performance – a very common problem in the 1930s – RAE decided that a much more intensive programme of research into the flat spin should be initiated. It had obviously been the cause of a number of inexplicable accidents. It was thought that turbulence generated by the tailplane as the aircraft rotated caused blanketing of the rudder resulting in it becoming ineffectual. This was proved by exhaustive tests in the spinning tunnel.

The first prototype for the RAF of an all-metal low-wing cantilever monoplane with a retractable undercarriage was the Bristol 133 built as a Private Venture but conforming generally with the ultimate Hurricane/Spitfire specification. Capt. Uwins flew it for the first time on 8 June 1934. He was very pleased and pronounced it a winner. A few modifications were made and by 8 March 1935 only the diving and spinning trials were to be carried out before it was flown to Martlesham Heath. Uwins carried out the spins and dives to a top speed of 310 mph (500 km/hr). It had achieved a top speed of 260 mph (419 km/hr) at 15,000 ft (4,572 m) and the useful rate of climb of 2,200 ft/min (670 m/min). Another Bristol test pilot, T.W. Campbell, took over from Uwins and climbed to 14,000 ft (4,267 m) to commence a right hand spin. Unfortunately the undercarriage had not been retracted; a flat spin developed. Centrifugal force caused fuel starvation so the Mercury radial engine stopped; for 8,000 ft (2,438 m) he struggled to recover and then decided to abandon the machine. His foot became trapped in the control column and, for what appeared to be an eternity, he hung head down from the crashing aeroplane. At 2,000 ft (610 m) he escaped from the trap making a safe landing as the 133 crashed and burned in a field near Bristol. No further work was done to develop the design.

One of the greatest pre-war British test pilots was John Lankester Parker of Short Brothers. His skill in testing flying boats was legendary. In 1933 Shorts built the R24/31 twin Goshawk-engined flying boat, a curious design with a cantilever monoplane wing cranked sharply upwards at the hull joint to lift the propellers out of the spray. The engines being at the knuckle of the wing, the unofficial name 'Knuckleduster' was bestowed upon it. Lankester Parker first flew it on a day when the Air Minister visited Rochester Works. Years later he commented to one of his successors, Tom Brooke-Smith, on one of the paradoxes of the test pilot's life. He said that, on this occasion, he was to fly the Minister back to the capital in a Calcutta flying boat which would alight on the Thames so that the great man could be ferried directly back to the steps of the House of Commons. During the morning he flew the Knuckleduster; it was a frightening experience, it would not climb so he staggered back to put it down again on the Medway. He commented to 'Brookie':

> 'On that trip I nearly killed myself for a paltry fee of £5; for the later flight to the House of Commons I was given a gold cigarette case with my initials in diamonds!'

The Goshawk evaporatively-cooled engine was bad news on every aeroplane fitted with it; it overheated and was most unreliable, the R24/31 being no exception. Flexing of the tail section of the hull was another problem; the design was abandoned after trials at the Marine Aircraft Experimental Establishment at Felixstowe.

Lankester Parker had one of his worst experiences in the Short Gurnard II, a naval aircraft which was the first to incorporate a new design of differential aileron control developed by Leslie G. Frise to lighten aileron load and to give a more even aerodynamic

Short R24/31 'Knuckleduster' flying boat.
(Aeroplane Monthly)

Short Composite aircraft separating near Rochester.
(Aeroplane Monthly)

effect on each side. It was, in practice, an extremely practical idea and is still in use. As soon as the Gurnard rose from the water it performed three 45 degree banks to each side with the control column thrashing from side to side, hammering the pilot's hands against the cockpit walls. Only by trapping the column between his legs and using all his strength to retain it could Parker manage to alight again after a total flight time of one minute. The ailerons were found to be over-balanced.

Another interesting project in which Parker was involved was the Short Mayo Composite aircraft; one which proved to have few technical snags in spite of its radical nature. One of the major aviation goals of the 1930s was non-stop flight across the North Atlantic. Sir Alan Cobham was working on in-flight refuelling whilst Major Mayo, technical consultant to Imperial Airways, suggested that a large flying boat, on the lines of the new Short Empire boats, should be built to carry a smaller aircraft on its back. So emerged *Maia*, the lower component and *Mercury* the mail-carrier seaplane with four Napier Rapier engines.

This aircraft was to be carried into the air at a loaded weight far beyond its solo take-off capability using the power of its own engines and the power of the four Pegasus engines of the lower component. It was not the first time that such an arrangement had been tried; in 1916 the flying boat designer, Cmdr John Porte, at Felixstowe had flown a Porte Baby flying boat with a Bristol Scout mounted on crutches attached to the centre section of the upper wing. The object of this test was to see if it was feasible to carry a Scout to within range of a Zeppelin. The test was successful but no further work was done with the project. In July 1937 Lankester Parker flew *Maia* for the first time with complete success; he took *Mercury* up for the first time in September. The two components were linked as a composite aircraft ready for taxying trials with Harold Piper in charge of *Mercury*; these were equally successful, the assembly even riding out a gale at the mooring on the Medway. On 20 January 1938 the two pilots made the first flight as a composite unit, minor problems prevented separation which took place on the third flight. There were no problems, the upper component climbing swiftly after launch to avoid the risk of collision. After further trials at various loadings and CG positions the two aircraft were flown to Felixstowe where the Short pilots made the first full load separation. Afterwards a jettison test of 1,000 gal (4,546 litres) of fuel was successfully carried out; the composite aircraft was handed over to Imperial Airways. On 14 July Capt. D.C.T. Bennett with a radio operator and an Air Ministry observer flew *Mercury* from launch near Southampton for a 12 hour flight over the Atlantic. A week later a launch was made at Foynes on the Shannon at an all-up weight of 20,800 lb (9,440 kg) the seaplane flying on to Montreal against an average headwind of 25 mph (40 km/hr); 2,930 miles (4,715 km) were flown in 20 hours 20 minutes. Several similar flights were made with complete success. The war ended further work on the project. Whilst it was a considerable technical success its scope was extremely limited as a lower component and a very large crane would have been required at each base. It is not likely that it could ever be cost effective. By the end of the war long-range aircraft and airfields with paved runways were available to serve most important cities throughout the world.

The rapid expansion of the Royal Air Force as a result of the almost fatal lack of perception of the German menace in the early 1930s led to the development of some innovative bombers. The great Barnes Wallis had designed the large airship, R100, built at Howden in Yorkshire by a subsidiary company of Vickers Ltd. After the fatal crash of her sister ship, R101 in 1930, resulting in the destruction of R100 and the abandonment of rigid airships in Britain, Wallis concentrated upon heavier-than-air machines. He introduced a structural system derived from his work on the airship. It consisted of a series of curved space frames with the structural members crossing like trellis-work to give a very rigid, light structure which required no strength-bearing outer covering. The first bomber was the single-engined Wellesley, which Mutt Summers flew for the first time on 19 June 1935. It was a promising design but, in July, the port undercarriage collapsed during a landing; the high aspect ratio wing was severely damaged so the aircraft was under repair for several months. At the beginning of 1936 Summers recruited F/O Jeffrey K. Quill as a test pilot mainly concerned with the new interceptor fighter under development at Vickers Armstrongs at Eastleigh. Quill became involved with the Wellesley and, in July 1937, at a fairly late stage of production, discovered a very nasty element in the character of the new bomber which had, hitherto, shown quite innocuous spinning characteristics. He was testing one of the production aircraft at the stall, a régime which he had already covered very thoroughly with the prototype. At 12,000 ft (3,658 m) over the southern outskirts of London, he waffled along at slow speed, writing notes on his knee pad; suddenly he entered a spin to starboard. Recovery action was ineffective and a dangerous flat spin developed

Vickers Wellesley bomber. Note the external fuel tanks. (Ken Ellis Collection)

which defied all attempts at recovery. At 3,000 ft (914 m) he decided to bale out, very disturbed at the prospect of the Wellesley crashing in a London built-up area. It hit an empty house; fortunately no fire broke out. Later Jeffrey told of a strange coincidence; 37 years later, his daughter, Virginia, was working for the BBC where she met a girl who asked;

'Was your father a test pilot?'

'Yes' said Virginia, 'Why?'

'Well, he dropped a damned great aeroplane on my mother's house!' An intensive investigation into the accident was inconclusive. Another mysterious crash led to the death of a Farnborough pilot, Flt/Lt Salmon who took off in a Wellesley to do stalling tests. It spun in, again no conclusions could be drawn. In service the Wellesley was efficient and well liked by its crews.

The famous successor to the Wellesley, the twin-engined Wellington, began its career with a disastrous accident. In June 1935 Mutt Summers flew the prototype B9/32 for the first time from Brooklands airfield. This was a rather more elegant aeroplane than the famous 'Wimpy', so familiar in the early years of the war. It had a well streamlined nose and tail without turrets. Its performance was outstanding and fully justified Wallis's claims for geodetic construction. After months of test flying by works pilots the prototype was delivered to Martlesham Heath for Service evaluation. In April 1937 Flt/Lt Maurice Hare and his observer LAC Smurthwaite, were carrying out diving tests. A sudden violent flutter of the tail unit occurred, the tail of the aircraft breaking away. The nose-down pitch hurled Hare out through the cockpit glazing whilst the unfortunate LAC lost his life in the crash. A major search for wreckage was immediately made along the flight path of the machine. A lump of lead was found which proved to be the mass balance of the elevator control, fitted, of course, to prevent control surface flutter. Production had already commenced, so suitable remedial action was taken.

Vickers B9/32 bomber prototype from which the Wellington was developed. 1936.
(Ken Ellis Collection)

A bomber contemporary with the Wellington was the Handley Page Hampden. This was an unusual design powered by two Bristol Pegasus engines; it differed from the Wellington and its other contemporary, the Whitley, in not having any power-operated turrets. As a result of this omission the fuselage could be made very slender with the crew grouped together in the forward section; its slim lines prompted the nickname 'the flying suitcase'. The tailplane and rudders were mounted on a slender boom but it was difficult to fit all the equipment inside it on the production line. The production engineers devised a neat solution by splitting the tail boom along its top and bottom centre lines so that the assemblies could be made and the two halves mated afterwards, the idea was employed later with equal success in the de Havilland Mosquito and is, of course, commonplace today. Major James Cordes flew the prototype from Radlett for the first time on 21 June 1936 and flight trials proceeded satisfactorily until 5 November when the landing gear warning buzzer switch failed. As no replacement was immediately available a concession was obtained to permit one more flight to complete the particular programme. As Cordes and his observer, R.S. Stafford, landed from this flight the starboard undercarriage collapsed. As the aeroplane subsided on its belly with the nose glazing breaking up in front of Stafford, the observer's only comment was 'There's a strong smell of grass in here'. Repairs were completed and a new starboard engine installed. On 13 January 1937 it flew again. Approaching Radlett airfield over Elstree there was a sudden violent bang from the front of the replacement engine as it shed its reduction gear and propeller; fortunately no fire broke out. Cordes was concerned lest the heavy DH variable pitch propeller had dropped into a housing estate so, on return to base he asked the works manager to telephone the police to report the loss, giving the rough location of a field which seemed to be a likely starting point. The police inspector said 'That's alright, sir, I'll send one of my chaps out on his bike to fetch it in!' A wisp of smoke rising in a field identified the point of impact but it took more than a copper on a bike to retrieve it!

In service the Hampden was a disappointment, it had a remarkable speed range, from 73 mph (118 km/hr) to 265 mph (427 km/hr) but its limited defensive armament was a serious handicap. The narrow fuselage was very cramped and, if the pilot was shot, it was extremely difficult to remove him from his seat.

Across the Atlantic Boeing was developing the 299 bomber into a four-engined airliner, the model 307 which was, in effect, a capacious fuselage to which was fitted the wings and empennage of the 299. On the last day of 1938 the Boeing chief test pilot, Eddie Allen with flight observers, flew the aeroplane for the first time; it was a successful design but, in March 1939 its career received a severe setback.

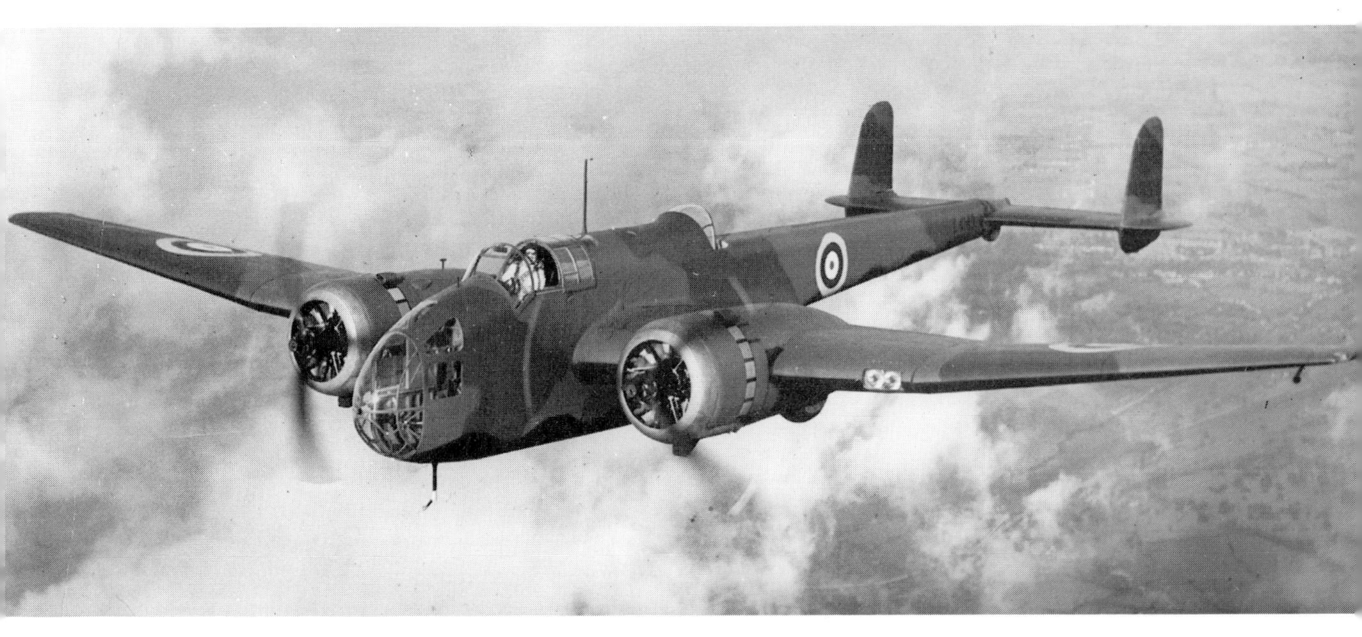

Handley Page Hampden being test-flown by Major Cordes.
(Handley Page Ltd.)

Boeing 307 prototype.
(Aeroplane Monthly)

A KLM mission was evaluating the type as a possible purchase for the Dutch airline's fleet. They decided that they must investigate what by any standards was an appalling situation for a pilot and a very dubious test procedure. With a Boeing captain, Julius Barr, and a KLM co-pilot two engines were cut on the same side and a yaw induced towards the dead engines. A stall was to follow immediately. At a speed only slightly above the stall the heavy transport departed into a spin. The pilots were able to recover into a dive but, in pulling out, overstressed the aircraft which broke up, crashed and killed all ten men on board. The investigation indicated that the fin and rudder of the 299 was not adequate for the job so a larger one was designed, also used on the 299 when it became the B–17E Flying Fortress.

The 307, which was named Stratoliner, was the first pressurised airliner to go into production. Ten were built for service with Pan American Airlines, TransWorld and the US Army Transport Command. They gave good service in their military role as VIP transports. By the end of the war the Lockheed Constellation and the Douglas DC–4 were leading contenders for airline orders so Boeing was forced to drop out until the Boeing KC–135 tanker in its Boeing 707 airliner role began its domination of the long-haul market.

The Royal Aircraft Establishment at Farnborough was the scene of many remarkable test flying sorties between the wars and a test pilot who had his fair share of drama was Arthur E. Clouston who had left the RAF as a Flying Officer to become a civilian test pilot. His C.O., Flt-Lt D'Arcy Grieg, the famous Schneider Trophy pilot, told him to get to know every aircraft on the Station and, for starters, taught him how to fly the Cierva C30 Rota autogiro, of which a small number was in service with the RAF. The experience was not a pleasant one, as he said:

> 'The rotor blades and propeller began to rotate faster and faster, the noise was so bad that I could not think. The vibration shook me like a jelly. The heavy control stick came down from the hub above our heads like the branch of a tree. Apart from the throttle and brakes this was the only control and it went round and round as if it was stirring porridge, whilst the machine rocked from side to side.'

He soon mastered the technique and began to enjoy flying autogiros.

The spirit and, indeed, the hazards of test flying in those pre-war days are well illustrated by some of Arthur Clouston's experiences. The scientists often showed scant respect for pilots' skills and opinions; on one occasion he was flying with one of them who asked him to land the aircraft at a speed below stalling speed. As he was already coming in at a speed which left the machine wallowing helplessly and likely to fall out of the sky he refused to do so. The scientist was offended and persuaded another pilot to do as he wished. Clouston was amused to see the aeroplane descend like a lift, wreck the undercarriage and disappear through a hedge.

He had a narrow escape from disaster in an aircraft specially built for RAE by the Miles Aircraft Company. It was capable of flying with differing wing thicknesses, thin, medium and thick. Speed runs were carried out along the railway line between Farnborough and Basingstoke until the farmers complained that the animals were suffering from the noise; the trials were then moved to a line on the south coast near Tangmere. En route to the test area one morning the weather was bumpy with cloud covering the South Downs. With his observer he decided to abandon the tests and return to RAE. He landed, slowed down and then opened the throttle to taxi to the hangar. To his horror he noticed that the port wing was trailing on the ground, the spar having been broken in the turbulence. Another few minutes of flight in those conditions could so easily have been their last.

Some of the most hazardous test sorties ever carried out were the responsibility of Arthur Clouston and his colleagues, among them S/Ldr C.R.J. Hawkins, 'Willie' Wilson, 'Spinner' White, 'Johnnie' Kent and Pat Fraser. With the strong possibility of war on the horizon two RAE scientists, Dr Ben Lockspeiser and Dr Roxbee Cox were investigating the feasibility of barrage balloons and their cables against modern metal aircraft. Roxbee Cox gave quite succinct instructions to Clouston:

'I want you to fly an aeroplane into the wire to see what happens.'

It was decided to follow on from Pat Fraser's earlier work with long strings dangling from a parachute. Fraser had appreciated the danger and had a thick felt crash helmet made. It fitted Clou who began work using a small Miles Hawk trainer built of wood and fabric; from it was thrown a very long fishing line attached to a parachute thrown overboard at

5,000 ft (1,524 m); at the end of the line was a fabric ball soaked in red paint to indicate the contact points of the line with the surface of the aircraft. The first approach was fairly uneventful, the line catching the wing in the right place with the aircraft skidding away slightly. Suddenly the line raced over the wing a few feet from the cockpit, the friction generating smoke as the line wrapped itself around the wing making a deep cut in the leading edge. It was soon found that the major problem was loss of control when the line caught in the aileron. On one flight it tangled with the propeller whilst the parachute gyrated astern at the end of the line which soon fouled the rudder and elevators. The Hawk was almost uncontrollable and a parachute jump seemed imperative. 'Jump!' yelled Clou to his observer, a young scientist on his first flight. The terrified boffin averted his gaze, 'Jump jump!' roared the pilot. The scientist, puzzled that anyone should wish to leap out of an aeroplane high above Farnborough just shook his head. Clou hastily scribbled a note 'Machine out of control *you must jump*!', tapped the observer on the shoulder and handed him the note. Ashen faced, he read it, released his safety harness and had one leg over the side when the parachute tore away leaving the Hawk under control again. Immediately, to the astonishment of the scientist, the order was vehemently countermanded. He continued to struggle out until, at last, Clou convinced him that the need had passed. Clou's ego was not enhanced when, after the landing, the young man said:

'I did not know what the problem was, I realised that the aircraft was a bit frisky but thought it was your flying'!

On the face of it there appears to be little difficulty in flying an aeroplane into a string suspended from a barrage balloon – the next stage of the research. The strings were made more visible by fixing streamers to them. The position of the balloon gave little indication of the location of the cable itself and a shift of wind could easily alter the angle so that the unfortunate pilot hit the cable before he was able to find the suspended string. Fortunately a ground party with radio was able to warn of such an event – if the radio continued to work.

As the preliminary trials with string built up experience with light wooden aeroplanes it became necessary to work with the actual steel balloon cable. Clearly this would remove the wing from the Hawk so the all-metal Fairey P 4 prototype – from which the Fulmar fleet fighter was developed – was used. Initially a long length of cable was dropped attached to a parachute. This was difficult to locate as it swayed from side to side. The aircraft often landed with hundreds of yards of balloon cable tangled around the tail wheel having created havoc and mayhem among telephone and high tension cables. On one occasion, when painters were on scaffolding working on the Mess building, as the P 4 came in the flailing cable wrapped itself around the scaffolding and deposited it and the painters firmly upon the ground. Fortunately no serious injuries resulted but, in modern parlance, industrial action was decided upon; no work was done when Mr Clouston was flying! An equally memorable event was the distribution over the Farnborough landing area of a number of bicycles, lately parked neatly in a rack near the Main Gate and gathered up by the trailing cable. These were two amusing occurrences in a programme fraught with the utmost peril for the pilots. On one flight Clou hit the cable at 170 mph (274 km/hr); it caught the tip of the propeller which whipped it around the fuselage flailing the nose, cockpit and wings, leaving deep gashes in the metal – one of them two inches from the head of the pilot whilst a small fire broke out behind the propeller. To guard against the high risk of decapitation a steel canopy was fitted to cover the cockpit.

On another sortie a balloon cable jammed in the aileron gap and forced the trim tab to maximum deflection, the P–4 entering a flat spin. With both arms and a leg Clou managed to force the column over to regain a measure of control and make a high speed landing in a dangerously banked attitude. After all this exertion he was hardly able to climb out of the cockpit.

These various hazardous flights caused the RAE to re-think the whole operation. It was decided that it was too dangerous to expose scientists in such missions so the pilot would fly alone. The only consolation implicit in such a concept of the pilot being more of a disposable asset than the scientist was that he could bale out more swiftly if he was on his own. Furthermore the experiments were to be carried out at a fairly desolate site near Martlesham Heath. To improve the identification of the wire suspended from the parachute a pair of large fabric squares was fitted on the wire, one above the other, so that the pilot steered for the gap between them. The next stage was to suspend the cable from a tethered balloon which gave it more stability but with more risk to the pilot because of the increased resistance when the wing hit it; resistance which caused the aircraft to yaw violently, requiring hard opposite rudder and aileron. Clouston spent weeks flying the P 4 into increasing lengths of cable until it cut so deeply into the main spar that the danger was increased substantially. The last few yards of wire wrapped right round the wing before release so it was assumed that an explosive device on the end of a cable would be fatal to enemy aircraft. Clou insisted that the scientists accepted that this was so rather than demand that he should prove it in the P 4.

Later, in March 1942, tests were carried out with multi-engine aircraft; S/Ldr C.R.J. 'Tiger' Hawkins was the pilot of a Wellington in the Research Flight at RAE which he commanded. Suddenly, as contact with the wire was made a cloud of dust, bits of fabric and other debris came forward into the cockpit area and the 'Wimpy' pitched upwards uncontrollably. The pilot did not realize that the violent yaw as the wing hit the cable had overstressed the fuselage to such a degree that it broke between the wing and tailplane.

Equally suddenly the machine carried out a violent pitch downwards, the pilot's harness being broken by the G forces. He was thrown forward and down into the bomb aimer's compartment amid all the debris. He struggled to return to his seat against the violent movement of the aircraft, he was then thrown there again and managed to escape; he thought that he had gone out through the top escape hatch but inspection of the wreckage indicated that Hawkins went out through the very small direct-vision window in the side of the canopy and, incredibly, must have passed through the arc of the still revolving propeller blades. Fortunately he had already throttled back. He was uninjured but black and blue from bruises for several days.

The practical outcome of this exceptionally hazardous test programme was the survival of many aircrew during the war. The combination of a strengthened leading edge and the Martin-Baker cartridge-operated cable cutter was a major contribution to the safety and morale of crews of low flying bombers. The great Jimmy Martin, (later to be knighted) perhaps better known for his work on ejector seats, had considered the balloon cable problem and decided that the tough cable could be directed along the leading edge to enter a special cutter where, for a second or two, it would rest upon an anvil; its entry into the device would fire an explosive charge which, in turn, activated a cutter to part the cable. 250,000 sets were made during the war.

As early as 1940 their value was proved by S/Ldr R.A.B. Learoyd and his crews who were briefed to make a low-level attack in their Hampdens to immobilise traffic in the Dortmund-Ems Canal. The operation commenced with two of the bombers fitted with cable cutters and one flown by Learoyd himself, going in to sweep the target area clear of balloons before the main force arrived. He was awarded the Victoria Cross for his gallantry.

In 1984 Air Commodore Clouston told the author that his work on protection from balloon cables was the most satisfying in his long career as a test pilot. For it he was awarded the Air Force Cross.

CHAPTER 3

The Inter-War Years - III

A mid 1930s programme in the civil side of the British industry produced one of the most elegant aeroplanes ever built, the de Havilland DH 91 Albatross. It was a direct descendant of the DH 88 Comet which won the Mildenhall to Melbourne Air Race in 1934.

Captain Geoffrey de Havilland and his board were dismayed to realise that the Comet, a specially designed racing aeroplane had been closely followed into second place by a Douglas DC-2 airliner of KLM, flown by two airline captains, Parmentier and Moll, with a load of fare-paying passengers. The DH board recognised this triumph as the beginning of United States domination of the world airlines and decided that DH must respond to this challenge.

They submitted detailed proposals to the Air Ministry for a high-speed airliner based upon the Comet design. In its customary myopic way the Ministry rejected it but, after many representations pointing out that the Handley Page 42 biplane was not really in the same league as the sleek DC-2, a contract was grudgingly placed for two high-speed mail carriers which could become the basis of the new airliner.

The structure was a remarkable departure from current practice. The fuselage was built upon a large collapsible jig with layers of birch ply forming the inner and outer skin with a balsa wood in-filling between them to stabilise the very strong structure which was bonded and compressed upon the jig by steel bands. This enabled a superbly streamlined fuselage to be constructed without expensive tooling. The one-piece wing comprised a spanwise wooden torsion box with leading and trailing edge sections attached. To achieve a high degree of aerodynamic efficiency the wing was very thin but it proved difficult to stow the retractable undercarriage legs in such a wing.

However, the many problems were largely overcome and the chief test pilot, Bob Waight, flew the prototype, E 2, later registered G-AEVV, for the first time on 20 May 1937. She handled well but the first of many undercarriage problems arose; it would not retract. Waight was killed in October flying the diminutive TK 4 racer designed and built by students at the DH Technical School. Waight was succeeded by Geoffrey de Havilland, the 27-year-old son of the founder of the Company, who continued the test programme and found that the inset rudders were inadequate to give directional stability in the climb. Larger rudders were then designed to be mounted at the ends of a new dihedralled tailplane. This solved the problem and an incidental benefit was a considerable improvement in the already beautiful lines of the aircraft which originated, as did the later Airspeed Ambassador, on the board of Arthur E. Hagg.

On 31 March 1938 Geoffrey was forced to belly-land E 2 due to the total failure of both electrical and manual undercarriage actuators. Damage was slight and, after repairs and the painting of G-AEVV on fuselage and wings, testing was resumed. In July the second mail-carrier, G-AEVW, was flown and was soon in trouble. On 27 August Geoffrey de Havilland was conducting trials at maximum overload. To avoid jettisoning water ballast before each landing he brought the aircraft in at full weight. The first two touch-downs strained the fuselage; in the third it broke across the rear entry door aperture. Fortunately the crew was uninjured and no fire occurred. De Havilland were naturally highly embarrassed and tried to avoid any publicity. A newsagent, whose premises overlooked Hatfield aerodrome, photographed the bent and unhappy looking Albatross and sold the print to one of the national dailies. It may be assumed that his sales of newspapers and cigarettes to de Havilland executives went into steep decline.

However, G-AEVV went to Martlesham where the heaviness of the elevator and rudder controls were criticised. The remarkable figure of 2.53 air miles per gallon of fuel was recorded which offered a range of 2,500 miles (4,024 km) against a 40 mph (64 km/hr) headwind. The fuselage of -VW went back into the jig for repair and was flown again within five weeks. In October 1938 the first true airliner version, G-AFDI, *Frobisher* was delivered to Imperial Airways after tests at Martlesham Heath. Finished in silver with pale blue lettering and trim she looked superb at Croydon among the Handley Page 42s and she even outshone the DC-2s which Swissair was operating. Unfortunately the literal Achilles heel of the type revealed itself in a most public and embarrassing manner in January 1939 as *Frobisher* taxied towards the terminal building after a flight from Paris. As she moved from the sodden grass to the edge of the concrete hard-standing the side load on the tyre caused the undercarriage leg to fold and the impact with the ground fractured the main spar outboard of the engines. This weakness and water soakage, bedevilled the short lives of the seven aircraft built; during the first year of the war they were used on communications

de Havilland DH 91 Albatross. 'Frobisher', the Imperial Airways flagship, is seen outside the terminal building at Croydon.
(British Aerospace, Hatfield)

Airspeed Oxford prototype. (Airspeed Ltd.)

duties but, being left in the open air was too much for the wooden structure and, by August 1943, all had been withdrawn from service. Their chequered careers were short but these beautiful aeroplanes left a priceless legacy of aerodynamic and structural experience that led directly to one of the outstanding aircraft of all time – the Mosquito.

Another British company with spinning difficulties was Airspeed at Portsmouth. The introduction of the new all metal military aircraft in the late 1930s produced pilot training problems. The only aircraft with even a limited resemblance to such 'hot-rods' as the Lockheed Hudson and the Bristol Blenheim was the venerable Avro Anson which was virtually vice-free and would fly itself – not the ideal aeroplane to accustom crews to the nasty habits of some of the new machines. Airspeed built the Oxford twin Cheetah engined trainer which filled the bill admirably, simulating most effectively the nasty habits of these aircraft and having a few of its own for good measure. Spin recovery came into this category.

The prototype was first flown by Flt Lt Cyril Colman on 19 June 1937 and the test programme was shared with his assistant, George Errington. Spinning trials were carried out by George over a deserted area of Devon and the characteristics were to be investigated with varying loads at different positions of the CG. With CG forward there were no problems; after eight turns pull out was satisfactory although the engine on the inside of the turn occasionally stopped. The spin was stable and it was possible to photograph the instrument panel on the way down. This was an early example of automated test recording – Airspeed was nothing if not innovative.

After 100 turns had been carried out the technical department was satisfied and the cabin load was moved so that the CG was aft of the specified aft limit. As there might be problems at this loading an anti-spin parachute was fitted. It was operated by a lever on the cockpit canopy roof framing. Release of the 'chute was effected by a lever alongside. As a further precaution Errington had a rope fitted from the cockpit to the door on the port side just aft of the wing root to assist him if he had to abandon the aircraft whilst in a spin.

Errington headed for Devon and climbed to 16,000 ft (4,876 m). He checked his parachute, started the stopwatch and initiated the spin with camera poised. After eight turns he took recovery action. The 'Ox-box' took no notice, with only 8,000 ft (2,438 m) to go before the commencement of boring operations into the Devon soil he decided to deploy the parachute; the Oxford ignored that too. George decided to get out and staggered towards the door. Suddenly the tail came up and the spin increased, the machine moving into a spiral dive. He rushed back to his seat to pull the parachute jettison lever on the assumption that the parachute had suddenly deployed. Again nothing happened, perhaps he hadn't pulled it hard enough. He had another go, pulling, as he said 'Hard enough to shame a Scot at a fruit machine'. The whole lever assembly then parted company with the cabin roof and swung dangerously upon its cables.

By this time the Devon soil was only 4,000 ft (1,220 m) away and shrouded in cloud. Discretion being seen as the better part of valour he made for the door again. Once more the aircraft began to recover, so he quickly returned to the seat with no time to do more than try to grab the control column over the seat back and hope to arrest the headlong rush to disaster. The altimeter showed about 1,500 ft (457 m) and he was still in cloud from which he suddenly emerged at high speed missing a hill-top by about 200 ft (61 m) flying straight and level with both aircraft and pilot trembling like jellies. Inspection proved that the parachute had deployed sideways and the shrouds had wrapped themselves around the tail.

The spinning problems of the Oxford were never solved; even a twin rudder layout was tried on one machine but it made little difference. One significant fact was established however; it was particularly sensitive to misalignment between the engine cowlings and the wing root fillets. A leather seal was designed and this certainly improved the situation. Spinning was prohibited at Flying Training Schools. Apart from this difficulty the test programme of the Oxford was remarkably free of trauma and few modifications were called for. The type served throughout the war at home and abroad within the Dominion Flying Training Scheme. It was in production until July 1945, 8,586 being built.

Airspeed produced another aeroplane which gave the test pilots food for thought on several sorties. Before the war the Royal Navy used for target practice the DH Tiger Moth converted to be controllable by radio. In this form it was of all-wood construction and named Queen Bee and could be fitted with wheels or floats. With a top speed of 109 mph (175 km/hr) it was hardly representative of the potential enemy aircraft likely to assail the British Navy, although it must be said that not many of the 380 built for the RAF were shot down. In 1935 Airspeed was invited to tender for a faster replacement which could be stowed with folded wings and launched from a warship. That consummate artist, Hessell Tiltman designed an elegant taper wing all-wood biplane powered by a 350 h.p. Armstrong Siddeley Cheetah radial engine. The sharp taper of the wings seemed an extraordinary decision in the case of an aeroplane which by reason of its role must have a high degree of inherent stability. However, it seemed to present no problems in that area. The type was known as the Queen Wasp.

The concept of remote control by radio was remarkably advanced at that time with an array of fail-safe devices to cope with every predictable malfunction. Basic control was by an air-driven gyro system operating pneumatic servos to the rudder and elevators. No aileron function was used in automatic flight. Coded Morse signals from the transmitter were fed into the gyro and limited throttle control was available from three positions; full open, cruise power and closed. A complex throttle over-ride protected it from the effect of acceleration forces on the gyro causing misleading signals to be received.

The elegant Airspeed Queen Wasp target seaplane with Armstrong Siddeley Cheetah radial engine. It was also flown with a wheeled undercarriage to the detriment of its appearance.
(via Aeroplane Monthly)

To land the Queen Wasp 'landing glide' was selected on the control panel on the ground. As soon as the speed dropped to the correct figure a servo motor lowered the flaps and the actual landing sequence began when a weight on the end of the trailing aerial touched the ground or the sea, closing contacts on the aerial winch which selected 'elevator up' and switched off the gyro. In bumpy weather aerial snatch could activate the landing sequence inadvertently so it was necessary to include a further inter-lock to ensure that the signal could not become operative before the 'landing glide' signal had been received. If a major control failure occurred the aircraft would be set into a gliding turn so that a reasonable landing could be made, hopefully, in a safe area. In the event of radio failure the glide turn procedure would be initiated if an interval of two minutes elapsed without radio signals.

One of the problems facing test pilots of radio controlled aeroplanes in the 1930s was revealed at a lunch in the de Havilland boardroom at Hatfield when Hessell Tiltman discussed the Queen Bee with the directors during the design stage of the Wasp. He told of a strange incident when a Queen Bee pilot had been briefed to carry out tests at Martlesham Heath to monitor the input signals. The Control Officer agreed that he would cease transmission at mid-day so that the pilot could return to the Mess for lunch. At noon the pilot was surprised to find the Bee becoming distinctly skittish and performing some rather advanced aerobatics which slowly diminished his interest in lunch. After twenty minutes of these gyrations he decided that, rather than ask an 'erk' to clean out the cockpit he should switch off and go home.

Ashen-faced on his return he challenged the Control Officer who was mystified, having ended the transmission at the agreed hour. Further tests were carried out and it was found that as soon as transmission ceased the receiver began to pick up a programme of dance music from Radio Paris. None of the DH men had heard about this but the story was soon confirmed when a Group Captain in the lunch party said, 'It is quite true, I was the pilot!'

Early trials commencing in June 1937 were very promising although some porpoising was experienced with the float version. Catapult trials followed the installation of launching spools and a little 'beefing up' to withstand the G forces at launch. Flt-Lt McDougall, a Farnborough test pilot, had good reason to remember the first one. The throttle was wide open when the catapult was fired and the Wasp rose gracefully into the air with the onlookers pondering upon an optical illusion as the pilot was no longer to be seen in the cockpit. The machine dived slightly, bounced a wheel and rose again to drop the other one.

After this bounce the wing tip dug in, the Wasp rolling over to wreck itself. Onlookers, fearful of fire rushed over to find the pilot shouting to be released from the rear fuselage. He was quickly removed, soaked in petrol but otherwise unharmed. The G forces had been too much for the seat fixing bolts which were still of mild steel, not high tensile steel as specified. McDougall was an extremely lucky man.

In a later chapter the story of the loss of George Errington in a deep stall accident to a DH Trident will be told. It is tragically ironic that George experienced the first recognisable deep stall in the Queen Wasp. He asked Tiltman, as chief designer, to accompany him so that he could demonstrate a curious stability feature which he had not previously experienced. At 2,000 ft (610 m) George said:

> 'I want you to check that we are at 2,000 ft over the edge of the aerodrome on the leeward side. Please watch carefully as I pull the stick back until the wings have an angle of attack right on the other side of the stall'.

Tiltman saw the ASI reading drop to 45 mph (72.5 km/hr) and, gradually drop to zero.

Tiltman told the author:

> 'In the meantime we were losing height very rapidly indeed, noticing the expression of anxiety on my face Errington assured me that the machine was under proper control which he demonstrated by putting on full aileron. The Wasp responded by rocking gently as it would under normal flying conditions. To get into the aerodrome the pilot had to put the nose well down and open up the engine to full throttle. We just skimmed the hedge. Whilst in this super-stalled condition we must have descended vertically, indeed I think that we were going astern in the ten knot wind. During the descent the attitude was normal, say plus five or ten degrees, but the angle of attack must have been nearer eighty degrees. This confounded the theory that sharply tapered wings are unstable in the stall. She was very stable laterally at all speeds with flaps up and rudder central.'

It was possible to reproduce this effect on this prototype K8887 but not on the second one, K8888 or subsequent production aircraft; pilots criticised these aircraft for having vicious stalling characteristics as one would expect with the wing plan; it remains a mystery why the two prototypes were so different. The contract for 90 Queen Wasps was cancelled when the Luftwaffe began to provide an abundance of targets.

The work of engine test pilots, which is valuable but often boring work is overshadowed in the public perception by their higher profile aircraft colleagues. The work of Capt. Norman Macmillan in earlier years was memorable in the context of the simple engines of that era; the modern engine test pilot has a much more complex job to do in the case of a large gas turbine, for example. The Miles Aircraft Company, as did Airspeed, perceived a need for a new trainer for the fast fighters such as the Spitfire and Hurricane and, as a private venture, built the very attractive Rolls-Royce Kestrel-engined trainer with retractable undercarriage and variable pitch propeller. It proved to be only 15 mph (24 km/hr) slower than the Hurricane at 14,500 ft (4,420 m), the actual top speed being 296 mph (477 km/hr) – a very creditable achievement in 1937. The manufacturer's trials having been completed the prototype was delivered to the Rolls-Royce test airfield at Hucknall, near Nottingham. The chief test pilot was Capt. R.T. Shepherd and he laboured under the ego-bruising view of his manager, Ernest W. Hives, later to become Lord Hives, that R-R was only a sophisticated garage and that test pilots were only flying testers, not the knights of the air which the aircraft companies considered them to be!

Ronnie Shepherd was noted as a gentleman with a very short fuse which was manifest on an occasion when he was taking off in the Miles trainer; the engine failed at about 100 ft (30 m), he belly landed in a field and ran on at speed until the machine came to rest against a hedge, most conveniently right opposite a public house. He demanded a pint of beer and sat in the cockpit drinking it. Within minutes the police arrived and demanded to be informed 'What was goin' on 'ere?' Shep was livid saying 'I can't even have a pint without the b——- police poking their noses in!' Another anecdote about him was told by Jock Bonar, one of his test pilots. It concerned a test flight in a Fairey Battle which had been fitted experimentally with a fully-feathering variable pitch propeller. Shep feathered the blades and dived past the group of technical onlookers, he climbed, unfeathered the propeller and began another dive, feathering the propeller as he did so; once again he climbed and pressed the button to unfeather. Nothing happened. Few things in life are more ineffectual than a single-engine aeroplane with a stationary propeller as it will have no hydraulic power and, thus, no powered flaps or undercarriage lowering facility. So Shep pumped the wheels down with a hand pump. Swinging round the airfield in his approach he carefully aligned the aircraft with his landing path but was unaware of the aerodynamic clean-ness of the Battle with no flaps; it hurtled on over the grass and touched down just before the further hedge which it ploughed through coming to rest on the road alongside it. Shep jumped down to the wing, slipped on the greasy surface and crashed to the ground, breaking two ribs against the cockpit. Jock Bonar arrived with the ambulance and said that it was possible to hear him swearing all the way to the hospital in Nottingham! These episodes are the happier aspect of test flying problems which could have had much more serious consequences.

One of the most valuable test aircraft in the Rolls-Royce fleet was the Heinkel He 70. In 1935 the only test aircraft were draggy biplanes such as the Hawker Horsley, which were useless for the type of development testing envisaged for the clean new high speed fighters under development. The fastest machine at Hucknall was the High Speed Fury which, at best, could only just exceed 220 mph (354 km/hr). The Heinkel was a very sleek aeroplane

Heinkel He 70 with Rolls-Royce Kestrel engine. This was one of the most significant contributions to engine installation development in the inter-war years.
(Rolls-Royce plc)

The Hawker Henley test-bed for the Rolls-Royce Vulture engine.
(Rolls-Royce plc)

capable of a top speed of almost 260 mph with the Kestrel engine originally installed. The story of this installation is an intriguing one. The Germans would not sell the He 70 with its standard 750 h.p. BMW VI engine which, together with its superb lines and finish gave it a maximum speed at sea level of 224 mph (360 km/hr) – faster than contemporary fighters. In 1935 an He 70G was fitted with an 810 h.p. Kestrel engine which Heinkel insisted should be installed at their Rostock works. When Capt. Shepherd visited the works some time after the delivery of the engine he noticed signs of oil leaks in various places. This was consistent with the engine having been bench tested and stripped down to see what could be learned from it. It was also believed that it had been flown in a prototype of the Messerschmitt Bf 109. However, registered G-ADZF, the He 70 proved to be a most valuable tool for the engine company as a flying test bed. It reached a maximum speed of 255 mph (410 km/hr) and served until 1944.

In one of its many test configurations it had an installation identical with the Miles Kestrel trainer. As a footnote to the Miles aircraft it was found uneconomical to reproduce in the works the elegant lines of the prototype and it was changed completely to go into service as the Master which proved to be an excellent trainer, in spite of a number of adverse comments by A&AEE test pilots, notably concerning its lack of stall warning and the ease with which it would stall during spin recovery.

A formidable aeroplane joined the R-R fleet when the ill-fated Vulture engine was built for use in the Avro Manchester bomber. This was the Hawker Henley, originally developed as a light bomber, designed to take the 1,000 h.p. Merlin I engine rather than the 2,000 h.p. Vulture with its four rows of cylinders in 'X' configuration. To keep the CG in the right position lead weights had to be fixed in the tail. The huge bomber's air intake on top of the cowling and the four large exhaust manifolds at the sides seriously obstructed the view. It was generally flown by Jock Bonar who thought it a complete menace to the pilot. Twice he had to force-land it in a field and he told the author that he lay awake at night when he had to fly it next day! The torque swing on take-off was violent so he had to commence the run almost 90° out of wind to compensate and build up sufficient speed for the rudder to become effective. Its landing speed was an alarming 120 mph (193 km/hr) so the forced landings must have been quite terrifying. However, Jock survived these and other equally dangerous test sorties with his characteristic sense of humour, to die, in bed, at the age of 90.

The two aircraft which can share the credit for the RAF being able to win the Battle of Britain and, consequently, save the free world were in development in the middle of the third decade. Specification F7/35 covered the requirement for a high speed interceptor fighter. Sydney Camm of Hawkers designed the Hurricane to meet it. R.J. Mitchell of Supermarine, designed the Spitfire to Spec F7/34. The common denominator was that they were both to use the new Rolls-Royce 1000 h.p. PV12 engine which was under development.

Both were low-wing monoplanes with retractable undercarriages and flaps; there the similarities ceased. Camm was a very conservative designer and would only innovate when he could be absolutely certain of the outcome. Effectively, the Hurricane followed the constructional principle proved over many years in the range of beautiful Hawker biplanes – Hart, Fury *et al.* This was a steel tubular space frame structure for the fuselage with fabric covered wooden formers and stringers, to achieve the clean aerodynamic shape required. It is almost certain that Camm was the famous designer to whom Neville Shute Norway showed the design of the Airspeed Courier in 1934. He responded by saying that the retractable undercarriage was not worth the trouble, weight and expense and would not be reliable! Nevertheless the Hurricane retracted the main wheels and, in the prototype, the tail wheel. Wisely Camm designed it with the oleo leg mountings well out on the centre section to give a wide track with plenty of room for housing the assembly in the thick wing root.

Mitchell was an innovator by nature as his successful Schneider Trophy seaplanes had shown in winning the Trophy outright for Britain. He had previously built a rather dreary design to meet Spec F7/30, one which showed none of his feel for elegance of line; it was, however a stepping stone to his ultimate masterpiece, the Spitfire, a name which prompted him to say, 'They would give it a silly name like that, wouldn't they?' It was a sleek all metal stressed skin aeroplane with a very thin wing which offered considerable difficulty in stowing the eight guns and, indeed the retracted undercarriage which, retracting outwards, gave a very narrow track for the wheels, a feature which provided considerable difficulty when the aircraft, as the Seafire, was used on aircraft carriers.

The Hurricane prototype, K5083, was first shown by P.W.S. 'George' Bulman on 6 November 1935. As development by de Havilland of the three-blade variable pitch propeller was not complete it was flown with a two-blade fixed pitch wooden one. After taxying trials Bulman took off and the undercarriage remained down for the duration of the flight. The low approach speed for the landing and the powerful ground effect of the thick wing section surprised onlookers from the factory. The next few flights confirmed the view of the chief test pilot that the Hurricane was an outstanding fighter; on one of them, probably the third on 23 November, Bulman was irritated because he lost his hat! Like the irascible Capt. Edgar Percival in later years he always flew in a trilby hat – on this flight the sliding cockpit canopy broke away and took the hat with it. Fortunately Bulman was not injured but some of the supporting structure and the escape panel under the rails on the starboard side were damaged together with the stringers and fabric covering at the rear of the cockpit. An additional stiffening frame was added to the new canopy. The undercarriage wheel fairings had a hinged flap fitted to each of them to close off the wheel-well after retraction. They became sloppy, dropped in operation and became known as the 'daisy cutters'; they were removed as was the retractable tail wheel so, in each case, valuable weight was saved and the fixed tail wheel required less maintenance with a marginal loss of performance. Camm had fitted struts from the fuselage to the cantilever tailplane. Roy Chaplin, his assistant, disagreed with them so, whilst Camm was in hospital for the removal of his appendix, the offending appendages were removed from his aircraft! His comments are not recorded but were doubtless pithy. The removal of these struts was helpful to other fighter pilots when trying to identify a possible adversary at long range; neither the Hurricane nor the Spitfire had struts but they were fitted to the Bf 109, so a useful identification feature was established.

On 7 February 1937 K5083 was flown to Martlesham Heath for RAF evaluation. Hawker had confirmed their satisfaction with the aircraft after only eight hours flying in ten sorties. The A&AEE were equally impressed by it but not with the new PV12 engine. Internal coolant leaks were the major problem with distortion of the cylinder heads due to the high temperatures generated in the engine. Many engine changes had to be made. Gp Capt. Sammy Wroath, who was a test pilot there at the time, told the author 'If someone had told us that the Merlin would be a world-beater we could not have believed it – it was one mass of trouble'. Test flying was severely limited both at Martlesham and at Brooklands when the aircraft returned there. Rolls-Royce decided to change the design of the cylinder head which had the so-called ramp-head combustion chamber; this affected performance and was prone to cracking. Additionally the two-piece Kestrel type cylinder block designed to make coolant leaks impossible was, manifestly, not a success. The major modifications required to the engine necessitated protracted rig testing by Rolls-Royce, followed by test bed running and finally flight testing at Hucknall.

All the mods were incorporated in the Merlin II and it became one of the most reliable engines ever built, enjoying the total confidence of the aircrews whose lives depended upon it.

As may be imagined these alterations provided an enormous work load for the engine test pilots, among them Ronnie Shepherd, Harvey Heyworth and his brother Jim, Peter Birch, from Bomber Command, Harry Bailey, an ex R-R apprentice fighter pilot who had served in the Battle of Britain, Tony Martindale of RAE and Rendell Stokes from Bomber Command, together with Service pilots posted to Hucknall and liaison pilots such as Ronnie Harker and Jock Bonar; they all did a first-class job to ensure that Rolls-Royce engined aeroplanes were as reliable as it was humanly possible to make them. The other engine manufacturers were equally assiduous in ensuring that their engines were equally reliable.

During the restricted flying period at Brooklands Philip Lucas carried out an investigation of the spinning characteristics of the Hurricane. They were not wholly satisfactory so trials were carried out with a scale model in the new Farnborough spinning tunnel. As a result of these tests a small fin extension was fitted under the tail and the rudder area increased to align with it below the fuselage. No further trouble was experienced.

Not until April 1937 was the first production aircraft with the new Merlin II engine flown. This had a number of modifications called for by the test flight programme incorporated; among them were a modified sliding canopy, the new Standard Blind Flying Panel in front of the pilot and full night flying equipment. Instead of the tedious hand pump to operate the undercarriage and flaps an engine-driven hydraulic pump reduced the pilot's workload considerably. Rolls-Royce had learned from their engine test programme that the ejection of exhaust gases rearwards through a suitable nozzle rather than directing them out sideways was capable of increasing the speed of the Hurricane by about 5 mph (8 km/hr) so ejector exhausts were made standard. No guns were available for the early deliveries, ring and bead sights were fitted temporarily whilst no radio equipment or vacuum pumps for the blind flying instruments could be fitted. Such was the state of the British industry after years of Government inaction in the area of national defence.

The first production aircraft, L1547, was used mainly for clearance of the compatibility of the de Havilland bracket type variable pitch propeller with duralumin blades with the Merlin engine. This was a two pitch installation initially but as soon as constant speed units were available in 1940 an urgent fitting programme was set in motion at fighter stations.

In October 1937 Philip Lucas had a grim experience during a very urgent test flight carried out in weather that was not suitable for flying; he took off into low cloud through fog and found that, when the tests were finished, the ground was totally obscured. He descended to the cloud top which, according to his altimeter, was at 2,000 ft (610 m). He reduced power to the minimum and flew level in the hope of finding a gap in the murk. He suddenly scraped the underside of the Hurricane across the top of trees in a wood and took off much of the fabric from wings and lower fuselage; he managed to reach Kenley where the aircraft was patched up. It was concluded that he misread the new Kollsman sensitive altimeter with its three pointers. In fact he was at 200 ft (61 m). Three similar accidents in service cast doubt upon this theory, with justification as it was proved. Tests were carried out to simulate the circumstances. When diving at 400 mph (644 km/hr) it was found that a static position error of 1800 ft (549 m) existed on the altimeter. This was due to the fact that in an aircraft with an open cockpit the static vent of the instrument is open to cockpit pressure. With a closed cockpit a totally different situation existed. The instrument pipe was then connected to the static side of the pitot static head feeding the airspeed indicator. There was no further trouble.

The prototype Spitfire at Eastleigh in April 1936. (Ken Ellis Collection)

The design of the Spitfire was both structurally and aerodynamically the antithesis of the very conventional Hurricane. Mitchell rejected the conventional wisdom of a thick, high-lift wing and produced the elegant thin elliptical wing which was a production engineer's nightmare but assisted in stowage for the eight guns and their ammunition. Overall the structural concept was far in advance of current production techniques and, indeed, the skill and experience of the workforce. Consequently there were many delays before the prototype K5054 was flown for the first time from Eastleigh on 5 March 1936 by 'Mutt' Summers. As a measure of the production problems, the first flight of the first production aircraft, K9787, was not made until 14 May 1938.

Tests of K5054 at Martlesham Heath showed that it was easy to fly and had no vices; a few alterations were made and the final judgement was that 'In general the handling of this aeroplane is such that it can be flown without risk by the average fully trained fighter pilot!' The only real criticism concerned the heaviness of the ailerons which, in combat service became a serious problem which had to be overcome by Jeffrey Quill and his team of test pilots who continued to develop the aeroplane to the Mark 47 Seafire which was in production at the end of the war.

The Merlin engine in the Spitfire shared the problem with the Hurricane of a power cut when negative G was applied in combat manoeuvres. This left both aircraft at a serious tactical disadvantage to the directly injected Daimler Benz engines of the Bf 109. This was overcome to a degree by a simple modification devised by a lady scientist/engineer at Farnborough. She devised a small disc with an orifice in it to restrict the fuel flow when G surges took place. Miss Tilly Shilling made the disc in her own workshop and it was known as 'Miss Shilling's Orifice'. Later versions of the Merlin, notably those with the Bendix Stromberg carburettor by which fuel was pumped in a low pressure spray, virtually solved the problem.

The fitting of constant speed units to the de Havilland and Rotol propellers of both British fighters improved performance and reduced cockpit workload. The remarkable saga of the development of the Spitfire from 1936 onwards by Jeffrey Quill and his team has been described in great detail by Quill in his book *Spitfire, a Test Pilot's Story* published in 1983.

Engine power was continually increased to meet operational needs and, as throughout its life the aircraft suffered from a tendency to longitudinal instability, the problems faced by Joe Smith, who succeeded R.J. Mitchell after his tragic death from cancer, were immense. The magnitude of the achievement can be best summed up in one of Jeffrey's favourite statistics 'The maximum all-up weight of the Seafire Mk 47 was the equivalent of the first operational Mk 1 of 1938 taking off with 32 airline passengers and their luggage'. The weight rose from 5,820lb (2,640 kg) to an overload weight of 12,500lb (5,670 kg).

One of his oddest test sorties was one when a contra-rotating propeller installation was in development. He was climbing fast when there was a bang and speed fell off very quickly to 140 mph (225 km/hr). Full boost and rpm were still shown and speed dropped still further. He wondered if he had managed to snag the towline of one of a gaggle of Horsas being towed behind Dakotas just receding into the distance. No, this was not the explanation but an immediate landing had to be made at full power at RAF Middle Wallop. On leaving the cockpit he could see no reason for the occurrence until he studied the propellers. The rear one was at full fine pitch. Removal of the spinner revealed that the translation unit which co-ordinates the pitch change between the two propellers had failed, the rear blades acting as a very powerful air brake.

Alex Henshaw, chief test pilot at the Castle Bromwich factory also had some difficult moments in the early years of Spitfire production. During the summer of 1942 he had three failures in quick succession: a fracture of the glycol tank which led to engine failure; an oil pressure loss; and what, at the time, was unknown but became very serious, failure of the skew gear which was part of the drive from the crankshaft to the camshafts and the magneto drive. Test pilots were in the nerve-racking situation of flying with one eye looking out for a convenient field in the event of the engine stopping without warning. Alex nearly lost his life on one such occasion flying from Cosford to Castle Bromwich in 10/10 cloud when the failure occurred. Below him was the Black Country landscape of pylons, factories, canals and back-to-back houses between two rows of which he tried to land in the back gardens. He lowered his seat to give him some protection and, just as he was about to touch-down the starboard wing stalled and was torn off as it hit a large oak tree. The nose then hit a house and opened up all the kitchen furniture to view. At that moment the port wing broke away and the fuselage rushed on in an avalanche of soil, vegetables and debris in a crescendo of noise. Miraculously Henshaw was only slightly injured. In his book *Sigh for a Merlin* which gives a detailed account of all these problems he quotes a total of 127 forced landings in the six years flying from Castle Bromwich. This includes Wellingtons, Lancasters, Spitfires and Seafires.

These very dangerous incidents in the lives of the Spitfire test pilots can be repeated at all production centres before and during the war where the pressures to save the country from the dilatoriness of pre-war politicians left Britain in such a perilous and unprotected state. The debt of the country to its test pilots has never been appreciated or paid.

It was appropriate that on 24 April 1993 Jeffrey Quill, supported by Alex Henshaw, unveiled at the RAF Museum, Hendon, a full size replica of the Spitfire prototype, K5054 resplendent in its original attractive pale blue finish, it was a moving occasion. The original cost of K5054 has been quoted as £15,776 and she flew for about 260 hours. Rarely can the nation have made such a valuable investment.

Alex Henshaw's Spitfire at Willenhall after engine skew-gear failure. (Alex Henshaw)

Westland Whirlwind.
(via Aeroplane Monthly)

The last Stirling built at Longbridge, LK619. Geoffrey Alington flew it from Castle Bromwich on 3 October 1944.
(Geoffrey Alington)

CHAPTER 4

The Second World War - I

The much ridiculed visit of Prime Minister Neville Chamberlain to Adolf Hitler at Munich in September 1938 had one positive result; it gave more time to develop the prototype aircraft so vital to the defence of this country.

One of the first prototypes to fly after this meeting was the Westland Whirlwind twin Rolls-Royce Peregrine-engined fighter. 'Teddy' Petter, the designer, was an exceptionally gifted and innovative man but, sometimes, his enthusiasm for innovation outstripped his judgement. The Whirlwind bore witness to this. There were great complexities such as a one piece Fowler flap from aileron to aileron which also controlled radiator cooling; the radiators themselves were very complex, the exhausts were carried through the fuel tanks; the monocoque structure was of magnesium alloy and all the skin panels were butt jointed longitudinally. The main reason for its failure was the use of the Peregrine engine in which Rolls lost interest as the market for it seemed limited.

Harald Penrose, the chief test pilot, flew the prototype from RAF Boscombe Down on 11 October 1938 after taxying runs had been undertaken. The hydraulic Exactor controls to the throttle were, as usual, spongy and not positive. After half an hour it was obvious that there were many problems to be overcome, particularly in the control of the aircraft. Petter had hinged the rudder at one side rather than on its centre line; it was uneven in effect, as might have been expected; with it free there was directional instability. There was a tendency to pitch nose down as speed increased, in tight turns there was a shuddering vibration which suggested interference between the fin and the tailplane mounted at the top of it. The engines ran too hot and Penrose was very apprehensive about the exhausts passing through the tanks, a feature which he had criticised to Petter who ridiculed his objections.

By the beginning of December only six hours flying had been logged whilst Petter would not accept that his creation was far from perfect until the machine had been flown at RAE. After two and a half hours flying the Service pilots confirmed that Penrose's criticisms were entirely valid. It was unfortunate that such a talented designer should take so little notice of his test pilot, particularly one with the experience of both aerodynamics and engineering which Hal Penrose could claim.

The stupidity of the location of the exhausts through the fuel tanks became apparent in June 1939 when, at 200 ft (60m) a violent lateral lurch caused Harald to instinctively apply full correcting aileron to compensate for the starboard one which became locked fully up, having become disconnected from the linkage. He climbed for height lest a parachute jump was necessary and investigated the behaviour of the aircraft in the hope that he might be able to bring the crippled Whirlwind back safely. In a wide, flat turn he gingerly approached the airfield making sure not to overshoot and rolled safely to a standstill near the hangar where it was found that, as he had predicted, the exhaust had burned through its duct and melted the aileron push rod; there was also a strong possibility of damage to the main spar. Miraculously the fuel did not ignite. At last Petter was convinced and normal stub exhausts were fitted.

The Whirlwind had many more problems; in five months only 29 hours of flying was logged. During this period 250 major and minor alterations had to be made to engines and airframe, not that this was exceptional at this time with such an advanced aeroplane. Diving trials revealed that it had poor stick-free stability at 400 mph (644 km/hr) and it nosed over into a steeper dive. Vibration at the tail remained a problem in tight turns and various types of fairing between fin and tailplane were tried. Eventually a streamlined bullet fairing solved the problem.

Ultimately the Whirlwind entered service with three squadrons and was successful as a long range escort fighter for low-level sorties across the English Channel, as a fighter bomber and for low level attacks on shipping. It remained in service until December 1943 and would undoubtedly have been developed further if Rolls-Royce had not abandoned work on the Peregrine engine.

The mainstay of the ability of the RAF to carry bombs deep into a potential enemy's territory was the trio of bombers built by Short, Handley Page and A.V. Roe. The first to be flown, the Stirling, was the only one to be envisaged as a four-engined aircraft, the other two being designed initially to be powered by a pair of the new 2000 h.p. Rolls-Royce Vulture engines – 24-cylinder 'X' layout liquid-cooled units. Short Brothers were noted for their marine aircraft and, at the time when the Stirling was in the design stage, work was proceeding on the Sunderland. A serious handicap to the designers was that the aircraft must be capable of entering a standard RAF hangar 100 ft (30.5 m) wide at the entrance. This required a low aspect ratio wing which, with the wing loading demanded, severely restricted the operating altitude of the bomber. The shoulder wing configuration and the large Gouge flaps necessitated a remarkable double decker undercarriage of great complexity and limited resistance to side loads. The bomb bay was also restrictive in size, being compartmental and able to carry bombs no larger than 4,000 lb (1,816 kg) in weight. The ground angle was very steep, the cockpit being some 24 ft (7.3 m) from the ground. In 1938 Shorts built a half-scale model of the bomber powered by four Pobjoy Niagara III 90 h.p. engines. It was built of wood and provided valuable data on control and aerodynamic problems. Tom Brooke-Smith, later chief test pilot, often flew the S31 as the model was known and provided experience for the Observer Corps who tracked what appeared to be a Stirling at twice the height at which he was flying; he also provided diversions for fighter pilots who intercepted what they thought was a large four-engined bomber only to find that it was the same size as their own aircraft. John Lankester-Parker decided that the tailplane of the S31 was not large enough and that a similar problem would occur with the bomber, the S29. So both were changed with considerable improvement in stability and control.

On 14 May 1939 Lankester-Parker flew the prototype, L7600, for the first time. This event followed a number of runs across the Rochester airfield on the previous day. On one of these he lifted off the ground for about 50 yds (45.7 m) to feel the elevator control and general trim. Parker, S/Ldr Eric Morton from MAEE Felixstowe and flight engineer George Cotton flew the bomber for about twenty minutes and were well satisfied. They approached for what was a perfect touch-down; suddenly the aircraft swerved, the huge undercarriage collapsing underneath it as it subsided in a cloud of dust. The crew members were uninjured but the new prototype was a write-off. It was found that one of the brakes had seized, locking the wheel.

Not until 3 December was the second prototype ready for flight but the Air Ministry had sufficient confidence in Shorts to take steps towards production. As the test programme was resumed there was little wrong with the machine apart from the notorious Exactor controls

The lift built at Castle Bromwich to move Fairey Battles from the erecting shop to the airfield. (Geoffrey Alington)

for the throttles which were characteristically spongy and indeterminate in action. Parker had decided, on the basis of his one short flight, that there were no untoward handling characteristics other than the powerful swing to starboard as the throttles were opened. Pilots soon learned to open the throttles with the starboard pair following with the port pair.

One of the most remarkable test flying episodes of all time concerned a production Stirling in which the crew had a miraculous escape from death. In 1941 the Austin Motor Company controlled a shadow factory at Longbridge, near Birmingham. The so-called aerodrome, built during World War One by shaving the top off a hill, was surrounded by houses and factories on three sides and a railway cutting on the fourth side. This cutting almost cost the life of chief test pilot T. Neville Stack when, on his approach in a Battle, a violent down-draught dropped him into the cutting, injuring him so severely that his test flying career ended there. Stack was succeeded by Geoffrey Alington, a well-known sporting pilot. From Battles and Hurricanes Longbridge graduated to Stirlings. It was, of course, only possible to fly the lightly loaded aircraft from the 400 yards (366 m) available at the factory 'airfield' so testing took place from Worcester aerodrome and, later, from Elmdon, the site of the present Birmingham International Airport. On 23 February 1943 Stirling BK660 was at Elmdon for slight modification after its flight from the factory. Geoffrey Alington was visiting a squadron so one of his pilots, Doug Cotton, was persuaded, fairly late in the day, to carry out a final check flight before delivery to a squadron next day.

Cotton and his flight engineer rushed out to the aircraft, being accosted on the way by an Irish labourer working on a new runway. Alington had given instructions that these men were not to be given flights but Cotton was persuaded to do so. The Stirling taxied out for take-off, the mag-drop checks were made and it roared across the aerodrome. The usual drill was to keep the elevators at neutral when the Stirling would fly straight off the ground into a gentle climb.

Cotton found that the climb angle was becoming excessive and tried to move the control column forward. It was immovable and the angle steepened alarmingly. Realising that the elevator locks had been put on as it was a gusty day he yelled to the other two men:

'The controls are locked, get up here quickly and put all your weight on the control columns as I stall-turn the aircraft, it is our only chance!'

The Stirling stall-turned and dived almost vertically as they pulled, to no avail. Cotton pointed out the local police station which they would hit if their efforts failed. Suddenly as he said 'Sorry, chaps, this is it!' a bang shook the airframe and the nose moved slowly upwards, as the lock was partially broken. By this time the ground was perilously close but fortunately the terrain was flat and in open country. Wheels and flaps were down and, as level flight was regained the six feet diameter wheels hit the deck breaking away and bouncing up to 200 ft (61 m) where they were seen by the pilot's wife who, having heard the engines from their nearby house, looked out of the bedroom window, rather uncharitably hoping that it was one of the ferry pilots at the controls.

As the bomber subsided to the ground at well over 100 mph (161 km/hr) four propellers detached themselves, followed by the Hercules radial engines. Ahead was a pair of massive oak gateposts supporting a gate which the farmer had, considerately, left open. They proved to be a most effective arrester gear which removed both wings to allow the fuselage to coast on a further few hundred yards, coming to rest battered but largely intact.

All that could be heard was heavy breathing from the shaken crew so miraculously preserved to fly another day. The labourer, who had most perceptively commented during the 45° climb:

'Streuth, these Stirlings don't 'arf climb, don't they?' suddenly observed 'Blimey, don't these test pilots put 'em through it?' Cotton, with some asperity shouted 'You silly b..... we've crashed, get out quick before it catches fire!'

Stirling BK660 after its flight from Castle Bromwich with the elevators locked. (Geoffrey Alington)

Not until they were well clear of the fuselage did they realize that the wings and all the fuel were some distance away. The destruction of a new Stirling was not a matter to be glossed over but it emerged that, in the rush to take off, the pilot had omitted to check the vital lock which would not have been in place but for the gusty weather. The affair proved that assumptions made in test flying can be fatal.

The Avro Manchester prototype L7246, was first flown by Capt H.A. 'Sam' Brown and his assistant Flt Lt S.A. 'Bill' Thorne from Ringway on 25 July 1939. There were high hopes for this heavy bomber which would probably have been realised but for the unreliability and failure of the Vulture engine to develop its anticipated power output.

In the air it handled well but was directionally unstable. To overcome this fault a third fin was applied as a temporary measure whilst larger fin and rudder assemblies were built for production aircraft leaving the line after those which first entered service in November 1940. The Vulture was developed to give 1,845 h.p. for the bomber but it was realised that the engine was unlikely to be fully successful. Alternatives were sought, one of them being a pair of 2,520 h.p. Bristol Centaurus radials; the 2,100 h.p. Napier Sabre 24-cylinder 'H' layout liquid-cooled engine was also studied. The prototype went to A&AEE for trials of accelerated take-off and arrested landing. Immediately war broke out A&AEE had been moved from Martlesham, the location of which was easily recognizable by enemy bomber pilots due to its proximity to the Rivers Deben and Orwell. RAF Station Boscombe Down was chosen for the new site and urgent action was taken to build up the facilities. Gp Capt H.J. 'Willie' Wilson was a Flt Lt in the Aerodynamics Flight when the Manchester was under test. He told the story of the assisted launch trials. After a few preliminary tests which proved satisfactory it was thought that the technique was sufficiently well developed to invite senior officers and other VIPs to witness a demonstration. The aircraft had a set of twelve rockets under each wing, inboard of the engines and wired to fire in pairs on each side in sequence. The pilot taxied out to a point just in front of the spectator enclosure, opened the throttles and, as the aircraft began to move, pressed the 'FIRE' button for the rockets. Unfortunately it had not been noticed that one of the brackets supporting one of the rocket packs was fatigued with a crack in it. Suddenly, all hell was let loose, the bracket failed and short circuited the cable to all the rockets, the sequence control being by-passed. All of them fired in a spectacular display as they hurtled through the propeller arc, the blades neatly slicing them into short lengths which were distributed in all directions including that of the VIP enclosure. They fled for their lives. This remarkable demonstration, in the best tradition of Murphy's Law, did nothing to encourage the VIPs to espouse the cause of Rocket Assisted Take-off any more than a later demonstration of arrester gear did.

Willie Wilson was to demonstrate this technique, again using L7246, which was fitted with an outsize arrester hook like a carrier-borne aircraft. Large concrete blocks had been sunk in the ground on either side of the landing path. These supported an oversize carrier arrester wire rig. Willie came in to catch the wires with his hook. Unfortunately the mass and acceleration calculations carried out to determine the size of the blocks left much to be desired. As soon as the load came upon the wires the blocks arose from the ground and were dragged along behind the aeroplane, some broke away and were projected towards the spectators who, once again, decided to bolt for their lives. The pilot, meanwhile, had some difficulty in maintaining a straight course with so much concrete hanging on the aeroplane.

As may be assumed, work on these schemes was quickly abandoned.

The Manchester prototype was involved in a rather hairy take-off which revealed the unreliability of the engines and the good handling qualities of the design. S/Ldr Jack McGuire, an old Martlesham hand and an exceptional test pilot, suffered an engine failure on take-off as the big-end bearings of the port engine began to break up. As the machine swung to port he ordered his co-pilot to feather the port propeller as he was fully occupied in controlling the bomber, which was turning towards the hangars and two large radio masts like telegraph poles. The co-pilot was not experienced in handling feathering propellers and pressed both buttons. Fortunately, the fuses in the feather pump motor circuits would not accept both operating at the same time so the mistake was neutralized as both blew. McGuire was then left with the dead engine and the unfeathered propeller but still had power on one side but at a speed little above take-off speed. He missed the hangars but the wing hit one of the poles at about half span on one side. Being a very well built aeroplane the pole broke, slowing the Manchester slightly but by this time it was over a valley and could gain some speed in a dive. He managed to make a safe landing.

The methodical progression of aircraft development practised in peace-time was not often part of the war-time scene; short cuts had to be made, sometimes, sadly, with fatal results. An example of this short-cut philosophy concerned S/Ldr McGuire and one of the new MkVI Wellingtons designed for high altitude flying with a primitive pressure cabin and 1,600 h.p. Merlin 60 engines. With 109 Squadron some of these were used for trials of the navaid 'Oboe'. Jack McGuire was called upon to test, as quickly as possible, one of these much heavier aircraft. There was no time to carefully build up to max. weight conditions, he was told 'Get on with it, as fast as possible!' It was urgently needed for an operation.

McGuire taxied out at full load using what little wind was blowing to get off in the meagre 1,000 yards (914 m) available. He opened the throttles to full power, held the aircraft on the brakes until the tail came up to the minimum drag position and let it go. At that weight every bump caused the wings to flex at the tips about a foot (0.3 m) as the pilot cooly judged the rate of acceleration and the distance to the boundary. He achieved a clean take-off a few yards from it. An engine failure would have been disastrous as the machine would have crashed into a parking lot of prototypes awaiting test.

On the face of it this type of flying appears reckless in the extreme but, as we had 'our backs against the wall' at this time there was no alternative. These pilots were professionals of the highest calibre analysing the risks and backing their judgement of the odds. Usually, as in the case of the Wellington, the risk came off and weeks of work were saved. Tragically, in some cases the outcome was disaster as, indeed, was the end of Jack McGuire's last heroic flight. He had been promoted to Acting Wing Commander to command B Flight, responsible for trials of bombers. A young New Zealand pilot, F/O Fleming, had been briefed to test a Liberator bomber. It became apparent that Fleming was not happy with this assignment; he reported various instrument and other malfunctions, not unusual in the Lib which was an early example of an all-electric aeroplane. He was quite correct to report the faults but McGuire decided that they were not sufficiently serious to hold up the test sortie. He decided to take command himself with Fleming in the right-hand seat; also in the crew were seven observers.

One and a half hours into the sortie fire broke out in one of the engines, the extinguishers were incapable of containing it so the captain ordered 'abandon aircraft'. He remained at the controls until the whole crew had clipped on their parachutes and jumped. As the last man left the fire burned through the main spar of the wing which broke away, the crippled Liberator taking this fine officer to his death.

As a footnote to the saga of the Vulture engine and the work of the engine test pilots Reg Kirlew, one of the Rolls-Royce pilots, was, in 1940, flying the prototype Vickers Warwick, K8178; the type was intended to be a replacement for the Wellington and shared its geodetic construction. It was powered by Vulture II engines. Kirlew experienced a cooling system failure which resulted in almost total power loss. With superb skill he made a

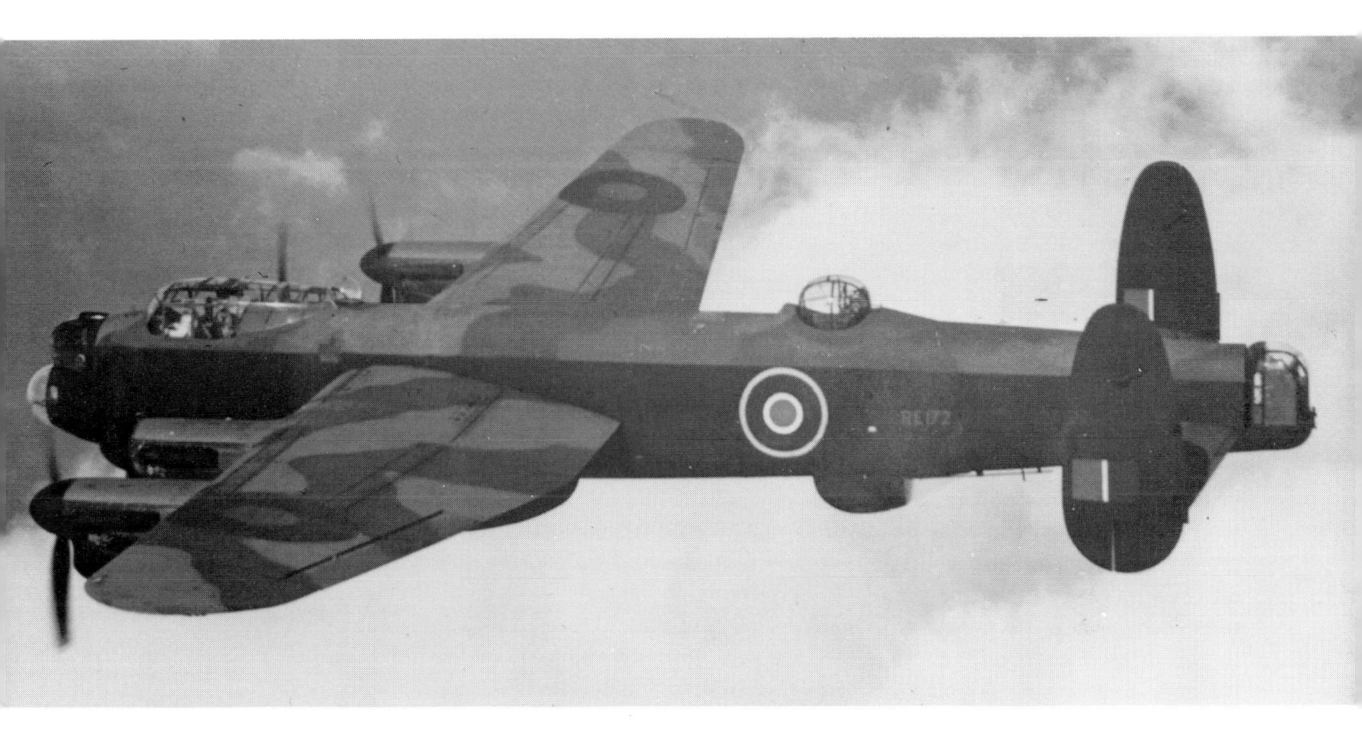

Avro Lancaster III.
(British Aerospace, Manchester)

perfect landing at the small grass airfield at Burnaston near Derby.

Time ran out for Reg Kirlew in 1941, when he had a similar failure flying a Manchester near RAF Tern Hill, in Shropshire. He tried to land at Tern Hill but could not reach the boundary, touching down in a field just outside and hitting a tree which tore the wing off; the aircraft bursting into flames immediately. Derek Brown, the flight engineer and the test crew of five managed to escape from the wreck but, tragically, Kirlew was trapped and died in the flames.

The demise of the Manchester, which went into service with eight RAF squadrons, was initiated by Avro's proposal for a Manchester III fitted with four Merlin engines. The prototype, BT308, a converted Manchester airframe, first flew on 9 January 1941 and showed stability problems which led later to the fitting of a larger tailplane and the large twin rudders. It showed great promise and went to Boscome Down for acceptance tests on 27 January 1941. From that time the Lancaster proved itself to be one of the greatest bombers ever built, ultimately being capable of carrying the huge 22,000 lb (9,980 kg) bomb.

The third of the new Bomber Command 'heavies', the Handley Page Halifax, had a chequered career at the design stage commencing with the issue of Spec P13/36 in September 1936. Two Rolls-Royce Vulture engines were called for; the performance was to be very high for the period and to give long range it was to be capable of catapult take-off in overload conditions. A powerful defensive armament with powered turrets was necessary and, if possible, it was to fulfil the roles of medium bomber, general reconnaissance and general purpose – which included troop carrying. It was also to be capable of carrying a torpedo and was to be sufficiently manoeuvrable to operate in the dive-bombing role at a 30° dive angle. After many discussions between Handley Page and the Air Ministry, a proposal was put forward by the firm in May 1937 that an unarmed bomber with two of the new Napier Sabre engines should be built. This was rejected but the point had been made, a point which paved the way for the remarkable de Havilland Mosquito.

After many more discussions and the power plants ranging from two Vultures to four Bristol Pegasus or Taurus, Napier Daggers or R-R Kestrels, the torpedo function was dropped and the suggestion made that four Merlins would show a marked improvement on previous proposals. This was provisionally accepted and both the dive-bombing and catapult launch requirements were withdrawn. So the project began to take the form of a sound bomber design. Two prototypes were built, one a shell for trials at Martlesham Heath, the other fully equipped. Radlett was considered too small to host the first flight of the prototype L7244 so it was dismantled and taken to RAF Bicester, the base of No 13 OTU.

Major J.L.B.H. Cordes carried out taxying trials and was very dissatisfied by the Lockheed hydraulic brakes which acted too slowly. He refused to fly until they had been changed to Dunlop pneumatic ones which he had always found most satisfactory. A three day and night panic operation permitted Cordes to make the first flight on 25 October 1939. The only major problem with the aircraft was a failure of one of the elevators along the line of the spar. Fortunately the centre of gravity was at mid-range and Cordes was able to return safely without imposing undue strain upon the weakened control surface. The second prototype with its military equipment fitted went to Boscombe Down where overbalance of the rudders was noted. To assist the pilot in overcoming the high aerodynamic forces on the rudders at speed it was necessary to build a section of the rudder area forward of the hinge line so that the forces on the rear of the area were partially overcome by the forces on the forward projection. If too much area was forward of the hinge line the rudder might lock over to one side or the other. This tendency was exacerbated in the case of flight with one or two engines out on one side. To investigate this further an early production Halifax I, L9515, was sent to Boscombe Down for further tests with S/Ldr W.J. Carr as a pilot and a scientist, Mr J.J. Unwin. They recommended that the leading edges of the rudders should be altered to a bulbous section and that the movement of the rudder trimming tab should be reduced. After this modification it was concluded that there was still the possibility to overbalance but it did not appear to be a dangerous situation. However, as the type entered service accidents occurred due to overbalance. The two prototypes and L9515 were not wholly representative of the later production aircraft so an almost new Halifax II, W7917, went to Boscombe Down for trials commencing at the beginning of February 1943 under the command of Flt Lt S. Reiss; Mr Unwin and a flight engineer completed the crew. On 4 February the machine was climbed to 12,000 ft (3,658 m); suddenly it dived and recovered into a flat spin in the course of which it hit the ground, breaking up but with no consequent fire. The crew died. It was found that the top section of one of the rudders had broken off in the course of an overbalance which was so violent as to overstress the structure. This was a very serious matter with Halifaxes coming off the line at an increasing rate. It was essential to carry out a quick fix, perhaps as an interim measure, which could be carried out at squadron maintenance bases. Two further Halifax IIs were allocated, one of which was to be fitted with the modified rudders suggested by S/Ldr Carr. The tests on this machine indicate the cold courage of the A&AEE test crews who, being aware of the fatal accident rate due to this problem and the fate of their own colleagues in W7917, simulated exactly the last flight of W7917.

At an indicated air speed of 150 mph (242 km/hr) it was not found possible, due to aerodynamic loads, to initiate a sideslip; at 130 mph (209 km/hr) full rudder could be applied without overbalance. At 120 mph (193 km/hr) as the pilot applied three-quarters rudder travel they both took over and hit the stops. He was unable to centralise them so the Halifax entered a spiral dive. Full throttle on the port engines was not effective either. As speed rose to 150 mph (242 km/hr) the rudders returned to control and recovery was effected.

After this experience the pilot climbed again to 12,000 ft (3,658 m) and repeated the test at 110 mph (177 km/hr). The result was similar except that full power on the port engines assisted recovery. The conclusion was that the rudder overbalance totally overpowered the ailerons so, on the approach to land, if a pilot used the rudders in a heavy-handed manner a spin would develop which would be fatal at that speed and altitude, 4,000 ft (1,220 m) of height being needed for recovery. Flight on only two engines, a frequent occurrence returning from ops, also left the crews in a most vulnerable situation in the dangerous low speed régime with heavy rudder deflection to compensate for asymmetric power. The condition became even more fraught when pilots were forced to 'cork-screw' in attempting to evade enemy night fighters.

Many experiments were made to overcome the problem by restricting rudder travel and even resorting to the time honoured method of cording the trailing edges of the rudders to make operation heavier for the pilot. None of them was successful but a recommendation was made to increase considerably the fin area of the aircraft. This design change was incorporated on the Mk II Halifax with almost rectangular fins and rudders, increased in area by 40 per cent. This was approved by A&AEE pilots and completely cured the trouble.

Handley Page Halifax VI. This version was similar to the Mk III but had extended wing tips, more powerful engines and increased fuel capacity. (Handley Page Ltd.)

Arthur Clouston was involved in a desperate bid to conquer the enemy bombers over Britain before adequate location systems were available. It was thought that high intensity flares on trailing wires would help to illuminate the raiders so, for weeks, Clou flew a Hampden over Salisbury Plain with a million candle-power flare trailing behind on 1000 ft (305 m) of wire. With a boffin in the back he was regularly shot at by Germans and British ack ack guns. The scientists decided that it might be better to fit the flares on the under-wing bomb racks. Clou was not too happy about this both from the point of view of fire risk and because he was now a much better target, being 1000 ft nearer to the flare. He asked to carry out the tests at Silloth on the north-west coast where, he had been told, enemy aircraft do not operate. So a Whitley was flown to Silloth to represent an enemy bomber. With his Hampden astern Clou called on the Whitley pilot to douse his navigation lights. The scientist pressed the flare ignition button and a pair of two million cp flares under each wing were ignited. The glare from the propellers and the vapour particles in the air was dazzling and Clou had to warn the Whitley pilot to dive to avoid collision. Once lit the flares burned for three and a half minutes.

Within seconds aerodrome control called him,

'An enemy aircraft has been detected alongside you. Please leave the area with all possible speed!'

Twisting and turning he fled to the coast with the ground for miles around lit up like a daylight scene. He felt as naked as the day he was born and just as helpless. In the meantime the German bomber made full use of the unexpected illumination to carry out an attack on Silloth where all lights had, unavailingly, been turned off. Clou, waiting for the accursed flares to burn out, cruising up and down the coast, heard the Whitley pilot receive permission from Silloth to land so he followed him in to be received somewhat coldly and told to take his experiments elsewhere.

An alternative scheme was tried out in Northern Ireland with a Douglas DB7 equipped with a crude projector in the back to shoot photographic flares in the direction of the enemy. With two junior scientists to feed the projector Clou chased the Whitley which was well illuminated. Suddenly a flare jammed and ignited in the tube, setting fire to others. Acrid choking smoke filled the fuselage; fortunately with admirable presence of mind and much courage the scientists dragged the smouldering flares out of the tube and threw them out of the aircraft. They returned to base with Clou feeling distinctly dispirited about the concept of illuminating the enemy.

CHAPTER 5
The Second World War – II

In 1937 the Hurricane was in production for the Royal Air Force. The Hawker design team, realising that this aircraft had limited development potential due to its obsolescent form of construction, was considering a successor using the modern technology of stressed skin construction which was essential for aircraft powered by the new 2,000 h.p. engines under development. Specification F18/37 was issued and a design emerged for a twelve-gun interceptor fighter with either the Vulture engine or the Napier Sabre. Due to the development problems of the high-revving and complex Sabre the Vulture-engined prototype, the Tornado was flown first, on 6 October 1939, by Philip Lucas. By this time the design was envisaged with four 20 mm cannon which were easily housed in the fairly thick wing, a wing section which proved to be a serious handicap to performance as an interceptor.

After the Munich crisis the Air Ministry demanded that top priority should be given to the Merlin engine for Hurricanes, Spitfires and the new Halifax bomber, so development work slowed down on both the Vulture and the Sabre. By 1941 only four Vulture engines had been delivered to Hawker. Attention was concentrated upon the Typhoon, as the Sabre engined machine was known. The prototype, P5212, was flown by Lucas on 24 February 1940. In its construction Camm retained his well-tried tubular steel front fuselage assembly but covered it with an alloy skin with a metal monocoque aft of the cockpit. The wings were metal covered and all the control surfaces were fabric clad.

Hurricane priorities played havoc with the test flight programme and delays were frequent. On 9 May 1940 Lucas experienced a major structural failure in the air when the monocoque section at the tail of the fuselage cracked. He was able to make a safe landing and was awarded a George Medal for saving the aircraft so that the reason for the failure could be established. In the meantime plans were going ahead to build the Typhoon at Gloster's Hucclecote factory. Michael Daunt was assistant chief test pilot to F/O P.E.G. Sayer and made the first flight of a Gloster-built machine on 27 May 1941. Michael, a very entertaining Irishman, had served with the crack No 25 Fighter Squadron prior to joining Gerry Sayer and had some pungent comments about the Typhoon. He told the author that:

> 'As an aeroplane, one of the most bloody ever! The things that were wrong with it before it went into the Air Force were appalling; the tail dropped off and pilots suffered from carbon monoxide poisoning due to exhaust gases being sucked into the cockpit. By the time we were able to measure the gas concentration several pilots had been killed. The aircraft vibrated as it went round corners – it was said to rattle the eyebrows. In the end the pilot's seat had to be mounted on springs to isolate him from the effect of it.'

Typhoon Ib. This later version is fitted with a tear-drop canopy. (Hawker Aircraft Ltd.)

Mike saw a camera gun film of a mock combat with a Spitfire, which appeared on the film as a biplane. Bill Humble, a droll Hawker test pilot joked that too much exposure to Typhoon flying would cause impotence. The story reached a 'Tiffie' squadron and caused one of the pilots to request a transfer in the interests of marital harmony! A letter from the Institute of Aviation Medicine at Farnborough was necessary to dispel his concern.

Many forced landings by Gerry Sayer and his team at Brockworth, the test base, were caused by the failure of the oil scavenge pump which had also been experienced by the Napier test pilots at Luton. Jock Bonar was particularly unlucky as will be seen in Chapter 9. Gerry and Mike Daunt had become accustomed to treat every landing as a forced landing aiming to stop the aircraft at a certain point. This skill served them well when the worst happened as it did with Mike when he lost every drop of oil, the engine blowing up. He made what was potentially a perfect belly landing in a small field but the four-blade 14 ft (4.3 m) propeller was bent into a good imitation of a pair of skis on which the Typhoon hurtled across the field heading for a high bank skirting a sunken road. Convinced that utter disaster faced him Mike was relieved when the machine shot between two trees which neatly removed the wings and fuel tanks as the fuselage carried on at reduced speed to stop by the road in a most convenient position for recovery by the salvage crew.

One of Daunt's worst experiences was in an extraordinary aeroplane built by Folland at Hamble for use as an engine test bed. Henry Folland, who had been Gloster's chief designer, could not afford to employ a test pilot so Gerry and Mike agreed to fly this machine, the F4/37, generally known as 'The Frightful'. Neither was keen on the prospect of diving trials as they tossed a coin; Mike lost. During one dive the tail broke away generating G forces sufficient to break the harness of the pilot and hurl him out through the canopy under an acceleration of 8G. His parachute harness almost strangled him and he landed very heavily, badly injured. The first helper to arrive was the local vicar who, poor man, was assaulted by this beefy Irishman to whom he intended to give succour.

Mike's account of this meeting must be one of aviation's funniest stories.

> 'The vicar was very kind and had a voice just like Robertson Hare (a famous comic actor with a plummy voice). I had a broken collar bone and wrist and was very violent, as sometimes happened if you are slightly strangled! I hit him hard and, in spite of this

he kindly visited me in hospital. I have never forgotten his comment, "When I picked you up you were muttering something which sounded like a rugger cry 'Oh shee, Oh shee". I had to explain that when you have a badly lacerated mouth it is difficult to articulate the letter T!'

Michael spent six months convalescing from this disastrous flight.

Hamble was the base of another aircraft which featured in a remarkable escape from a violent death. In March 1940 the Armstrong Whitworth Albemarle bomber prototype made its first flight with AW's chief test pilot Charles Turner-Hughes at the controls. This was a hybrid construction, part metal and part wood, and incidentally, the first large British aeroplane with a tricycle undercarriage. After a satisfactory first flight it was flown to the company base at Baginton for tests which resulted in the wing span being increased from 67 ft (20.4 m) to 77ft (23.47 m). There was a degree of directional instability which was cured by an increase in the area of fins and rudders. An A&AEE pilot disgraced himself by becoming lost in the Albemarle and landing it in field, doing slight damage to the underside.

Early in 1941 the pilot heard a noise which he diagnosed as engine trouble. He switched it off and immediately entered a spin from which recovery seemed impossible. The two flight observers were ordered to abandon the aircraft – one of them became trapped under the fuselage and, when he deployed his parachute, this became wrapped around the tail where it acted as an anti-spin 'chute allowing the pilot to recover control. He then realised that his original problem was noise made by air over the wing which had lost part of its upper skin. It was clear that he would have to make a high speed landing but was unaware of the unfortunate man hanging underneath, who tried to climb the rigging cords but was too cold to do so. As the aircraft descended to about ten feet (0.3 m) from the ground he released his harness and fell into some bushes on snow covered ground, miraculously surviving but with serious injuries. The prototype was burnt out, the pilot escaping with minor injuries. The Albemarle was a mediocre aeroplane with a few virtues and vices. The introduction of the big four-engined bombers left it with only a limited function. It was relegated to glider towing in which role it gave good service in all the European airborne operations.

Folland F4/37, 'The Frightful', fitted with a Bristol Hercules engine. 1942. (Ken Ellis Collection)

Another aeroplane which made its debut in the first year of the war was the Fairey Barracuda. As usual the Lords of Admiralty required it to enter the Fleet Air Arm and carry out every imaginable function with high efficiency and, as so often happened, the aeroplane was ruined. Its Merlin engine was inadequate in power and the drag of the girders which constituted the undercarriage made a full load take-off an extremely hazardous affair. A bawdy Fleet Air Arm song began 'Tearing down the runway with ....-all on the clock.....', reflecting the dislike of many crews for the machine which, in its torpedo dropping function, displayed a distinctly user-unfriendly habit. As the torpedo dropped and the pilot reefed the machine round in a climbing turn to avoid a close approach to his target the Barracuda often rolled over and followed the torpedo into the sea.

The early test flights in the hands of Chris Staniland revealed problems of buffeting when the large Youngman flaps were lowered to the dive bomb position. The tailplane was originally low mounted and was finally lifted four feet (1.2 m) to a point near the top of the fin. Lt Eric 'Winkle' Brown, an outstanding naval test pilot encountered the Barracuda at RNAS Arbroath in 1942. As the designer of it was the Belgian Maurice Lobelle, Eric expected to see an elegant descendant of the Battle and Fulmar. He was shocked to see the extraordinary display of hardware disgorged from the fuselage and wings as one made its approach, transforming, as he put it 'the pedestrian and unappealing into what could only be described as an airborne disaster'. He felt that there were events which he could await with more pleasure than taking this quaint contraption into the air.

By the end of 1943 'Winkle' was a Lt-Cdr with 1,500 deck landings on 22 carriers in his log book. In 1944 he was posted to RAE Farnborough as chief naval test pilot with the primary objective of investigating the feasibility of operating the DH Mosquito from a carrier. By this time five Barracudas had crashed in mysterious circumstances during torpedo-dropping exercises. At RAE was a most competent and courageous lady test observer, Mrs Gwen Alston; her husband Peter also a test observer, had been killed at Martlesham Heath in February 1939 when, with S/Ldr Robert Cazalet as pilot, the first Harvard trainer to arrive in Britain entered a spin from which Cazalet was unable to recover; both died and Gwen decided to continue with her work at RAE flying many hours and carrying out valuable experiments. Her husband's work is commemorated by the annual award of the Alston Medal for Test Flying, established by his wife and administered by the Royal Aeronautical Society. Eric Brown and Gwen Alston carried out several flights simulating the dropping of a torpedo from the Barracuda. They commenced the tests with a check on sideslip characteristics at various speeds, deliberately inducing a rudder stall. As soon as the overbalance point was reached the nose dropped as it did when the flaps were set to neutral at the bottom of a high speed dive. The instrument recording cameras were switched on and, at a safe altitude, the precise technique of torpedo release was carried out. At the limiting speed for flap retraction Eric set them to the cruise position and kicked on full starboard rudder. The Barracuda instantly entered an inverted dive which, of course, at normal operating height would have been fatal. Operating procedures were amended pending the design and fitting of a larger fin and rudder.

The Barracuda was first flown in the same year as a far more distinguished aeroplane, the de Havilland DH 98 Mosquito. Its wooden construction was, initially, the butt of all the prejudice of which the Air Ministry and, indeed, the RAF was capable. Only the support of Air Marshal Sir Wilfrid Freeman enabled the design to reach the prototype stage. It became known as 'Freeman's Folly'. The author was fortunate enough to be at Hatfield on 24 November 1940 when Geoffrey de Havilland Jr. and his observer John Walker carried out taxying trials and made the first flight on the next day. It was an unforgettable sight as this beautiful aeroplane, W4050, in a chrome yellow finish took off on a 30 minute flight a

The de Havilland DH 98 Mosquito prototype just before its first flight at Hatfield in November 1940. The sleek lines achieved by the moulded plywood construction are apparent.
(British Aerospace, Hatfield)

mere eleven months after design work had commenced. The undercarriage was retracted and the Handley Page slots were locked. These had been fitted as a safeguard against wing drop at slow speed on the approach. No such problem arose and Geoffrey reported most favourably upon the handling qualities of the aeroplane. Some tailplane flutter was recognised on later flights and a form of slat was mounted on the inner aft section of the nacelles in an attempt to smooth out the airflow. This was unsuccessful so a dihedralled tailplane was fitted. This, too, was unsuccessful. Airflow was studied by means of wool tufts applied to the nacelles which, in the prototype, terminated in a radius at the trailing edge of the wing. The shape of the rear of the nacelle proved to be too blunt so it was extended aft of the trailing edge. This also necessitated a major change to the flaps which were in one piece from fuselage to aileron, the rear of the nacelle being attached to the flap and retracting into the nacelle when the flap was lowered. The flaps were re-designed to suit the fixed aft end of the nacelle which, in their lengthened form, improved the already beautiful lines of the machine.

Another problem arose from designer R.E. Bishop's continual quest for perfection in streamlining. The exhaust manifold on each side of the nacelles of the Merlin engines terminated in a single ejector with a small and shapely cooling shroud over it. This was inadequate and much larger manifold shrouds became necessary.

The prototype was flown to Boscombe Down on 19 February 1941 after only 35 hours test flying. There were still a few minor problems to be worked out but its remarkable performance met predictions of a top speed of 386 mph (621 km/hr). The staff at A&AEE showed no great urgency in flying the new aeroplane until the OC, Gp Capt. Allen Wheeler flew it and realised that it was a war-winner. From that time all the stops were pulled out and the true potential of the Mosquito emerged. It was 30 mph (48 km/hr) faster than the fastest known German fighter and 100 mph (161 km/hr) faster than any comparable bomber whilst its handling characteristics were far from those which might be expected from a 'hot-rod'.

On 24 February S/Ldr Charles Slee had flown it and as he taxied across the rough surface of the airfield the tail-wheel castoring device failed, jamming the wheel assembly. At the same time the pilot noticed that the controls seemed to become much heavier. The station engineer officer began an immediate investigation; there appeared to be no failure associated with the control runs and the episode was somewhat mystifying. Suddenly the cheerful voice of an 'erk' on the starboard side of the aircraft broke in,

'It's all right, Sir, it ain't the controls at all, she's broken 'er bleedin' back!'

And so she had – tail-wheel shimmy had caused the failure of the castoring device which, in turn, had stressed the rear fuselage until it cracked near the starboard access door. A hardwood strake over the top edge of the door was fitted as a standard modification and W4050, with a new fuselage, flew again three weeks later. To avoid the shimmy problem a Marstrand tail-wheel with two tracks moulded on the outside of the tyre was fitted. Unquestionably the Mosquito was one of the finest aeroplanes ever built – it could be said to have been the first multi-role combat aircraft with no fewer than 38 different versions in service. In all, 7,781 were built. It is sadly ironic that a Mosquito cost the life of Sir Geoffrey de Havilland's youngest son, John who, on 23 August 1943 was flying a Mosquito which collided with another one flown by another DH test pilot George Gibbins. Both pilots and their observers, Nick Carter and John Scrope were killed. Sir Geoffrey's eldest son, the chief test pilot, was killed in another DH machine, the 108, as is recorded in Chapter 9.

The outbreak of war saw the RAF without a dive-bomber. The remarkable success of the Junkers 87 Stuka in the Spanish Civil War and the assault on France and the Low Countries persuaded the British Government that this was an error of omission which should be rapidly rectified. The British aircraft industry was too heavily involved with the priority work of building fighters and bombers to bother with what appeared to be a fringe design with limited application at that time. So the British Purchasing Commission in the United States investigated the purchase of an American aircraft. Earlier requirements formulated by the French Government had led the fairly small Vultee Company to design a suitable dive-bomber, the V–72, for which orders were to be placed by the French. Their defeat in 1940 left these orders in limbo so the British Purchasing Commission showed interest. The V–72 was designed with twin rudders and was fully stressed for dive-bombing with slotted surface wing flaps and dive brakes. The Vengeance, as the British version was called, a name also used by the USAAF, reverted to a single fin and rudder and had a 1,700 h.p. Wright Cyclone 18-cylinder twin-row radial engine. It became a tough, strong weapon, built like a tank as one pilot described it.

Unusually, the contract specified the test flying procedure by both the contractor's pilots and the RAF Resident Technical Officers. Two prototypes were available at Vultee Field, Downey and the first one was evaluated by Gp Capt. 'George' Bulman, who was the Head of the Test Branch of the Purchasing Commission. W/Cdr Mike Crossley RAF was also involved in the flight test programme. To increase the production facility for the Vengeance the Northrop Corporation was contracted to build the machine in addition to Vultee.

American responsibility for test flying rested with the famous Vance Breese who was responsible for the change from twin rudders to a single one after taxying trials had proved his earlier contention that two rudders would give inadequate control on the ground. In July 1941 Vance Breese made the first flight. He was not satisfied with the dive brakes and recommended that holes should be punched over the surfaces as was done with the Douglas Dauntless. The suggestion was rejected by the engineers, but the orientation of the slots was changed. An interesting aspect of the Vengeance programme was that it was almost certainly the first time that telemetry was used to record by instruments on the ground data obtained from the aircraft in the air. During the stalling checks it was found that, although the stall was fairly innocuous and aileron control held it laterally stable throughout, there was a degree of buffeting at high accelerations which caused concern for the integrity of the tail structure. Strain gauges were fitted and the information being transmitted to the ground receiver could be heard in the form of tones in the pilot's headphones. Frank Davis, on the departure of Breese, took over responsibility for the tests and made one stall for each reading of the strain gauge; he would then manually switch to the next gauge ready for another stall. It required several hundred stalls from 1 G to 6 G to cover all the permutations. The tests proved the integrity of the structure without modification. A problem arose with the rudder control which was considered too heavy for a dive-bomber in which quick and easy directional changes must be made to achieve accurate aim. This was overcome by installing a spring tab at the trailing edge of the rudder. Recovery from a high speed dive was another contentious area. As speed built up the aircraft tended to tuck under and required excessive stick forces for recovery. On one occasion Frank Davis was diving to test an oil system valve for negative G when rudder flutter occurred and the surface tore away behind the hinge line. The balance area forward of the hinge line was still under pedal control but tended to be fully over one side or the other including yaw. Davis was able to hold it on the stick and the fin gave sufficient directional stability to land safely. This was another example of the hazard of fabric-covered surfaces in high speed flight. The rudder was altered to have an all-metal skin. This also solved the problem of heavy pull-out forces from the dive as it was decided to modify the elevators similarly. By the end of 1941 most of the bugs had been eliminated from the new dive-bomber which the RAF was looking forward to operating. Unfortunately for their desires the Japanese attack on Pearl Harbor on 7 December 1941 completely altered the situation. The Americans realised that they would need many more aircraft so delivery schedules were completely altered, but that is another story. The 1,200 which were delivered to the RAF gave extremely good service, mainly in Burma with Hurricanes giving top cover to their attacks.

Building on their success with the Douglas DC-2 and -3 commercial airliners, Douglas had, with Lockheed, begun to develop four-engined long range aircraft. The first to fly was the Douglas DC-4E, a very large aircraft with accommodation for 42 day passengers or 30 sleepers. There were many problems with it and its sheer size was against it when it first flew in June 1938. A new DC-4 was built; smaller and much more efficient, it had a pressurised fuselage and as soon as America entered the war it became a military transport. Lockheed's beautiful Constellation airliner was rather later and only a few went into service with the USAAF. Both aircraft, of course, were the mainstay of the world airline fleets after the war.

Boeing, having had little commercial success with the Model 307 airliner, turned their attention to a replacement for the B–17 Flying Fortress in the form of a very long range bomber capable of flying in the lower stratosphere. In the summer of 1942 the prototype of the B–29 was ready for chief test pilot Eddie Allen to commence the test programme. Allen was one of the finest test pilots in the world with experience at Martlesham Heath, Langley Field and with most of the leading American aircraft manufacturers. This complex aeroplane could not have been in better hands. The B–29 was well in advance of any other aircraft in the world; it was powered with four entirely new 2,200 h.p. Wright R–3350 18-cylinder engines, it had high aspect ratio wings for maximum aerodynamic efficiency, pressurisation of the crew locations in the fuselage, powered controls and an electronic fire-control and armament system. At a loaded weight of 105,000 lb (47,628 kg), and a range of over 5,500 miles (8,851 km) with a bomb load of up to 10 tons (10,170 kg). Its maximum speed was 360 mph (579.6 km/hr). The first prototype flew in September 1942 after a long series of taxying tests during one of which he lifted off to a height of 15 ft (4.6 m). These

Boeing XB–29 with experimental ram-jet underneath.
(Flypast)

tests proved that the undeveloped engines left much to be desired. However, on 21 September Allen took off on a 75 minute maiden flight during which the aircraft behaved impeccably. Thus begun the painstaking work of getting all the minor bugs out of the aeroplane and the major ones associated with the engines. During the first 26 flying hours of the programme 16 engine changes became necessary.

Eddie Allen flew the second prototype on 30 December. During the sortie an outboard engine caught fire, the propeller could not be feathered and the CO2 fire extinguishers were found to be useless. Fortunately Allen, with great skill, managed to return to the airfield trailing flames and smoke. In the meantime the first prototype was still plagued with engine trouble; forced landings were a regular occurrence.

On 18 February 1943 Allen and his co-pilot Bob Dansfield took off with a crew of nine test observers to check the powerplant cooling system and propeller operation. Having climbed to 5,000 ft (1,524 m) an outboard engine caught fire; this time the propeller could be feathered and the fire doused with CO2. Allen radioed back to base that he was returning after an engine fire. Many Boeing executives turned out to see his return and were horrified to see, as he flew at 1,500 ft (457 m) over Seattle that a second engine was on fire. Allen radioed the field asking for all the fire appliances to be ready as he was landing with a wing on fire. He continued his approach to be runway trailing debris and smoke as the pilots struggled to remain airborne. Just outside the field the flames reached the fuel tanks and the aircraft blew up falling on a meat processing plant where 20 people died as well as the whole of the crew.

The engine problems were finally blamed upon detail design failings and poor quality control at the engine builder's plant but there was more to it than that; they were troublesome as late as the 1950s when the RAF operated some B–29s, re-named Washington, as a replacement for the ageing Lincoln. When John Allam, at the time a Vickers test pilot, was using one for weapons trials, he had several experiences of engine fires.

Engine fires were a problem with the only strategic bomber built by Germany during World War Two; the Heinkel He 177 was designed to a 1938 specification for a heavy bomber to carry a 4,410 lb (2,000 kg) bomb load to a target 1,000 miles (1,609 km) away at a speed of 310 mph (500 km/hr). Siegfried Gunter, the designer, decided that to achieve the low drag necessary to meet this demanding spec. he would have to use two 2,000 h.p. engines – shades of the Manchester saga. As no such engine was available in Germany he compromised by mounting two 1,000 h.p. Daimler Benz DB 601 engines side by side in each of the two nacelles. The resulting power unit was known as the DB 606 and could develop 2,600 h.p. for take-off. It might have been assumed that the use of two well proven engines like the DB 601 would guarantee reliability but it was not so. The close coupling and cowling of the two engines produced almost insurmountable problems of cooling. Initially evaporative cooling was used to eliminate the drag-producing radiators, Heinkel having had some success with an earlier aircraft, but it was not suitable for this much larger one. So, in 1939, it was decided that orthodox radiators would be fitted. These increased drag and reduced range so, to make up the shortfall in range, the fuel load had to be increased with further deterioration of performance. At the last moment the *Luftwaffe* decided that the He177 must be capable of performing the role of a dive-bomber – an absurd proposal for such an aircraft, with a wing span of 103 ft (31.4 m) and an all-up weight of 68,343 lb (31,000 kg).

The prototype was first flown from Rostock on 19 November 1939. The engines began to overheat so the pilot, *Dipl Ing* Francke, the chief of the *Luftwaffe* test centre at Rechlin, terminated the flight after twelve minutes. His report on the sortie was generally favourable although he commented on inadequate empennage area, flutter at the tail and some propeller shaft vibration. The second prototype was soon flown by another Rechlin pilot, *Flugkapitän* Rickert. After preliminary flights he began diving trials, during one of which severe flutter developed and the aircraft disintegrated. After this disaster the tail surfaces were increased in area by about 20 per cent. All machines being built were modified. The third aircraft went to Rechlin for evaluation and the fourth continued with the diving tests terminated by the crash of No. 2. With *Flugkapitän* Ursinus at the controls this machine also failed to recover from a dive, killing the crew.

leinkel He 177 four-ngined bomber. This one 'as captured and is being valuated under RAF olours.
ia Aeroplane Monthly)

The fifth prototype was the first machine to carry full military equipment. It experienced a double engine fire in the air, crashed and exploded. After this disastrous start to the test programme the priority was clearly the investigation of the very serious engine problems. The first 35 aircraft were allocated to development testing and operational trials.

The He 177 went into operational service in mid 1942, Bristol having the dubious distinction of being the first British city to be visited by one of them. Many modifications were made to the engine installation but the problems were never solved. The engines were moved forward to give more room in the nacelle and a gutter was fitted between the engine pairs to catch oil drips which would otherwise fall upon the red hot exhausts; these showed only minimal improvement in accident rate due to fire. An important part of crew training concerned the drill in the event of an engine fire to ensure that the necessary actions be taken quickly before the wing spar was severely weakened, as happened on several occasions with fatal results.

By the time the type had moved its operations to the Russian front in 1944 the many modifications made had considerably improved serviceability and safety and the engine fires were generally due to inexperienced crews failing to follow the proper engine handling procedures. The Heinkel 177 was undoubtedly one of the worst and most unreliable aeroplanes ever to go to war, an embarrassment to the proud Heinkel organisation.

It is appropriate, at this stage, to mention the next Heinkel type number, the He 178. This was the first aircraft in the world to fly under the power of turbojet. The young RAF officer F/O Frank Whittle had, in 1930, taken out a patent for jet propulsion of aircraft by means of a gas turbine. The sad and sorry saga of official indifference to his brilliant ideas is well known. A luckier engineer was the German Hans von Ohain who, whilst studying at Göttingen University in 1934, designed a simple turbo-jet engine. He patented it and soon interested Ernst Heinkel. In March 1936 he joined the Heinkel organisation to develop his ideas. Official interest in Germany was only marginally greater than in Britain and Heinkel was not popular in the higher echelons of the *Luftwaffe* and the Government. In March 1937 a demonstration engine operating on hydrogen gas had been built, developing a thrust of 550 lb (249.7 kg). Ohain's work was unknown to Whittle who, at the time the German demonstration engine had been run, had just commenced running his first WU engine, the actual date being 12 April 1937. von Ohain developed a new engine to run on kerosene to develop a thrust of 1,100 lb (499 kg) and Heinkel designed the He 178, the world's first gas turbine propelled aeroplane.

The first of two prototype engines was flown under a piston engined He118 in 1939 whilst the second engine was fitted to the He 178 which was first flown by *Flugkapitän* Erich Warsitz on 27 August 1939 after a number of taxying trials and short hops. Flying from Marienehe airfield the undercarriage failed to retract and a bird strike caused the engine to fail soon after take-off. A safe dead-stick landing was made. The test programme continued until November 1939 when the *Luftwaffe* hierarchy, Milch, Udet and Lucht were persuaded to see the He 178 fly. The speed achieved was not particularly noteworthy due to engine problems and directional instability developed at about 390 mph (628 km/hr). Production of current aircraft was top priority so no major moves were made to give official support to von Ohain. Heinkel, however, was sufficiently convinced to design a twin jet fighter prototype, the He 280, which first flew on 2 April 1941 with new Heinkel engines developing 1,102 lb (500 kg) of thrust. Prior to this first flight, in the hands of Fritz Schafer, the machine had been flown as a glider, towed into the air by a Heinkel He 111. Handling was good and it was fitted with perhaps the first ejection seat, operated by compressed air. The turning point in *Luftwaffe* interest was the demonstration of the He 280 on Marienehe on 5 April 1941. Junkers took over turbine development and Messerschmitt began work on the brilliant Me 262 twin-jet fighter, one of the outstanding aircraft of the war. It first flew on 18 April 1941 with a 1,200 h.p. Junkers Jumo piston engine and propeller as the turbines of the thrust required were not available. The small Heinkel turbines from the He 280 were fitted but their thrust of 1,000 lb (454 kg) was not sufficient to lift it off the ground. Later, two BMW Spandau engines of 990 lb (450 kg) thrust were fitted as well as the piston engine. There were turbine failures both on take-off and, later, in the air. The first flight of the definitive Me 262 with Junkers 109 engines of 1,852 lb (840 kg) thrust was made on 18 July 1942 but, in August it was badly damaged during a take-off accident at Leipheim with *Dipl Ing* Beauvais, a Rechlin pilot, at the controls. It was rebuilt but, after a few flights, it crashed and killed its pilot.

For such a radical design the Me 262 test programme proceeded relatively smoothly. The outer wings had leading edge slots, which tended to open slightly due to wing deflection, causing drag. Aileron flutter occurred at Mach 0.8 with aeroelastic deformation and compressibility effects causing a nose-down pitch with increased elevator load. Ultimately the machine was cleared to 621 mph (1,000 km/hr) in the dive. The maximum level speed at 22,966 ft (7,000 m) was between 539 mph (868 km/hr) and 510 mph (820 km/hr) dependant upon air temperature. The main problems with the test programme were the tendency of the turbines to flame-out at altitude with compressor stall at high speeds and high altitude. The turbines in this aeroplane were of axial flow type whilst Whittle concentrated upon the less efficient but more reliable centrifugal flow compressor. The German engines were unreliable and had a time between overhauls of only 10 hours with a life of only 25 hours. Another major hazard for the pilot was the single-engine safety speed of 180 mph (290 km/hr), so an engine failure on take-off at an airspeed below this figure was often fatal. The night fighter version with its heavy load of radar gear was even more lethal. Nevertheless there can be no question that the Me 262 was one of the finest aircraft of the war and it was fortunate for the Allies that the constant diversions caused by Hitler's demands for it as a bomber rather than a fighter held up production for many months. It was fortunate for the pilots of the Allied bomber fleets that it came into service too late to make a major impact on the success of the bombing raids deep into Germany.

Messerschmitt Me 262 in process of being re-finished. (Flypast)

Messerschmitt Me 163B being prepared for a test flight. The small constant speed propeller on the nose drives a generator to provide in-flight electric power. The nose cone is made of 15 mm armour plate and the windscreen of 90 mm armoured glass. Early models had two 20 mm Mauser cannons which were later replaced by 30 mm Rheinmetall-Borsig weapons. They were installed in the wing root.
(Aeroplane Monthly)

CHAPTER 6

The Second World War - III

The Me 262 was the second radical fighter to be developed by Messerschmitt designers; the other was the Me 163, a product of the brilliant Dr Alexander Lippisch's advanced aerodynamic research and that of the designer of the rocket engine Helmuth Walter. The Horten brothers had proved the feasibility of swept wing gliders with no horizontal stabilizer and, through various research projects by these eminent engineers, the design of the Me 163 emerged as a very high speed interceptor with a phenomenal rate of climb for an extremely short duration. One of the research aircraft gave the pilot an unpleasant shock. A Heinkel 112 piston engined fighter was used as a test vehicle in 1937. It was equipped with a rocket motor powered by liquid oxygen and methyl alcohol in, of course, two separate tanks with the combustion chamber in the tail. Test pilot Erich Warsitz from the *Luftwaffe* test centre at Rechlin prepared for take-off at the Kummersdorff test airfield by opening the throttle of the Jumo engine; as he followed with the throttle of the rocket motor a violent explosion blew the aeroplane apart, the engine and components raining down among the spectators. Miraculously, Warsitz was hurled out of the cockpit sustaining only slight injuries. A further 112 with a DB601 engine was converted, this time the first flight was successful but the duration was only 30 seconds. On the third flight, with full fuel tanks, Warsitz closed down the rocket engine, immediately smelling burning and finding the cockpit filling with smoke. He was about to bale out but realised that he was too low so came in for a crash landing. To his embarrassment it was found that the fire was only a small quantity of residual fuel left in the tail pipe after shut-down.

A new fuel was developed, this was a mixture of hydrazine hydrate, methyl alcohol and a solution of cupracyanide in water. This component was known as C-stoff, the other component, T-stoff was a hydrogen peroxide solution; a violent reaction occurred in the combustion chamber as soon as these two elements met. Unfortunately an equally violent reaction took place outside the combustion chamber, this characteristic proving to be extremely hazardous to ground crews and pilots of the Me 163. The design progressed via a series of experimental gliders and research aircraft until, in the spring of 1941, two prototypes were delivered from the Augsburg works of Messerschmitt to a nearby *Luftwaffe* base, Lechfeld, where a much larger airfield was available. The rocket engines, designed to be controllable by the pilot between 331 lb (150.3 kg) and 1,655 lb (750.5 kg) thrust and capable of being re-lit in the air, were not yet available so test pilot Heini Dittmar carried out preliminary trials towed to altitude behind a Bf110. These were most satisfactory, the machine having a gliding angle of six degrees, but as speed increased in the dive the rudder fluttered dangerously at 225 mph (362.3 km/hr) and, at 325 mph (523.3 km/hr) the ailerons developed flutter. Adjustment of the mass balances on the control surfaces cured this problem and the design was soon seen to have very agreeable flying characteristics; even as a glider it could achieve the remarkable speed of 528 mph (850 km/hr).

Not until 13 August 1941 was a new prototype flown at Pennemünde by Dittmar. Rudolf Opitz, a leading test pilot, was sent there to share testing with him. Take-off was made with a twin-wheel bogie under the fuselage, which was dropped as soon as a height of about 30 ft (9.1 m) was reached. There were instances of the bogie bouncing back into the air and hitting the aircraft with disastrous results. The landing was made on a spring mounted skid. Opitz was briefed to make the third powered flight. He was so amazed at the spectacular take-off performance that he forgot to jettison the bogie before reaching 100 ft (30.5 m) so decided to leave it in position and land on it rather than drop it and break it. He made a very good landing to the surprise and relief of the onlookers who were apprehensive of serious directional instability, the bogie not being designed for landing purposes.

The success of the first three flights persuaded the team to make an attempt upon the target speed of 1000 km/hr (621.4 mph). On 2 October 1941, Opitz, flying a Bf110, towed Dittmar to 13,000 ft (3,962 m); he cast off and fired the rocket engine soon reaching 1003 km/hr (623.26 mph) – Mach 0.84. At that point the aircraft encountered compressibility effect and began to pitch down fairly violently, the fuel supply being cut off due to the negative G generated. Dittmar soon regained control as speed decayed and made a safe landing.

By this time it had become apparent that the aircraft offered potential as a high-speed interceptor and Ernst Udet was very enthusiastic about such a project. Messerschmitt put forward proposals which would lead to the formation of a fighter group early in 1943. Top priority was given to it but much of the momentum disappeared when Udet committed suicide in November 1941. His successor, Erhard Milch was less enthusiastic about the rocket interceptor and gave it a low priority – fortunately for the Allies. Work proceeded on a new version with armament and appropriate military equipment. Various prototypes were flown as gliders as the engines intended for them were not ready. Not until 29 April 1941 was one flown with the correct engine designed to develop 3,310 lb (1501.4 kg) of thrust.

To assist in the test programme another pilot, *Hauptmann* Wolfgang Spate was drafted from the Russian front. After an initial flight in which, on take-off, the 163 was seriously affected by the uneven surface of the airfield and he was hurled into the air with insufficient flying speed, Spate confirmed even more forcibly that the bogie was allowing severe porpoising to occur, hydraulic dampers were built into it.

The rudder and elevons were virtually inoperative until a fairly high speed had been achieved, rotate speed was 174 mph (280 km/hr). Approach speed was 137 mph (220 km/hr) and the landing was made at 99 mph (160 km/hr). The wing loading was 42.82 lb/sq ft at take-off and 21.93 lb/sq ft on landing. The top speed was about 600 mph (966 km/hr) at 30,000 ft (9,144 m). It was soon realised that some form of high altitude chamber would be necessary to condition pilots to the violent changes in altitude at high speeds, it being possible to reach 30,000 ft (9,144 m) in 2.6 min. One had been captured from the Russians and was installed. Pilots were taken to a simulated 40,000 ft (12,192 m) at increasing speeds. They were also fed a special diet to reduce the incidence of problems with internal gas.

A major difficulty which emerged from the test programme was the absence of adequate springing on the bogie – already Dittmar and Opitz had suffered spinal damage due to travelling over rough ground on the skid. Investigations indicated that 'G' forces of between 15 and 30G would have been necessary to have caused their injuries so, as it was not practical to improve the springing of the bogie, the seat was mounted upon springs.

Engine failure after take-off was a fairly regular occurrence. Opitz experienced it just after take-off when the aircraft was crossing the boundary at 240 mph (386.4 km/hr). By very clever flying he was able to return to base for a safe landing full of the very dangerous fuel. Any rupture in the tanks would have spelt disaster as soon as the two chemicals met each other. Another hazard which faced Me 163 pilots was the certainty that if a fuel leak penetrated the cockpit and reached the skin the pilot would literally be dissolved. Special protective overalls were supplied but they were not entirely proof against burning.

On the next flight he had another engine failure on take-off. This problem was found to be due to a venting system which did not operate correctly when the aircraft was fuelled and was in the inclined angle for take-off. The G forces on take-off and related turbulence at the T-stoff outlet sucked bleed air out causing the auto fuel control to shut down the engine. This was soon rectified. The training sessions supervised by the test pilots ran into a bad patch. One of the pilots, Joschi Pöhs, took off on 30 December and released his bogie prematurely, which bounced up to hit the aircraft, damaging one of the fuel lines. Power was reduced so he banked around to return for a landing. He took too much time to lower the flaps and the skid so lost so much height that he could not avoid a flak tower on the boundary. The Me 163 hit the tower which caused total loss of control, the aircraft crashing and killing the pilot.

In another accident one of the trainees, Alois Wörndl, reached altitude and, as the fuel was exhausted, dived towards the field and zoomed up again ready for another dive. He did not realize his distance from the airfield and found himself too far away to glide to it. He touched down on rough ground. The Me 163 overturned, hurling Wörndl out of the cockpit. The aircraft exploded and the pilot was found to have his legs and neck broken.

The distinction between test flying and operational flying became blurred with this aircraft as, initially, only the test pilots could train new pilots who did not have the advantage of a two-seat version. There were cases of pilots who made a rough landing with a quantity of each fuel in the tanks and feed lines. This could result in a catastrophic explosion and quite often did. Hanna Reitsch, the legendary German aviatrix, became a test pilot during the war. One of her most courageous sorties was in a V1 flying bomb which, under development, was showing disturbing signs of instability and unreliability. She suggested that a cockpit should be built into one of them which she would fly. She did so and the problem was solved. Her involvement with the Me 163 was as a test pilot for the unpowered pre-production aircraft. On one such flight the bogie refused to drop on release so she decided to land with it in position. At 100 ft (30.4 m) the machine stalled and crashed. Reitsch suffering six fractures of her skull and a displaced jaw bone.

A British pilot who had an opportunity to fly the Me 163 was Lt-Cmdr Eric 'Winkle' Brown, now Capt. R.N. (Rtd), a pilot of vast experience who, for a time was chief naval test pilot at Farnborough. As a fluent German speaker he was a member of the British team in Germany studying their aviation technology. He was intrigued by the concept of the Me 163 and wanted to fly one. He had met Hanna Reitsch who had painted a depressing picture of its dangerous peccadilloes. He was in the process of flying all the German aircraft which could be found in airworthy condition. He talked to the Me163 instructors who were not markedly more encouraging than Hanna. As the real problem seemed to be the lethal fuel rather than the aeroplane he flew several of them at Fassburg in the gliding mode, hoping to fly the powered version which had been taken to Farnborough. He was disappointed to learn that it had been decided that no powered flights should be undertaken. He watched a demonstration by the designer of the rocket motor, Dr Walter. He took a glass rod and dipped it in T-stoff, another rod was dipped in C-stoff. He let both drops fall to the floor, when they met there was a violent explosion. As Capt. Brown said in his book *Wings of the Luftwaffe*:

'I might not have agreed with the boffins' decision not to risk powered flight in the air, but at least now I understand it!'

The Germans admitted that 80 per cent of all accidents to the Me 163, known as the Komet, resulted from take-off or landing crashes. Only 5 per cent were combat casualties. Eric Brown first flew one at Fassburg in 1945 and was very impressed by its flying characteristics. His first flight in the Farnborough aircraft was a year later, at Wisley, Vickers airfield, when he was towed to altitude by a Spitfire and flew for 25 minutes. Again, he was very impressed commenting upon the delightful harmony of the controls and thoroughly satisfactory stability characteristics. It was difficult to detect any facet of handling that characterised the aircraft as tail-less.

Not until September 1947 was Eric Brown able to fly it again. He carried out a series of sorties to establish its fast landing characteristics: Wisley was too small for this programme so the trials were carried out at RAF Wittering. He built up the speeds from 133 mph (214 km/hr) without flaps. A later sortie brought him in to land at 158 mph (254 km/hr). As he landed the skid collapsed, came up into the fuselage and rammed the oleo supports up into the cockpit jamming the rudder bar to port. The aircraft veered round to port with the pilot's legs jammed up into the instrument panel. The port wing hit the ground and bits of the aeroplane were being shed as it travelled 610 yards (558 m) coming to rest just short of the airfield perimeter. Eric was trapped by his legs in the cockpit and it took some time to release him. He was extremely concerned about the possibility of spinal injury but, fortunately, heavy bruising from the base of his spine upwards and cuts and abrasions were his only injuries. The aircraft never flew again but it left Capt. Brown with the conviction that it was one of the most sensational aircraft of the war. It was of little operational significance because of its very high closing speed and limited duration of four minutes. His judgement of the Me 262 was equally complimentary. He said:

> 'In my view it was unquestionably the foremost warplane of its day; a hard-hitter which out-performed anything that we had immediately available . . . It was a pilot's aeroplane which had to be flown and not just heaved into the air . . . it was thoroughly exciting to fly'.

There can be no question whatsoever that if Frank Whittle had received the support in Britain that Ohain enjoyed in Germany the RAF would have had at least one jet fighter in action well before the *Luftwaffe*. With limited finance and in spite of scepticism in high places his patent of 1932 bore fruit and, by 1938 he had overcome many problems and had run an experimental engine, the WU, (Whittle Unit) at 16,500 rpm for thirty minutes. The visit of David Pye, Director of Scientific Research at Air Ministry initiated support for the production of an engine for flight trials.

George Carter, chief designer of Glosters, was consulted by Whittle. Carter was very impressed with the concept which Whittle outlined and showed him the design of a twin boom Sabre-engined fighter which seemed ideal as a project for jet power. Initially the engine would be test flown in a small experimental aircraft, the E28/39, of which two would be built. In the meantime Whittle and his engineers were working to squeeze the last ounce of thrust out of the experimental engines. The prototype, semi-officially known as *Pioneer* unofficially christened at Glosters, the *Squirt* was ready, on 7 April 1941 for taxying trials at Gloster's test airfield at Brockworth in the hands of the chief test pilot Flt Lt P.E.G. 'Gerry' Sayer. The engine had been restricted to a maximum of 13,000 rpm instead of the design figure of 17,500: Gerry was surprised to find that the aircraft did not move until the rpm reached 12,000. It was not appreciated that the thrust of a gas turbine

Gerry Sayer in the cockpit of the Gloster E28/39. (Michael Daunt)

builds up slowly to its peak in the last few thousand revs. Up to 13,000 rpm acceleration was poor but controllability on the ground was good. On the following day the rpm was allowed to rise to 16,000 giving a ground speed of 60 mph (97 km/hr). There was insufficient power in the elevators to lift the nosewheel in spite of the tailplane being larger than usual to compensate for the absence of propeller slipstream. At 16,000 rpm three short hops were made. Sayer was very impressed with the smoothness of the engine which ran well although most of the effective power was controlled by a small movement of the throttle at the top end of the quadrant, this gave the impression of coarseness.

After modifications to the undercarriage to increase the length of the nosewheel leg and various other small matters arising from the taxying trials the E28 was taken to RAF Cranwell for the first flight from the long runway there. The degree of official interest in the aircraft was manifest by the fact that there was no official cameraman to photograph or film this historic flight. The only record of it is a group of photographs taken by Michael Daunt with his own small camera. During the evening of 15 May Gerry Sayer opened the throttle and began his take-off; after 500-600 yards (457-549 m) run the E28 lifted off and climbed to 1000 ft (305 m), she was an attractive sight as Sayer banked round to return for his landing 17 minutes later, he appeared to be completely confident of the aeroplane. Frank Whittle was naturally very tense to see the satisfactory culmination of his hard work and battle for support. It is said that as the E28 left the ground another member of the group watching slapped him on the back exclaiming,

'Frank, it flies!'

He curtly responded,

'Well, that was what it was bloody-well designed to do, wasn't it?'

The success of this flight aroused interest at Government level and work began in developing a twin jet fighter, the Gloster F9/40, later to become the Meteor.

A major programme of flight test of the E28 prototype, W4041, began. The second one, W4046, soon joined the programme and, by mid 1943 two years of test flying had proved beyond doubt the value of Whittle's work which was, by that time, being evaluated at RAE Farnborough. On 27 July W/Cdr Charles McClure, OC Engine Flight, was to climb to 30,000 ft (9,144 m) where the air temperature would be about -33°C; after 52 minutes in the air he refuelled and took off again to climb to 35,000 ft (10,668 m). This sortie was satisfactorily completed. His next flight was to investigate the response of the airframe and the engine to negative G at an altitude lower than 10,000 ft (3048 m). He performed loops during which no problems were experienced; during negative G manoeuvres the engine ran roughly but soon recovered.

Next, McClure entered a stall turn, the aircraft going onto its back in a dive. During recovery the rudder jammed at full deflection, the pilot was able to centralize it but it then moved over to the other full lock, the engine flaming-out. He managed to recover and made a hasty gliding return to Farnborough where a close inspection revealed only a piece of loose fabric. It was suspected that the sub-zero temperature had affected the aileron controls so little more could be done other than dismantle them and check everything. W/Cdr H.J. 'Willie' Wilson, the OC of the Aerodynamics Flight, was quoted as saying:

'The E28 was the first aeroplane I have ever flown where you could see the fuel gauge needle moving the whole time the engine was running!'

His assistant, S/Ldr W.D.B.S. Davie, was briefed to carry out an investigation of the aileron problem on the following morning. During his climb to 37,000 ft (11,278 m) he noted a degree of backlash in the ailerons; reaching his ceiling, the control column would only move about half of its normal travel and a further attempt to move it locked it solidly half way to starboard. Suddenly the E28 went violently out of control hurling Davie through the canopy without oxygen mask or goggles and with only one glove at 33,000 ft (10,058 m). He had the presence of mind to put the emergency oxygen tube in his mouth and landed, shaken and frostbitten near Guildford. An investigation of the wreckage indicated that the control cables had slackened due to differential expansion of the steel strands and the light alloy wing, this difficulty being compounded by the use of the wrong lubricant on the cables within the compressed and bonded fabric fairleads. The whole of the test programme now rested upon the hard-worked first prototype. At this stage it became evident that, as jet propulsion allowed operation or altitudes far in excess of those currently considered appropriate, the physiological problems faced by pilots would be of great importance. The Institute of Aviation Medicine at Farnborough had, for years, been studying all aspects of the subject so a greater degree of urgency was conferred upon their work. It is appropriate to refer to the little-publicised work of the doctor pilots and others in the Institute. In 1932 Cyril Uwins, chief test pilot of the Bristol Aeroplane Company established a new world altitude record of 43,976 ft (13,404 m) in a Vickers Vespa open cockpit biplane. This was the first time that an Englishman had held this record. Before the flight he had consulted the Physiological Laboratory where he was allowed access to the decompression chamber at RAE to experience hypoxia which would be a possible hazard during his flight wearing standard RAF oxygen equipment but breathing pure oxygen. Later developments allowed S/Ldr F.D.R. Swain to climb to 49,957 ft (15,227 m) in 1936 and F/Lt M.J. Adam to reach 53,937 ft (16,440 m) in 1937, both pilots flying the special high altitude Bristol 138 monoplane. In these flights full pressure suits were worn by the pilots.

The test programme of the E28/39 was interrupted by the death of Gerry Sayer in a collision between two Typhoons. Michael Daunt, just recovered from his disastrous experience in the Folland 'Frightful' who had worked closely with Sayer, was appointed chief test pilot and was responsible for the first flight of the new twin-engine W9/40 which was delayed by problems with production of the two Whittle engines, for the prototype. The Rover car company was initially responsible for production of these engines to be known as the Rover WB Series 3 with a thrust of 1,500 lb (681 kg). The de Havilland Engine Company was developing Frank Halford's H 1 gas turbine which differed from the Whittle design in having a single-sided compressor impeller, the air being entrained only at

The pilot being assembled into the pressure suit before flying the high-altitude Bristol 138A seen in the background. (British Aerospace Airbus, Bristol)

the front. Whittle drew in air for his double-sided impeller at the front and rear of the engine via the nacelle shell which was smaller in diameter than the H 1 nacelle. The delay with the Rover engines led the Air Ministry to insist that the H 1 be fitted for the first flights, so nacelle alterations were necessary.

During engine runs at Bentham, Michael Daunt had an alarming experience which could have been fatal. He was wearing a leather flying coat which was unbuttoned, he leaned forward to peer into the nacelle to check for fuel leaks when the coat tail was sucked into the intake, Michael following immediately, head first. Fortunately the engineer in the cockpit moved very swiftly and closed the throttle and Daunt had the presence of mind to keep his mouth tightly shut until he was dragged out very shaken. His comment was:

'I was the third thing to be sucked in, the others being a hat and a tea tray'.

Steel guards were then used across all intakes during engine running; they became known as Daunt screens!

The first flight was made on 5 March 1943 by Michael Daunt. RAE had suggested that instability in pitch might result from the effect of the jet efflux upon the tailplane, so it was decided to run the engines at 8,000 rpm giving less than 1,500 lb (681 kg) of thrust for this take-off, which is of vital importance in any test programme. From the first lift-off the feel of the controls is analysed and the landing speed, obviously greater than the take-off speed, is assessed. As speed rose to 180 mph (290 km/hr) the aircraft behaved perfectly, then suddenly a violent yawing caused the rudder bar to oscillate with such force that Mike could not hold it, so an immediate landing was made. Even on this short flight much had been learned. Daunt had identified an out-of-balance nosewheel; he had carried out experiments to trace the origin of the directional instability and a fault had been detected in the undercarriage shock absorption system – all this in three and a half minutes. As Michael said afterwards:

'The job of the test pilot at that time is that of a diagnostician, later it changes into a very, very intelligent monitor.'

– a somewhat tongue in cheek observation!

Brockworth was too small for the Meteor test programme so a base was established at Moreton Valence RAF Station, south of Gloucester, which already had a runway capable of extension to 2,000 yards (1,830 m); after completion of the extension the flight test department moved there. The yaw problem was cured by the time-honoured expedient of taping a length of cord to each side of the rudder trailing edge. Single-engine handling proved to be satisfactory although, with the H 1 engines, performance was inadequate. A further prototype, fitted with Metropolitan Vickers F2 axial-flow turbines was delivered. The two Meteors and the E28/39 fitted with the Whittle W2/500 engine enabled good progress to be made. The work of the Gloster team was supported by the engine test pilots at the Rolls-Royce test flight facility. A Merlin engined Wellington II was converted to mount the Whittle W2B, later to become the Welland, gas turbine in place of the rear turret. The test engineer was incarcerated in the tail, his name was Clarke, generally known as 'Gassy'. During the regular 'flame-outs' of the engine the poor man, muffled up in thick clothing to give slight protection against the freezing outside air temperatures, was almost choked with the dense kerosene fumes until he could cut off the fuel supply. Jim Heyworth the test pilot, later to become chief test pilot when his brother, Harvey, retired, judged when this had been done by the cessation of gasping and choking noises in his intercom. Rolls-Royce also flew a Meteor prototype with the W2B engine. As Hucknall was too small for the aircraft the flights were made from nearby Church Broughton. On a hot day so much power was lost that all of the 6,000 ft (1,830 m) available run was needed to coax the Meteor into the air and over the low fence along the Uttoxeter road – all traffic was halted whilst a take-off took place.

The Type Test of 100 hours was passed giving a thrust of 1,600 lb (726 kg) for a weight of 850 lb (386 kg). These engines powered the few Meteor Is that were built. The top speed was about 410 mph (660 km/hr) which was only as fast as the Spitfire IX. The Me 262 was already flying at over 500 mph (805 km/hr). The Welland was re-designed to become the more powerful W2B/37, later the RB37 Derwent. This was fitted to the Meteor III with 2,000 lb (908 kg) thrust. This increased the speed to 470 mph (756.7 km/hr).

Wellington Mk II with Whittle W2B jet engine installed in the tail. (Rolls-Royce plc)

Avro Lancastrian flying test-bed with de Havilland Ghost turbines in outer nacelles. 1947.
(British Aerospace, Hatfield)

During the Gloster test programme two serious problems emerged. The engines surged and there was aileron instability. Surging usually began on the climb at about 14,000 ft (4,270 m) with violent 'hiccupping' which could result in structural failure. On one flight Mike Daunt's port engine began to surge at 25,000 ft (7,620 m). He descended in a shallow dive at 320 mph (515 km/hr); at this speed the ailerons showed a serious overbalance. Between 20,000 and 15,000 ft (6,100 and 4,570 m) they were satisfactory again although speed had increased to 360 mph (580 km/hr).

Many modifications were made to overcome the problem but none worked at both low and high altitude. Directional instability also re-appeared. During dives at high speed aileron flutter was apparent; internal mass balancing cured this. A streamlined bullet at the fin/tailplane intersection was successful in improving directional stability but was not the whole answer.

At Boscombe Down 'T' Flight was set up under a new Ministry of Aircraft Production Department, H.J. 'Willie' Wilson, by then promoted to Wing Commander, was in command charged with the evaluation of the early jet engines and the aircraft to be fitted with them; these were the Meteor and de Havilland Vampire with the Halford H 1 engine.

Although they were initially slow to accept the value of jet propulsion the Americans had, in fact, had in circulation as far back as 1923 a Technical Report covering the principles of the new prime mover. The NACA Laboratory at Langley Field revived it in 1939 as rumours of progress in Europe circulated. Research work on an engine was planned by General Electric whilst the German and British work carried on in great secrecy. In 1941 General 'Hap' Arnold, chief of the US Army Air Corps, was touring UK military establishments and heard, to his astonishment, that the first flight of the Gloster Whittle E28 was only weeks away. He immediately arranged for drawings to be sent across the Atlantic; later, a Whittle W IX engine was despatched to the GE Laboratories at West Lynn, Massachusetts.

The USAAF invited the Bell Aircraft Corporation to develop a jet fighter with a GE 1-A engine developed from the Whittle W IX. The XP-59 Airacomet first flew on 1 October 1942, thirteen months later. Thirteen were built, one being tested in the large wind tunnel at NACA Langley Field; tests which were the precursor of a major transonic programme at Langley. None of the Airacomets entered squadron service; one was tested at RAE Farnborough, the remainder were tested in USA and were used to familiarize pilots with jet propelled flying techniques.

Bell P-59 Airacomet.
(Wright-Patterson U.S.A.F. Base)

It was the precursor of the first American jet fighter, the Lockheed P-80 Shooting Star powered initially with the de Havilland/Halford H1 engine designed for the Vampire. During 1943 ground running trials it was found that Lockheed had used thin gauge metal for the intake ducts which collapsed at full throttle, the bits were sucked into the engine so DH generously sent over the engine destined for the second Vampire. Test pilot Mich Burcham was so astonished by the performance on the maiden flight that he turned it into a display of spectacular aerobatics, much to the dismay of the senior officials. It was tested at the Muroc Lake Test Centre in the Californian Mojave Desert where unlimited space was available for take-off and landing and problems of security were manageable. This later became Edwards Air Force Base. Testing began at Muroc in 1945. A curious phenomenon became apparent at 35,000 ft (10,670 m) when directional instability developed with a rumble in the intake whenever a sideslip was induced. On one of these sorties the engine flamed-out during a particularly violent sideslip and the pilot, Larry Clousing, was unable to re-light. He prepared for a dead-stick landing on the dry lake bed. As the engine had failed the hydraulic pump was inoperative as he was forced to attempt to lower the undercarriage on the hand pump, at this point he discovered the design of the system left much to be desired and had to make a belly landing. After repair, the tests continued a year later. The Shooting Star became a successful fighter with considerable combat time in the Korean War. Over 1,700 were built.

Michael Daunt and his test team encountered some dangerous situations in the test programme of the Meteor. One take-off ended violently when a compressor disintegrated with a tremendous bang, the debris being ejected, fortunately, through the upper cowling. On another sortie an impeller disintegrated at 5,000 ft (1,524 m), again the debris emerged through the upper cowling seriously damaging the nacelle and tail. The aircraft became laterally unstable and Daunt jettisoned the canopy preparatory to baling out. As speed dropped he realised that there was a chance of saving the machine in spite of the limited control available to him. He made a belly landing in a potato field dismissing the episode in his dry way with:

'This is how we tried out for the first time the Whittle-Daunt potato-lifter-chipper-cooker!'

Both of these engine failures were caused by resonance problems.

Apart from Mike Daunt's own very hazardous experiences which so affected his health that an early retirement from test flying became necessary, two other tragic accidents decimated the highly skilled team of Gloster and RAE test pilots. John Crosby-Warren, whose 6ft 4in (193 cm) frame was difficult to fit in a fighter cockpit, was flying a Meteor on low-level fuel consumption and stability tests. The aircraft suddenly dived into Minchinhampton Common and totally disintegrated. The Farnborough Accidents Investigation Branch carried out their customary meticulous investigation and told Gloster to look for an aileron tab, only an inch or so wide. It was found in a wood; its loss had made the aircraft uncontrollable.

Another victim was an outstanding RAE pilot, S/Ldr Douglas Davie who, on 4 June 1944, took off to fly a series of high speed runs, deputizing for his CO, W/Cdr Willie Wilson who had a serious cold. Onlookers heard a strange noise in the air and looked up to see the Meteor, which was powered by the Metropolitan Vickers Beryl axial-flow engines diving inverted and tail-less. Davie baled out but was unable to open his parachute; he fell through the roof of an RAE shed.

From the trail of wreckage several miles long it was deduced that the port engine compressor had disintegrated at about 15,000 ft (4,572 m) damaging the airframe; the dive completed the airframe disintegration and led to the death of a fine test pilot who had made a major contribution to the technology of flying jet aircraft.

Prolonged diving trials by Michael Daunt, during the course of which rivets popped out of the airframe in a pull-out, the limiting speed of the Meteor was judged to be M 0.76 to 0.77 later increased to 0.84 still considerably inferior to even the Spitfire IX, diving trials of which are recorded in Chapter 9.

By the end of 1944 wind tunnel tests at Farnborough had been carried out to attempt to increase the limiting Mach number. It was suggested that the engine nacelles should be lengthened. This was done with a standard Mk I whilst the more powerful W2/700 engines with 2,000 lb (908 kg) thrust were fitted. There was still insufficient power to achieve high Mach numbers in level flight so all the work was done in dives, a dangerous operation carried out partly by RAE pilots, notably F/Lt Philip Stanbury, a veteran of the Battle of Britain who had been posted to Gloster – presumably for a 'rest', to carry out work started by the unfortunate John Crosby-Warren.

Stanbury found that the aircraft handled well at speeds as high as M 0.84 although the nose began to pitch up as speed rose towards this figure. Normally this pitch was expected to be

Lockheed P-80 Shooting Star.
(Gene Furnish, via Wright-Patterson U.S. Air Force Base)

downwards so it was a bonus as there was an intention to attempt the World Air Speed Record after the war; this was to be flown at very low level. He had a very alarming experience in a Meteor which had been fitted with a pressure cabin. At 40,000 ft (12,192 m) a widescreen panel blew out and the stabilised cockpit atmosphere of around 24,000 ft (7,315 m) instantly changed to his present 40,000 ft (12,192 m) height. He began to lose consciousness and instinctively closed the throttles. Beginning to recover at 28,000 ft (8,535 m) he found that the Meteor, which had a smaller rudder than usual, was in a violent and uneven spin with his head being violently jerked from side to side by the motion. He was severely disoriented and the rudder was inadequate for recovery. Only by applying bursts of power on the inner engine was he able to recover at 3,000 ft (914 m). He felt so ill that he delayed his landing upon a runway which seemed to be rocking from side to side. He spent months in hospital but never entirely recovered from the experience. After the solution of the instability problem he ultimately became the first pilot to achieve 600 mph (972 km/hr) in level flight.

After the war Gp Capt. E.M. Donaldson established a World Record in a special Meteor at 616 mph (992 km/hr).

The prototype Merlin-engined Mustang in 1942. In the background is a Hawker Henley engine test-bed.
(Rolls-Royce plc)

CHAPTER 7

The Second World War – IV

During the period when the Meteor was under development the Americans were building one of the most impressive aircraft of the war, one which was instrumental in saving the lives of hundreds, if not thousands, of aircrew as they flew their bombers deep into enemy territory; this was the North American P–51 Mustang. The Company had received from the Air Ministry in 1938 an order for 200 Harvard I trainers; ultimately over 5,000 were supplied to the British Commonwealth Air Forces; North American had, therefore, a good reputation with the British Purchasing Commission who were keen to procure another fighter to support the Hurricane and Spitfire in RAF service. Building the Curtiss P–40 under licence was briefly considered and rejected. J.H. 'Dutch' Kindelberger, the president of North American, was sure that the firm could offer a superior design so was invited to tender. It was specified that, in view of Britain's desperate position in 1940, a prototype must be completed in 120 days. The NA design team headed by Raymond H. Rice and chief designer Edgar Schmued worked day and night to produce general arrangement drawings for submission. The Commission members were impressed and an order for 320 machines was placed.

The design was of advanced aerodynamic form with a unique laminar-flow wing, powered by an Allison liquid-cooled engine of 1,150 h.p. A major contribution to drag reduction was the radiator located under the centre of the fuselage near to the trailing edge of the wing. The form of the interior ducting was such that drag was reduced and some thrust gained from the entrained air from the radiator matrix. A remarkable feat of organisation achieved completion of the prototype 117 days after the commencement of detail design and the Mustang required only 200 more man-hours of labour to build than the much less complicated Harvard trainer.

On 26 October 1940 Vance Breese, by then chief test pilot of NA, took the machine for its first flight. Initially the V–1710 engine tended to overheat and, on 20 November, it cut out whilst being flown by Paul Balfour who made an error when switching fuel tanks. In the resulting forced landing the aircraft overturned; fortunately Balfour was not seriously hurt and the machine was not a write-off. After repair the flight test programme continued with very few problems. The first production aircraft for the RAF made its first flight on 16 April 1941, the second one was shipped to UK and delivered to Boscombe Down for evaluation. The machine proved to be faster than any contemporary Allied fighter although performance at altitude was inadequate due to limited supercharger power.

The turning point in the fortunes of the Mustang reflected considerable credit upon Ronald W. Harker who was the senior liaison test pilot at Rolls-Royce during the war. He worked closely with the squadrons flying aircraft powered with Rolls-Royce engines. W/Cdr Ian Campbell-Orde was known to him as they both served in the pre-war Auxiliary Air Force. Campbell-Orde commanded the Air Fighting Development Unit at Duxford in

1942 where an Allison-engined Mustang I was under evaluation. Having flown it himself he invited Harker to do so. He was immediately impressed; it had a number of advantages over current fighters. Its fuel capacity was three times that of the Spitfire; the .5" calibre machine guns were highly lethal; the great power of the ailerons gave it a spectacular rate of roll and the airframe with its laminar-flow wing generated low drag which was manifest in the remarkably high top speed.

Ronnie Harker immediately envisaged it with the new Merlin with the two-speed, two-stage supercharger, the 60 series, in which configuration it would be a very effective long range fighter – just what the heavy day bombers needed to stop the carnage over Germany. He asked the Hucknall performance engineers to calculate the performance of the Mustang with this engine, and was impressed to learn that the speed would be increased by 60 mph (96.6 km/hr), whilst the rate of climb and the range would be increased by a useful amount. He immediately visited Ernest Hives (later, Lord Hives) the chairman, and put his case, supported by the performance projections. He asked if a Mustang could be allocated to Hucknall for the conversion to be made.

Hives accepted the wisdom of the suggestion and arranged with Air Marshal Sir Wilfrid Freeman at the Air Ministry to have three aircraft delivered. Conversion began in August 1942 and the first flight took place on 13 October of that year, piloted by Capt Ronald Shepherd. All the predictions were confirmed and the machine was a complete success. The news soon reached Washington when large orders were placed for the USAAF and the RAF. New factories were erected to produce the machine. Over 15,000 were built at the two NA plants. The effect upon the morale of the hard-hit 8th Air Force crews of Fortresses and Liberators flying to distant targets like Berlin when they were escorted all the way by Mustangs can be imagined. Casualties among these heroic crews were very high but would have been immeasurably higher without this brilliant fighter in the form conceived by a perceptive British test pilot.

The very effective running mate of the Mustang in the air war was the Republic Thunderbolt. The Republic Aviation Corporation was originally the Seversky Company which had developed a number of advanced monoplane designs with powerful radial engines. A contract for a high performance fighter for the USAAF was placed in 1940. It was to have two 0.30" machine-guns in each wing and a pair of 0.50" weapons in the fuselage. The all-up weight was to be 6,150 lb (2,790 kg) and the top speed 400 mph (644 km/hr) at 15,000 ft (4,572 m), to which height it must climb in four and half minutes. An Allison engine was envisaged. Battle experience in Europe in 1940 proved that the armament would be inadequate and that vital elements such as fireproof tanks and crew protection armour were sadly lacking in US military aircraft. Moreover, it was considered that the liquid-cooled Allison engine with its vulnerable radiator plumbing system was not the best solution.

Republic decided to commence a new design around the new 2,000 h.p. Pratt & Whitney XR2800 radial engine, so designer Alexander Kartveli produced the drawings of the Thunderbolt to meet the Spec. and produced the heaviest single-engined fighter ever built. The original designation was XP–47B and it had six 0.50" guns, a top speed of 400 mph (644 km/hr) at 25,000 ft (7,620 m), an altitude which could be reached in 5 minutes. The weight was to be 11,600 lb (5,273 kg), nearly twice that of the original design. The complications were daunting. The turbo-supercharger was to be fitted in the fuselage behind the pilot and its ducting presented some formidable aerodynamic and structural problems. It was necessary to use a four-blade propeller to absorb the great power of the engine; it was the first such unit to be fitted to a US fighter. It was almost 13 ft (3.96 m) in diameter so the length of the undercarriage legs to give adequate ground clearance was yet

Republic P-47D Thunderbolt.
(Ken Ellis Collection)

another difficulty. Retraction was only possible by arranging for them to be shortened by 9" (22.9 cm) before retraction.

On 6 May 1941 Lowery L. Brabham, Republic's chief test pilot, flew the prototype from the Farmingdale runway. It was highly satisfactory so production plans were immediately initiated; the first production aircraft, effectively the second prototype, was sent to Wright Field for evaluation by the Army Air Force. Several other aircraft joined the test programme which was marred, on 26 March 1942, by one of them flown by George Burrell, a Republic test pilot, crashing on a Long Island golf course. The pilot was killed and the aircraft destroyed. Examination of the wreckage proved that part of the tail had failed in flight. Restrictions were imposed upon the flight envelope for all test work on the XP–47B pending a full analysis of the accident data. It was found that the fabric covering of the elevator had ripped causing ballooning of the rest of the fabric through suction forces, so the elevators were skinned in light alloy. Another Republic test pilot, Joe Parker, was soon in trouble near New York when he lost all elevator control; this too was in an aircraft with a fabric-covered elevator. He was able to bale out, splashing down in Long Island Sound.

The production Thunderbolt was 650 lb (295 kg) overweight and the rate of climb was not up to the level required but, on the credit side, top speed was nearly 30 mph (48 km/hr) faster at 429 mph (690.7 km/hr).

In squadron service the problems of compressibility were soon experienced and there were a number of teething troubles, inevitable in such a radically new and complex aeroplane. Diving speeds of over 400 mph (644 km/hr) were reached very quickly and pilots found that at high speed the aircraft 'tucked under' as the centre of pressure moved aft, it was fatally easy to induce structural failure in pulling out. In some cases complete loss of control occurred; this could result from either compressibility effects or, in some cases, the failure of the rudder assembly which was down on strength and rigidity. A completely new fin and rudder was fitted but still accidents occurred. Strict limits were applied to diving speeds, initially a limit of 250 mph (402 km/hr) was set above 30,000 ft (9,144 m); this could be increased progressively at decreasing altitude to a maximum of 500 mph (805 km/hr) at 10,000 ft (3,048 m).

On Friday 13 November 1942 Lts Comsrock and Dyar of the USAAF were briefed to carry out high speed runs in P–47Cs. The first was at 35,000 ft (10,668 m) flying at

400 mph (644 km/hr) after which they dived to the next level. They were suddenly locked in a compressibility trap with an indicated air speed of 725 mph (1,167 km/hr). After suffering violent buffeting they reached lower levels where the warmer air allowed them to regain control. The actual air speeds were in the region of 500 mph (805 km/hr).

Slowly all the operational bugs were eliminated from the 'Jug', short for 'Juggernaut' as it was affectionately known. The cost was considerable, during Service tests 41 aircraft were lost, killing 13 pilots. Nevertheless it proved to be a 'crashworthy' aircraft, pilots surviving crashes which would have totally destroyed most fighters, together with their pilots. By the end of 1945 over 15,000 of the type had been built and the Jug created for itself an enviable reputation once its pilots had become accustomed to its great size. It was, unquestionably, one of the great aircraft of the war.

Development work on the new W34 naval fighter, later to be named Wyvern, was commencing in the shops when, in September 1944 Petter had a disagreement with the Board over a question of management policy and resigned to join English Electric at Warton where his remarkable design ability was responsible for the Canberra and the Lightning, both outstanding post-war military aircraft.

An important event of great significance to test flying standards was the formation of the Empire Test Pilots' School in 1943. Since then the ETPS has gone from strength to strength and its example was followed by the Americans who formed a similar School at Patuxent River, Maryland under the control of the US Navy; the USAF have one at Edwards Air Force Base in California. After the War the French School at Istres, the Italian one at Rome and the German School at Manching were opened with syllabi similar to that of ETPS.

A display by Martin Baker at the 50th Anniversary gathering of the ETPS, which recorded that over 6,000 lives have been saved by Martin Baker ejection seats, was a reminder of the risks taken by those men such as Bernard Lynch who carried out the first live trials of these remarkable life-saving devices. Chapter 2 records the work of Sir James Martin in the development of cable cutters to protect bombers from balloon cables. His work on ejection seats is said to have been inspired by a tragic crash which killed his partner Capt. Valentine Baker. In 1938 Martin Baker built a simple fighter, the MB 2, powered by an 805 h.p. Napier Dagger engine. The undercarriage was fixed and faired with trouser-type fairings. It was Britain's first eight-gun fighter and had a very creditable performance which would have been of considerable value in the Battle of Britain in supporting the hard pressed Hurricanes and Spitfires. The Air Ministry rejected it, probably because the firm was not a member of the all-powerful Society of British Aircraft Constructors – 'The Family' as those who were not members derisively called it. Martin Baker followed it with a new design, the MB 3 powered by a 2,000 h.p. Napier Sabre engine. Again, simplicity of manufacture and maintenance was a prime feature of the aircraft. Its performance was very promising but its potential was not to be realised. On 12 September 1942 as Val Baker took off the Sabre engine failed; in trying to save the MB 3 by a very difficult forced landing he crashed into a field and was killed. Later came the outstanding MB 5 with a 2,340 h.p. Griffon engine driving contra-rotating propellers. This handsome aeroplane with a distinct resemblance to the Mustang was well ahead of contemporary fighters in its performance with a top speed of 460 mph (736 km/hr). It, too, had the merits of easy assembly and maintenance but officialdom was not interested. The famous Polish test pilot Jan Zurakowski carried out an outstanding demonstration at the 1946 Farnborough Show and those RAF pilots who flew it regarded it as a brilliant design.

So, after the tragedy of Val Baker's death and the frustrations with the aircraft, Jimmy Martin decided to concentrate upon life-saving devices. As fighter speeds rose it became clear in 1943/44 that some form of assisted ejection for pilots was essential. After flirting

Martin Baker MB 5.
(Martin Baker Ltd.)

with a primitive lever hinged near the fin to literally lift the pilot out of the cockpit a Defiant turret fighter was converted to carry such a device and Rotol's chief test pilot, Bryan Greensted, carried out some dummy ejections in May 1945. It soon became clear that such a design was of little value in many aircraft so Martin decided that the answer lay in the forced ejection of the pilot's seat. The problems of such an arrangement were physiological rather than technical as it was not possible to ascertain the maximum 'G' force which the human form could withstand in a rocket-propelled departure from the cockpit. An inclined ramp was set up at the Martin Baker works along which the seat could be propelled at varying speeds and accelerations using dummies to assess the forces. It soon became necessary to ask for human volunteers; an experimental fitter, Bernard Lynch, came forward to experience the first ride and, on 24 January 1945 he was fired up to a height of 4 ft 8 ins (1.42 m); three more tests took him to a height of 9 ft 11 ins (3 m) at which stage acute physical discomfort was experienced. The series of tests continued to the stage of live ejections by Bennie Lynch. 180 live ejections were made from the Defiant by Lynch and officers from the RAF, the Navy and the Ministry of Aircraft Production. The Institute of Aviation Medicine was deeply involved in monitoring the physiological aspect of the work and gave valuable advice. A/Cdre E.A. Lumley, the Principal Medical Officer of Fighter Command and W/Cdr W.K. Stewart of the IAM, referred to earlier, were among the first officers to eject.

Investigations into the circumstances under which one man sustained a crushed vertebra led Martin to obtain a human spine and carry out tests upon it. This led to the conclusion that ejections must take place with the spine erect and the vertebrae absolutely square to each other with peak accelerations limited to 20 G. The ejection guns were developed within these parameters. It soon became necessary to increase the aircraft speed to simulate ejections from current fighters so a Meteor was converted. On 24 June 1946 a dummy was ejected at 415 mph (668 km/hr). This introduced other problems which were satisfactorily overcome, Benny Lynch making the first live ejection from this aircraft at 320 mph (515 km/hr) on 24 July 1946 flying at 8,000 ft (2,438 m). It was entirely successful, Lynch reporting that no aerodynamic shock was experienced on ejection, proof of the smoothness of the ejection gun.

The US Navy showed keen interest in the work and soon set up its own programme using a test rig built by Martin Baker at Philadelphia Navy Yard. Space precludes reference to the dedicated development work carried out by the Martin Baker team until the ultimate 'zero-zero' seat was developed which Benny Lynch proved when he ejected from a Meteor at take-off speed on the runway – a remarkable example of cold courage on – 3 September 1955. The aircraft was being flown by S/Ldr Fifield who was the Martin Baker test pilot. Two classic cases of the value of this facility will be recorded later in the book, George Aird ejecting from a Lightning at a height of not much over 100 ft (30.5 m) near Hatfield and Bill Bedford ejecting at a few hundred feet from a crippled P–1127 when a lift nozzle broke away in flight.

The dangerous work carried out by Benny Lynch and his colleague, W.T. 'Doddy' Hay under the direction of Sir James Martin and his team cannot be over-rated in terms of its effect upon the morale of air crew flying military aircraft at high speeds and low level, to say nothing of the knowledge that even in a take-off accident they still have a very good chance of ejection and survival. It must also be most comforting for their families to realise the level of protection which the ejection seat can offer. In 1948 Benny Lynch was awarded the British Empire Medal; some might consider that a higher award was fully justified, Sir James was, of course, knighted for his work on many valuable projects over many years.

Military gliders offered an unusual form of activity for war-time test pilots. The Airspeed Horsa provided some memorable sorties from late 1942 onwards. George Errington made the first flight towed by a Whitley piloted by Flt Lt W.R.H. Carter, a Royal New Zealand Air Force officer. Some of the flying was carried out at Fairey's Great West Road airfield, now part of London Airport. On one flight the Whitley climbed too fast and when Nick Carter reduced height again the long tow rope sagged into a huge bow which scraped across the telephone wires bordering the Great West Road making a loud scream audible for a great distance. The effect on the telephone system remains a mystery.

Full load trials were carried out at Baginton and Honiley, near Coventry where the usual Midlands smog handicapped the pilots, particularly in the autumn and winter. On one full-load flight the two aircraft wallowed laboriously upwards, the throttles of the Whitley being fully open, suddenly they unintentionally rose above the cloud base. George Errington admitted afterwards that it was one of the worst experiences of his career; at first he was able to follow the tunnel-like vortices streaming off the propellers of the tug, he then lost contact and fell far below it. Nick Carter had to use all his strength and both hands to hold the control column forward to prevent a disastrous stall. For a moment he wondered if George had forsaken the controls of the Horsa for the Elsan, fortunately as the two aircraft staggered through the sky they descended below the cloud base again.

One of the problems of the Horsa was the jettisonable undercarriage; it did not always depart cleanly, one of the leg assemblies remained suspended from its anchorage, likely to go at the least provocation. Flying from Netheravon with three tons of concrete ballast, Nick Carter's crew were not amused to be ordered to jettison it so that a safe landing could be made alongside a hill as one of the legs remained in position. On another flight one of the units bounced off the ground and hit the tailplane removing a large piece of that important component. Following a decidedly 'big dipper' flight path a safe landing was made. On another occasion one of the legs hung up during a Saturday afternoon flight, later falling into the garden of a country house where a wedding party was grouping for a photograph. The leg assembly hurtled to earth between the photographer and the family – Nick pondered upon the expressions on the faces of the subjects if the photographer had the presence of mind to record the moment! Yet another leg fell into an Army camp and was recognised as a new type of bomb. The area was wired off and the Bomb Disposal team summoned.

The use of a Wellington as a tug for the Horsa led to the controls of the bomber becoming extremely stiff. Investigation revealed that the absence of heavy longerons in the geodetic 'trellis-work' fuselage had lengthened it appreciably due to the drag of the glider. A much more serious problem arose when Ron Clear was testing the performance of the Horsa in a dive with the massive dive brakes deployed. Descending very steeply he found it very difficult to pull out. He discovered that the tail plane, which had a single strut to the fuselage was twisting under the aerodynamic loads and negating the effect of the elevators. A most urgent programme to replace the single strut with a 'vee' assembly was initiated to ensure that the planned military operations would not be hazarded.

Airspeed Horsa military glider taking-off towed by a Halifax. For landing the undercarriage assemblies were jettisoned and the landing made on the skid seen between the wheels. (via Aeroplane Monthly)

The war-time carrier-borne aircraft provided their own problems for test pilots, the Firebrand being one of them, built by Blackburn at Brough – a company not esteemed for the merit of most of its designs. The Firebrand was a very large torpedo fighter with a single 2,305 h.p. Napier Sabre engine. Built like a battleship – some said that it had the flying characteristics of such a vessel – there were many problems. The second prototype, first flown in 1944 by Flt Lt Arthur Thompson suffered engine failure and, in a belly landing, hit a heavy telpher suspension cable which nearly decapitated him. Peter Lawrence, the chief test pilot, investigating aileron flutter at 25,000 ft (7,620 m) found the wing tips flapping through three feet (0.9 m). The skin fractured on the wings and fuselage whilst the cockpit side window broke. Lawrence slowed down to 100 knots preparatory to baling out, when fortunately the flutter ceased and he was able to make a safe landing. On another sortie he initiated a spin at 22,000 ft (6,706 m). After the customary three turns he could not recover, after 22 rotations he deployed the anti-spin parachute and recovered at 5,000 ft (1,524 m).

Lt-Cdr Eric 'Winkle' Brown, the naval chief test pilot at Farnborough, had a number of memorable experiences; on one occasion he was flying a Seafire from the catapult and took off with the catapult carriage still attached to the aircraft; a safe landing was made. On another catapult launch in a Grumman Avenger torpedo bomber he suddenly realised that as it left the carriage the wings were beginning to fold, he closed the throttle and the large aeroplane just hit the ground and rolled on until the brakes brought it to rest, leaving the pilot highly embarrassed!

Lt-Cdr Brown proofed all the Royal Navy carrier aircraft on all the carriers and was the first man to land a twin-engined aircraft on a carrier; this was a Mk VI Mosquito suitably modified with an arrester hook and suitably strengthened to accept the deceleration loads. On one landing he suddenly realised that the bolt retaining the hook forging had failed as it caught the wire. He opened the throttles and took off again, dropping to a few feet above the sea en route to RNAS Macrihanish.

On 3 December 1945 he landed the third prototype of the de Havilland Vampire jet fighter, which had been fitted with an arrester hook, on the deck of HMS *Ocean*. As a result of a successful trials programme the aircraft went into limited production for the Royal Navy.

This type was involved in an experiment to determine the value of landing a naval jet fighter upon a rubber deck so that the heavy undercarriage could be eliminated. Eric Brown conducted trials at Farnborough on a rubber deck laid upon a mat of fire hoses. On the first occasion the arrester hook of his Sea Vampire bounced off the ground as he approached the mat, the Vampire then dived into the mat, penetrating it. The technique was refined to the point where over 200 landings were made by different pilots, some of whom had not flown a jet aircraft before. With the end of the war no further work was carried out.

Avro York of BOAC.
(A.V. Roe & Co. Ltd.)

CHAPTER 8
Post-War Developments

The end of the war in Europe led to frenzied activity among the aircraft builders to establish a presence in, particularly, the civil market which, at the transport end of the spectrum, was already dominated by the Americans who had concentrated upon military transports whilst Britain and its other Allies built combat aircraft. The US Forces were operating mainly, the ubiquitous DC-3/C-47, the DC-4/C-54 – a first-class four-engined aeroplane, tailor-made for the long-distance routes and the Lockheed C69, to be called Constellation, of which only 15 had been delivered at the time of the Japanese defeat. Britain had to be content with the Avro York, a rather inelegant workhorse which had been built from the components of a Lancaster attached to a new high capacity fuselage. The Lancaster itself saw service as the Lancastrian, stripped of its military equipment and fitted with a few seats for the passengers who were frozen at altitude and deafened at all times. Some Halifax bombers were converted to passenger service as the Halton whilst the Sunderland flying boat saw service in the role originally intended for its progenitor, the Short Empire class transport. A number of DC-3 Dakotas were also used for BEA's European services.

Vickers soon launched the Viking with its tubby geodetic fuselage and main components from the Wellington. This gave good service on the routes of British European Airways. Handley Page, Bristol and A.V. Roe were busy on long-range designs, the Avro Tudor four Merlin engined aircraft was the first to fly on 14 June 1945. Sir Frederick Handley Page, ever impatient with delay, heard that Bristol had flown their workhorse Bristol 170 Freighter/Wayfarer on 2 December 1945. On 3 December 1945 the HP chief test pilot, Jimmy Talbot, who had succeeded Major James Cordes, and his co-pilot, E.A. 'Ginger' Wright taxied the new Hermes out for take-off from Radlett. Because of the urgency of the flight the taxying trials held the previous day, had been curtailed, tragically, as it turned out. As soon as G-AGSS was airborne it was clear that Talbot was in trouble with longitudinal instability, the aircraft diving and climbing to the stall with the pilots frantically trying to control it. Before safety height had been reached the Hermes stalled and dived, inverted, to hit the ground three miles (4.8 km) south of the airfield, narrowly missing a disastrous crash into Radlett itself. The pilots were killed and the aeroplane totally destroyed.

The enquiry into the accident decided that it was due to elevator over-balance and that the forces generated were far in excess of the ability of the pilots to maintain control of the aircraft. S/Ldr Hedley G. Hazelden, a very experienced Boscombe Down test pilot, was appointed to succeed Talbot. Work proceeded on the military version, the Hastings, whilst major design changes were made to the Hermes, changes which ultimately led to the Mk IV which went into service with BOAC in 1950. During his development work on the first Hermes IV, G-AKFP, 'Hazel' had a very disturbing experience. Handling tests were in progress from the long runway at the de Havilland airfield at Hatfield. Weight was

Handley Page Hermes 4 in BOAC livery.
(British Airways)

increased to 75,000 lb (34,020 kg) and a new spring tab was fitted to the elevators. In flight a violent flutter developed and the tailplane on one side began to disintegrate. He was able to control the aircraft to a safe landing.

By this time BOAC had become sadly disillusioned with the Avro Tudor. There were many problems with the early marks, problems which were not entirely the responsibility of A.V. Roe. The airline was continually changing its corporate mind and, at a development meeting on 12 March 1946, called for over 340 alterations. The order for the Tudor I was cancelled in April 1947 but still the design and development departments struggled on. Capt. H.J. Orrell was the chief test pilot with S.A. 'Bill' Thorne as his assistant. In March 1946 the prototype Tudor II had made its first flight from Woodford and showed the same defects and performance problems as the Mk I. On 23 August 1947 it taxied out for take-off with Bill Thorne at the controls, Roy Chadwick, the chief designer and Sir Roy Dobson, the Avro managing director, were also aboard. A red lamp fron the control tower halted the aircraft and a messenger came out to call Dobson to take an urgent telephone call. He instructed the pilot to continue without him. Shortly after the lift-off the aircraft banked, increasingly steeply until it plunged into a pond outside the airfield. Chadwick and Thorne both lost their lives and the other crew members were seriously injured. An inquiry established that during the previous night some modifications were carried out which necessitated the removal of the aileron control cables. These had been replaced in the reverse sense and no tests had been carried out before flight, consequently, when Thorne attempted to correct the initial bank he increased it – at low altitude this was fatal.

The second prototype of the Tudor I was converted to be powered by four 5,000 lb (11,000 kg) thrust Nene 5 jet engines. It became known as the Tudor 8 and was the first aircraft in the world to be powered by four jets. Its tail-dragger configuration limited its value as the jet efflux battered the tailplane and scoured the runway surface. It was a unique experience for Jimmy Orrell who recalled the fascination of the first flights, for which there was no precedent, the greatly increased altitude and speed with the absence of propeller drag resulted in an entirely different flying procedure. He realised that he had entered an entirely new world of aviation, 'The smoothness and quietness of the flight made it so different and so pleasant'.

Jimmy's unique experience with the Tudor 8, later called the Ashton, suggested that he was the ideal man to go to Canada where the new Avro Canada Jetliner with four jets was almost ready to be flown. The first flight was faultless; the second one was to check all the services and its stability under all conditions of trim. Selection of 'undercarriage down' was unsuccessful and the operation of the two emergency systems was equally unavailing. A 'radio conference' with the design staff at the Malton control tower was equally unhelpful so Jimmy was forced to the conclusion that a belly landing was inevitable. This was the first time that such an event had occurred and, as he crossed the threshold, he realised that the ground cushion effect was likely to cause a long float across the airfield; a few judicious fish-tails soon dropped off some speed and a smooth touch-down did so little damage that the aeroplane was flying again within six weeks.

Avro Ashton Mk 3.
(Ken Ellis Collection)

Jimmy's wife, Nan, was in the unhappy position of being in a departmental store when the local radio station picked up the dramatic conversations in which her husband was the central figure!

The Bristol Aeroplane Company was building the giant Brabazon with its eight 2,500 h.p. Bristol Centaurus XX radial engines and a wing span of 230 ft (70 m). This aircraft was first flown by A.J. 'Bill' Pegg from Filton on 4 September 1949. G-AGPW was a magnificent sight in the air and presented few problems during its short test programme of only 400 flying hours, after which it was abandoned.

Data gathering was a considerable task in those early days. Twelve cine cameras filmed continuously the twelve separate instrument panels with over 1,000 separate dials monitoring every aspect of the operation of the aircraft. Analysis of the data took hundreds of hours for each flying hour. David Davies who was the Air Registration Board test pilot associated with the project told the author of his astonishment when, on one test flight at around noon, Bill Pegg handed over the controls to his co-pilot, left his seat and said to Davis:

'Come along, we will have lunch now'!

They went aft where a section of the passenger accommodation had been fitted out. A uniformed steward served their lunch on a spotless white tablecloth with attractive plates and cutlery!

After one flight with a group of newspaper representatives on board Bill Pegg was leading them from the Brabazon to go to lunch. Nearby C.T.D. 'Sox' Hosegood, the chief

Bristol chief test pilot Bill Pegg in Brabazon I, the only one to fly.
(Bristol Aerospace Airbus, Bristol)

helicopter test pilot, was commencing his take-off in the new Sycamore chopper. He saw it lift off and, to his horror, heard a bang as the rotor blades disintegrated and the fuselage fell to the ground, fortunately only a short distance. He hoped that the newshounds had not noticed. One had and said:

'What on earth is going on there?'

Bill looked across and said, as nonchalantly as he could

'Oh we are just doing some ground resonance trials on a new helicopter!'

Hosegood was also responsible for Bristol's later twin rotor Type 173. The first flight took place on 3 January 1952. This revealed a totally unexpected problem. Theoretically the twin rotors should have cancelled out the torque effect which necessitated the use of a tail rotor on a single rotor design. In this case, as 'Sox' accelerated along the runway, the machine drifted away to starboard in spite of a bootful of port rudder. Raoul Hafner, the designer, was following in a jeep and was shouting loudly, but in the noise and general commotion the observer could not hear him. As the runway intersection was reached they were able to proceed along another one until the 173 was brought safely back to earth. Hafner rushed up and announced that they had a problem; he had already worked out that each of the main rotors would have a tendency to turn the aircraft in the direction of their rotation so a turning couple was established. The axis of rotation of each shaft was canted sideways and no further trouble was experienced.

Trials with the RAF version, the Belvedere, showed problems in hovering rearwards at low altitude. Hosegood found that the nose dropped and he had insufficient speed or height to do anything about it. The ASI probe dug into the soil but little damage was done. The Belvedere was one of the first helicopters to be fitted with duplicated power controls. As with the Sycamore some ground resonance problems were experienced, which were overcome by modifications to the rotor-hub drag dampers and landing gear.

The Royal Navy showed interest in the Belvedere and carried out an evaluation programme resulting in a number of modifications and a substantial order which was soon cancelled in favour of the Westland-built Sikorsky S58.

Bristol 173 helicopter in British European Airways colours.
(British Aerospace Airbus, Bristol)

Cierva W.11 Airhorse at Eastleigh.
(Ken Ellis Collection)

The original Alvis Leonides engines were replaced by the 1,650 h.p. Napier Gazelles which improved performance substantially. Proof of the general excellence of the design was a record-breaking flight made in June 1960 when S/Ldr C.B. 'Cyclops' Brown flew XG452 to Tripoli at an average speed of 130 mph (209.3 km/hr). Tropical trials carried out there and high altitude trials at Chambery gave few problems and the type was ordered for service with the RAF. Twenty-four were built and were flown until March 1969. The Bristol Helicopter Department was taken over by Westlands so no further development was carried out.

The Cierva Company built, in 1948, the giant AirHorse helicopter with three rotors driven by a 1,620 h.p. Merlin engine. One of Britain's leading helicopter pilots, Alan Marsh made the first flight on 12 December 1948 in the machine which was described by S/Ldr Basil Arkell as looking like an elephant in the air but flying like a pig! To ensure blade interchangeability the rotors turned in the same direction which gave a rather odd flight characteristic. To counteract torque they were set at an angle; it could be turned easily to starboard but was difficult to turn to port.

During a routine test flight on 13 June 1960 a fatigue failure in one of the rotor assemblies caused the AirHorse to dive into the ground, killing the crew including Alan Marsh and S/Ldr F.J. 'Jeep' Cable, another leading 'chopper' expert.

Two important post-war British airliner projects were the Airspeed Ambassador and the Vickers Viscount, both intended for service with British European Airways. They were built to meet the recommendations of the Brabazon Committee which sat during the war to consider post-war needs of the airlines. The Ambassador was to be fitted with two Bristol Centaurus radial engines, later to have two Rolls-Royce Dart gas turbines. The Vickers Viscount was to have four Darts at the outset.

The beautiful Ambassador, designed by the artistic and talented Arthur E. Hagg who had, in 1936, designed the equally attractive de Havilland Albatross, was first flown from Airspeed's Christchurch airfield on 10 July 1947 by George Errington, the chief test pilot. The flight lasted fifty minutes and was very satisfactory apart from the centre rudder shedding its trim tab.

The test programme was be-devilled with accidents and incidents which were only occasionally the fault of the aeroplane. After fifty hours flying the bolts holding the hydraulic actuation ram of the port undercarriage leg failed as the prototype, G-AGUA, was flying at high speed. The leg dropped and locked down, fortunately without tearing the wing off. The loss of hydraulic fluid in the system prevented the flaps being lowered for landing so Errington was forced to make a high-speed touch-down on one leg. The high wing layout proved its worth in terms of 'crash-worthiness', the aeroplane flying again within three weeks. The Ambassador showed remarkable characteristics in single-engine flight; at the 1948 Farnborough Show Errington took off, flew and landed with only one engine operating.

On 13 November 1950 the first production aircraft, G-ALFR, came to grief in the hands of Ron Clear. The ARB had asked for tests to check the outcome of a BEA requirement that the permissible CG limits be moved forward. The landing was the critical factor. A stabilized approach was to be made from 1,000 ft (305 m) in the full flap-down, power-off configuration. To allow the characteristics to be quantified a desynn indicator was fitted in the cockpit to show the pilot the position of the elevator in relation to the total elevator movement available. Ballast was then to be moved forward for the next flight.

Airspeed Ambassador. (Airspeed Ltd., via Ken Ellis Collection)

'Finished with engines!' Airspeed Ambassador G–ALFR, after the accident at Christchurch, 13 November 1950. (Airspeed Ltd.)

Ron Clear made a number of landings, checking elevator angle and stick force during the approach and touch-down. Finally, as the stick force approached the maximum desired, 50 lb (22.68 kg) the elevator desynn confirmed that about 4° of elevator movement remained. Ron approached and commenced his flare-out at about 50 ft (15 m), to his dismay he realised that there was no more elevator power to be used and that he was in a hopeless position for a satisfactory landing. He immediately applied full throttle. True to form the Centaurus engines coughed before bellowing forth at full power and the delay deprived the elevators of slipstream which might just have saved the situation. The violent impact of the nose wheel compressed the oleo strut which immediately recoiled, hurling the nose into the air just as the engines developed full power. The undamped accelerometer in the aircraft recorded an impact acceleration of 14G, two and a half times the maximum design value. The outcome of this situation was that the engines left their bearers and flew straight on. As Ron Clear so memorably put it:

'The glider climbed over them to a height of some 40 ft (12 m) with the control column now on the forward stop and the CG well aft of the aft limit'.

A safe landing was made before the end of the airfield was reached, all the tyres were flat and the aircraft was four tons (4,062 kg) lighter.

Clear's skill in handling such a potentially catastrophic situation enabled the Ambassador to fly again three weeks later. The investigation revealed that a series of related minor factors was responsible for the incident. The effect of the last four degrees of elevator movement which should have initiated the flare were ineffective as, at that angle, the surfaces were stalled. As the air speed indicator was independent, no balance pipe was fitted so there was a slight position error which was accentuated by a gusty cross-wind 60° to the landing run. This caused the captain's ASI to read high so the true air speed was lower than intended. At a works dinner a few weeks later George Errington congratulated Ron on his masterly handling of the affair and presented him with a small model of a ship's telegraph – the handle was set at 'FINISHED WITH ENGINES'! In the spirit of the times it disappeared from his office a few weeks later.

Airspeed, already a subsidiary of the de Havilland Company, found itself in a quasi-competitive position with its own parent who were too heavily involved with the Comet airliner development to have much time for the Ambassador. The Vickers Viscount had caught up due to the delays which had occurred in development. Nevertheless from March 1952 to July 1958 the BEA fleet carried 2,500,000 passengers on 90,000 flights altogether, one thousand million passenger miles at an average load factor of 67.5 per cent. G.R. 'Jock' Bryce joined 'Mutt' Summers' test team at Weybridge after service in Coastal Command and the Atlantic Ferry Organization during the war, also flying C-54s in Transport Command. Afterwards he was posted to the King's Flight.

Mutt and his assistant George Lowdell were pilots of the old school, to a degree, 'seat-of-the-pants' merchants, so Jock's experience on modern multi-engined airliners was invaluable. The Viscount was developed from a smaller version of it, the Vickers 630; it was absolutely right from the commencement of its test flying programme which soon became the sole responsibility of Jock Bryce when Mutt Summers retired.

An unusual and interesting section of the programme concerned the establishment of airframe drag at its true level. This was a vital factor in determining the economy of the aeroplane. Rolls-Royce were not, at that time, able to quote a figure for the thrust contribution made by the tail pipe of the Dart engine so Jock and Hugh Hemsley, the flight test manager, prepared a series of tests to find the answer. Sorties were carried out at speeds ranging from 100 kts (184.9 km/hr) to the designed diving speed of 295 kts (545.5 km/hr) in increments of 10 kts (18.5 km/hr) with all propellers feathered. Auxiliary batteries had been fitted so that they could all be unfeathered without pain and grief. A weather restriction was imposed so that flights could only take place in clear weather. The distance to descend from 25,000 ft (7,620 m) to 10,000 ft (3,048 m) was carefully calculated so that the sortie ended over Boscombe Down airfield and, at 10,000 ft (3,048 m) a warning bell sounded to indicate that immediate action should be taken to re-start the engines. Jock was surprised to find that to meet the requirements of the test procedure the run had to commence at Cardiff, nearly 100 miles (161 km) away. The sorties took months to complete but produced a mass of technical data.

Vickers Viscount 808.
(Aer Lingus)

Jock said that the Viscount programme taught him valuable lessons in test flying:

'The Viscount was right from the word 'GO'!, it was breathtaking'.

It went on to become one of Britain's most successful airliners and was sold to many overseas customers.

Bristol's other post-war contribution to civil aviation was the Britannia, built for service with British Overseas Airways Corporation on their long haul routes. It was powered by four Bristol Proteus propeller turbines. Bill Pegg flew the prototype, G-ALBO, on 16 August 1951 and found that elevator control was far too light and over-sensitive, giving a phugoid, switchback, flight path. When the undercarriage selector was set to DOWN no green light appeared for one of the main wheels and one of the four-wheel bogies failed to rotate to the landing position. Suddenly smoke appeared through the flight deck floor. An immediate landing had to be made with the crew hoping that the bogie would rotate. Fortunately, just before touch-down, it did so. The smoke came from an overheated motor in the systems bay.

Later it was found that during taxying excessive heat was transmitted to the main bogie bearing which was seizing up on the shaft. During the next flight the nosewheel failed to lock down so Bill Pegg landed with the nosewheel held off as long as possible in case the leg remained retracted; fortunately, as the main wheels made contact the green light came up on the indicator.

The second prototype met with a very serious incident on 4 February 1954. It had flown for 54 hours and was airborne with the chief pilot and vice-president, engineering, of KLM Dutch airlines who were interested in evaluating the type. Dr A.E. Russell the chief designer and the Bristol sales manager were also aboard. Ten minutes into the flight Pegg decided to shut down No 3 engine, the oil temperature of which was causing concern. This was excused to the visitors as a demonstration of how well the Britannia flew on three! Perhaps, rather rashly, he then decided to re-start it, run at low rpm and watch the temperature. It rose immediately so another shut down was initiated. Suddenly there was a loud bang and Dr Russell saw a hole appear in the cowling alongside his seat; through it a long flame extended back to the tailplane. Pegg shut off the other engine on that side and shortly afterwards the remaining engines stopped. The two flight engineers, Gareth Jones and Ken Fitzgerald, quickly realised that the fire had actuated the crash switches which cut off all electric power. Fitzgerald operated the over-ride manual control and the engines re-started. The aircraft violently swerved to starboard under this excess of asymmetric power. The fire drill was entirely ineffectual and their situation was dire, over the Welsh mountains at 10,000 ft (3,048 m) with 2,000 gal (9,092 litres) of fuel in the tanks. Bill Pegg was in an appalling dilemma, the answer to which meant, quite literally, life or death to twelve people to say nothing of the reputation of the Company. How long would the wing spar withstand the flames? – would the aileron control go first? – should he attempt a crash landing on the high ground, highly likely to be disastrous or should he try to return to Filton? Possibly the mud flats of the river Severn might offer a chance of survival. Burning metal began to pour out of No 3 engine.

If he decided upon Filton would the wing hold – what state would the undercarriage be in? – could he lower it? – would the flaps work properly? If the actuators on the starboard side were damaged by the fire the Britannia would roll into the ground. If they were not used and the brakes were inoperative, even if the tyres had survived the petrol filling station on the main road at the end of the runway, it seemed a dangerous stopping place for a blazing airliner. The chief designer said to the sales manager:

'I have heard of a few engine fires in my life in aviation but none which had burned so long without the wing coming off!'

Mk 101 Britannia on the mud flats of the Severn Estuary.
(British Aerospace Airbus Ltd., Bristol)

Bill, unaware of this encouraging analysis of their situation, saw that the tide was out and decided that an 'arrival' on the mud between Avonmouth and Sharpness offered the best chance of survival. As he came in at 200 mph (322 km/hr) with flaps and undercarriage up, both port engines stopped due to a short circuit. Ahead was a deep gulley across the mud which offered a serious hazard; once again Jones and Fitzgerald came to the rescue and re-started the engines to enable Pegg to fly over the gulley and put down in the mud where the Britannia ran smoothly for 400 yards (366 m) before stopping. The shaken party staggered across the glutinous mess to a brickyard on the bank to await rescue vehicles. Pegg stayed on to await a technical team and was amused to be offered an order for a substantial tonnage of bricks by a caller!

The reason for the disaster was a failure of a reduction gear pinion probably due to resonance; relieved of its load and low pressure, the turbine had run away and disintegrated to shed parts in all directions except, mercifully, towards the cabin and the fuel tanks. The oil tank was hit and this caused the fire. Not surprisingly, perhaps, KLM did not buy the Britannia, splendid aircraft though it proved to be.

To maintain the momentum of the flight test programme the prototype, G-ALBO was modified to comform with the latest all-up weight specification of 140,000 lb (63,506 kg). In May 1954 whilst being flown by W.F. 'Bill' Gibb a flap torque tube failed during stalling tests and the aircraft half rolled before Gibb, could regain control. An overload of 3 G was applied. A major problem which delayed the entry into service of the Britannia was engine flame-out in icing cloud; this was a particularly difficult one to solve and was ultimately overcome by hot air jets in the air intake and glow plugs in four of the eight combustion chambers to ensure an automatic re-light if the engine flamed-out.

The type had a very good safety record, one tragic event concerned G-ANCA under test from Filton on 6 November 1957 with a crew of 15 including technicians. It dived into a wood at Downend, near Bristol, from low altitude and killed all on board. The cause was identified as a runaway auto-pilot caused by an electrical fault. Eighty-four Britannias were built and over two million flying hours were amassed before all were phased out of service.

The big prop-jets were built at a time when the economics of the pure jet aircraft were rather suspect. The DH 106 Comet and the Boeing 707 sounded the death knell of propeller driven airliners on the long haul routes.

On 27 July 1949 Gp Capt. John Cunningham first flew the beautiful and revolutionary DH aeroplane for 31 minutes returning to say that he was very satisfied with its flying characteristics. The intensive test programme which followed proved that the Comet had met all the targets right through the performance envelope. The powered flying controls were the subject of criticism as they had little 'feel'. The symmetrical wing section necessary to achieve high speed was capable of being stalled on take-off if a pilot rotated too early and in too high an angle of attack. In this case the aircraft would not take-off, as happened to a BOAC Comet at Rome in 1952 and at Karachi in 1953. At Rome there were no casualties but at Karachi the whole crew and technician passengers died. Later marks were built with a drooped leading edge. The two disastrous accidents when Comets disintegrated in the air in 1953 and 1954 totally wrecked the prospects for this trail-blazing air liner which put Britain several years ahead of the Americans who were able to build into the Boeing 707 all the lessons learned from the fatigue failures which finished the Comet I. de Havilland, almost ruined by the disasters, gritted their corporate teeth and built the Comet 4 which gave good service with BOAC and others but, as an airliner was outclassed by the larger Boeing 707 which, with the massive resources of Boeing behind it, gave the Americans dominance on the world's airlines.

de Havilland DH 106 Comet Mk I.
(British Airways)

The Wyvern was the last fixed-wing aircraft to be built by Westland and it bore the triple burden of being a new airframe powered by a new and under-developed engine, the 3,500 h.p. Rolls-Royce Eagle H Type engine like an enlarged Napier Sabre driving a complex new propeller system. These three elements, to a test pilot, represent the worst of all worlds, yet, by devoted effort and the tragic deaths of several pilots the W34, as it was first known, eventually proved to be a useful fleet fighter in the service of the Royal Navy.

The Eagle was the largest piston engine ever developed in Britain and, to the designers, appeared to have the development potential appropriate to the new fighter. To achieve adequate absorption of this immense power and give adequate propeller ground clearance Rotol designed a twin four-blade contra-rotating propeller whilst de Havilland followed

Westland Wyvern with Rolls-Royce Eagle 24-cylinder flat-H type engine of 2,690 hp. The Wyvern was later fitted with the 4,030 ehp Clyde prop-turbine and, finally, the 4,110 ehp Armstrong Siddeley Clyde prop turbine. Both piston engine and turbine versions had contra-rotating propellers. (Rolls-Royce plc)

with a twin three-blade unit which was flown on the third prototype.

In parallel with the Wyvern, W.E.W. Petter was busy with a twin-jet bomber which showed considerable promise. Disagreement over a question of Company policy led to his resignation in September 1944 and his departure to English Electric where his bomber design became the Canberra. Arthur Davenport, the chief designer, was appointed technical director with John Digby promoted to chief designer and work on the W34 was completed. For Harald Penrose it was the last prototype Westland aircraft he was to test fly. Both he and his assistant pilot, S/Ldr Peter Garner had taken a deck landing course with the Navy to learn the mysteries of this esoteric art.

The first flight of the W34 was at Boscombe Down on 16 December 1944. Harald reported that the machine had been generally satisfactory although marginally unstable in a dive. The chord of the tailplane was increased to overcome this problem. Model tests in the RAE spin tunnel had indicated that the aircraft might not recover from a spin so this manoeuvre was banned pending further investigation. It became clear that the destabilising influence of the large eight-blade contra prop was more than anticipated so modifications would be necessary to the area of the horizontal and vertical stabilisers.

The propeller installation itself was another unknown quantity. A major difficulty in the early contra-rotating propellers was lubrication of the thrust race which moves along one of the shafts between the propellers to act as a translation unit conveying the movement of the blade actuating piston to the links connected to the blades of the two propellers. Stiffness of the shafts was another one. It was an engineering nightmare which caused many problems and even cost lives. To simplify the W34 system no feathering facility was included, so the area of the eight blades in fine pitch, when the engine failed, became a powerful airbrake which could only be compensated by the pilot entering a steep dive to maintain flying speed and required very careful judgement of the point of flare-out for landing.

Penrose experienced this early in 1947 when flying at 16,000 ft (4876 m). The single drive shaft to the magnetos sheared so he lost all power. The overcast cloud base at 3,000 ft (914 m) gave little decision time whether to bale out or follow the compulsion of all test pilots to bring back a valuable prototype whatever the risk. After several anxious minutes a small rift in the clouds gave a glimpse of the radio masts near Dorchester. That gave orientation to the aerodrome at Warmwell, so he decided, in spite of the vital steep dive, to try for a landing. The margin was infinitesimal but he cleared the derelict hangars by 50 ft (15 m), lowered flaps and undercarriage by the emergency air bottles and felt the wheels lock down as they went through the waist-high grass.

When the retrieval party from Yeovil eventually arrived one of the cars hit a concrete block hidden in the grass. Further inspection revealed lines of them, buried in 1940 to prevent safe landing by enemy aircraft in the event of invasion. The wheel tracks of the Wyvern ran right through the gaps between the blocks.

On another occasion Penrose was on 'finals' over Yeovil when the aircraft suddenly flicked upside down and plunged towards the tightly packed roofs in the town. His reflexes, conditioned by many hours of aerobatic flying, were instantaneous and effective; with the houses only 500 ft (152 m) below he recognized a major control aberration and thrust the control column diagonally forward to the far corner of the cockpit and kicked on maximum rudder, shuddering the Wyvern lifted its inverted nose and flick rolled to a correct flying position but on the brink of a stall, slowly and carefully he gained altitude and saw that both ailerons were hard against their up stops. The whole hideous experience had taken only five seconds. As Harald said in his autobiography:

'Few had escaped from so close a call as this'.

He was able to make a perfect landing to find that one of the aileron control rods had failed. He later commented, ruefully:

> 'Had we dived in when the aircraft whirled uncontrollably inverted, the verdict would have been 'An error of judgement whilst performing aerobatics at a dangerously low altitude' instead of mechanical failure'.

By now Peter Garner was proving to be a valuable member of the team testing Seafires and the Wyvern. He had already been 'blooded' by a forced landing in a field when the engine of his Seafire failed. Penrose had advised him:

'Always land as near to a road as possible, help can more easily reach you in the event of a pile-up'.

A sad irony in view of what happened later for, in October 1947 the Wyvern claimed its first victim. John Yoxall, of *Flight* came to Yeovil to take air-to-air photographs. Harald and Peter Garner tossed a coin to decide who should fly the fighter. Peter won and flew away to rendezvous with the photographic aeroplane. Fifteen minutes later the crash alarm outside the office sounded. The Fleet Air Arm Station at Yeovilton had phoned to report the Wyvern descending in difficulties with the propellers stationary somewhere south-east of Yeovil. Alan Bristow, the Westland helicopter pilot, immediately took off with Penrose, a nurse and a first-aid man in the firm's helicopter to search the countryside, but it was all too long before they spotted a wisp of smoke rising from the Wyvern lying on its belly in a field. They landed alongside but the pilot was dead in the blazing cockpit. So, not for the first nor, indeed, the last, Penrose had to face the agonising duty of telling the pilot's wife that her husband had made his last flight.

The circumstances of the accident can only be guessed at; it appears that the initial failure was in the propeller translation unit and Garner would have been faced with the enormous drag of the stationery blades necessitating a steep dive to maintain flying speed, so he may have begun to flatten out a fraction too late, as the machine hit the ground hard he was thrown forward against the windscreen knocking him unconscious.

This tragic death left a serious gap in the Wyvern team and there were no volunteers for the job as the Wyvern had gained a reputation as a dangerous aeroplane. Potential recruits felt that the pay and the risk were totally incompatible. Eventually Rolls-Royce recommended one of their engine test pilots, S/Ldr Mike Graves, who was familiar with the Eagle engine; he was engaged in 1948.

There were now six Eagle Wyvern prototypes shared between Westland at Yeovil, Rolls-Royce at Hucknall, the A&AEE at Boscombe Down and RAE, Farnborough. Rolls-Royce decided to abandon the Eagle engine as the Clyde propeller turbine of 4,300 equivalent horse power (ehp) was showing considerable promise. The 4,000 ehp Armstrong Siddeley Python was also a candidate but had not been developed as far as the Clyde which, installed in a TF2 Wyvern and fitted with a Rotol six-blade contra-rotating propeller, was flown at Boscombe Down on 18 January 1949. The maiden flight, with Penrose at the controls, was his shortest ever. Immediately after take-off dense smoke filled the cockpit apparently indicating that fire had broken out, even the instruments, two feet away, were invisible. Opening the hood made things worse, so, with a careful approach because of no forward vision, he managed to return to the runway he had left four minutes earlier. It was found that the smoke was due to a leak of fuel upon the turbine exhaust pipe.

The Clyde was developed to a maximum output of 4,500 ehp with water methanol injection but it was not a reliable power unit so the Python became the favoured engine though with another crop of technical problems to be discovered and overcome. A Lancaster and a Lincoln flying test bed were fitted with Pythons in their outboard nacelles enabling useful data to be acquired by the Rolls-Royce test team under S/Ldr Jim Heyworth, the chief test pilot. The first Python-engined Wyvern was flown on 22 March 1949.

From this time major problems with propeller/engine speed controls were experienced, particularly in the deck landing phase when an immediate engine cut was essential; over-sensitivity of control in the dive was totally unacceptable as there would be a serious risk of over-speeding. S/Ldr Graves, whom Penrose had permitted to make the first flight for experience of the unknown also reported heavy engine surging at a level worse than with the Clyde whilst the alterations made to the fuselage to accommodate the larger diameter of the Python had caused various changes in stability. Dihedral was subsequently incorporated in the tailplane and the fin and rudder were enlarged.

The engine surge problem was a direct result of the deck landing requirement to be able to cut power instantly by connecting the propeller pitch control to the throttle. This, however, caused the release of energy stored in the rotating components of the engine and, thus, the violent surges. Hundreds of high speed dives were made by the Westland pilots to check whether there was a risk of a catastrophic overspeed. The engine and propeller company test pilots were also heavily involved in this programme which represents what was probably one of the most complex and demanding test flying effort in matching an engine and propeller installation, with the gravest risk to the pilots on every sortie.

The next problem to be faced was the resolution of spinning limitations suggested by the RAE spinning tunnel tests with a model so an anti-spin parachute was installed in the tail. Penrose approached the stall cautiously at an appropriate altitude investigating stalls and the violence of wing drop, initiating spins with the rudder and checking before development and then on to a full turn, two turns, four and so to six. Recovery from a full spin was totally abnormal, the motion being violent and unstable. When rudder was reversed for pull-out the heavy fighter flipped onto its back and continued to spin in this attitude. Normal spin recovery techniques were useless but a solution had to be found. Once again his aerobatic experience saved his life. He pulled the control column back and dived out inverted, the half loop to normal flight leaving him too close to the ground for comfort.

Spin recovery was clearly totally unacceptable, discussion between the aerodynamics department and RAE led to the sharp leading edge of the wing being replaced by a blunter one. This was an improvement but a degree of instability remained. Graves was given the opportunity to try a spin and Harald flew alongside in another Wyvern to analyse the erratic motion.

In September Penrose flew the Python Wyvern to Farnborough for the SBAC Show and, afterwards, left it there for evaluation by the RAE test pilots.

The propeller control seemed an intractable problem. On one occasion power fluctuated so violently on take-off from Yeovil that Harald had to fly dangerously slowly at a mere 100 ft (30 m) to Merryfield, twelve miles (19 km) ahead. On another occasion the engine flamed-out at altitude and could not be re-started. Fortunately he was able to dive steeply to overcome prop drag and reach Merryfield yet again.

Soon the Wyvern claimed another life. Mike Graves, who seemed to be increasingly confident and was settling in well was given the task on 31 October 1949, of demonstrating the Python Wyvern to visiting Naval and Ministry personnel at Yeovil. He took off and climbed to 1,500 ft (457 m) at which point Penrose was shocked to see the propellers stop. Graves immediately turned right with the intention of landing downwind; he misjudged his height, crossed the threshold at 200 ft (61 m) and touched down at high speed three quarters of the way along the runway, hurtling through the boundary edge and into a housing estate where the Wyvern destroyed a house, killing the occupants and the pilot. Once again the chief test pilot had the sad task of visiting another young widow.

Three other later victims of this aeroplane were Lt Hamson RN, an A&AEE pilot who crashed near Stonehenge in 1952; an American, Lt-Cmdr Kapruski in December 1953 and Eddie Griffiths, Armstrong Siddeley's chief test pilot who died in May 1954 when the machine crashed near Rugby during engine-out tests. There were also several 'near shaves', generally due to propeller control problems or translation unit lubrication failures.

Not until 1951 did Armstrong Siddeley and Rotol finally solve the engine control problem so that the aircraft could be released for land-based operations and only in 1954 were carrier operations commenced with the S4 version, five years after the first flight of the W34 prototype. When No 813 Sqdn embarked its Wyverns aboard HMS *Albion* still further difficulties were encountered when flame-out occurred due to fuel starvation during high 'G' catapult launches. By 1955 a fuel recuperator had been fitted to ensure a sustained flow regardless of the 'G' force.

A number of Fleet Air Arm squadrons operated the Wyvern and its effectiveness as a weapon and popularity with those who flew it is an eloquent tribute to the devoted work of Harald Penrose and his team and also the engine company, propeller company and the RAF test pilots who worked, and, indeed, gave their lives, in this endeavour which must have been one of the most difficult and complex technical development programmes in the industry so soon after the war. To develop a new airframe and an innovative new engine with an equally new and complex propeller system is a nightmare scenario for technicians and pilots alike. Harald Penrose expressed the view that the Wyvern almost became a very good aeroplane. It was the last fixed wing type to be built at Yeovil, the 390th type he had flown and the last in his 25 years as a test pilot. In 1953 he became the Company's Group Sales Manager and Special Director, holding these positions until he retired in 1968.

Another test pilot with experience of the vicissitudes of Wyvern flying was S/Ldr Cliff

Rogers who joined the Rolls-Royce test team from Bomber Command where he was awarded a DFC and from Transport Command where he was well acquainted with the Merlin engine. One of his first assignments was to fly the Eagle Wyvern. On one occasion he was briefed to carry out a full-throttle test run at 25,000 ft (7,620 m). At this height a sudden rapid rise in oil and coolant temperature accompanied by steam necessitated an immediate shut-down and quick identification of an emergency landing site. Looking down he recognized, as an ex No 5 Group bomber pilot, Lincoln Cathedral and the Saracen's Head, a popular war-time watering hole. He decided to head for the disused airfield of Skellingthorpe, to the west of the City recalling that the wind at take-off had been 25 knots and gusting. With a need for 125 knots over the fence with this heavy aeroplane the landing without power was not likely to be an easy one with the massive eight-blade propeller as a highly effective airbrake, he also recalled recent accidents under similar circumstances.

Cliff's first thought was to get out swiftly, but this posed problems, not the least of which was his duty to bring the Wyvern back for investigation of the trouble. So he lowered the undercarriage and steered for the totally inadequate 1,400 yard (1,280 m) runway with a wood and a lake obstructing the approach path. Diving to maintain flying speed he made a perfect touch-down and rolled to a standstill. Pausing to recover his composure he suddenly saw the control column moving across the cockpit for no apparent reason. He looked out to see a gentleman in rustic garb thumping the wing with a heavy stick and waggling the aileron. Cliff was extremely annoyed to see his Wyvern, unmarked after a very dangerous experience, should be assaulted in this manner. He opened the canopy to be informed with some asperity by the visitor, a local farmer, that under no circumstances would he allow the Lincoln Flying Club to operate from Skellingthorpe, he had bought the field and proposed to farm it without let or hindrance! Rogers persuaded him that the Wyvern was not an elementary trainer or a private owner's machine and the landing really had been a fire emergency! The farmer, suitably mollified, took him to his home for a splendid lunch and allowed Cliff to shoot over his ground for several years. It could, perhaps, be said that this was the only element of humour which illuminated the Wyvern test programme.

Four months later he was flying the Wyvern over the Derbyshire hills when the engine blew up. This time he again invoked his episcopal navigation system and used Lichfield Cathedral as a pointer to another disused airfield. This time the situation was markedly less encouraging, ominous and expensive noises were coming from the engine which soon caught fire. Down went the undercarriage as he headed for one of the runways, this time he missed it and landed on the grass where the local football team was playing, although he ran from corner flag to corner flag none of the players was touched. Cliff still has a vivid recollection of green and red shirted players laying flat on the grass! The RAF fire crew moved off smartly as the burning Wyvern approached and chased it, extinguished the fire and undoubtedly saved the valuable prototype. Rogers was extremely angry to discover that the corporal in charge of the appliance was to receive a reprimand for leaving the Fire Station without permission. He visited the Commanding Officer to ensure that justice prevailed.

After two very dicey experiences with this interesting flying machine Cliff pondered upon whether he would have been better advised to take up chicken farming! Nevertheless he went on to a distinguished career as chief test pilot of Rolls-Royce, following a series of top class incumbents in this post, R.T. Shepherd OBE, Harvey Heyworth AFC and his brother Jim Heyworth DFC. Cliff retired in 1984. Awarded the OBE in 1968 he was delighted to be awarded an Honorary Fellowship of the International Society of International Test Pilots in 1992.

CHAPTER 9

The Dangers of the Transonic Years

Not until the later years of the Second World War were pilots exposed to the mysterious forces identified as a result of compressibility problems. The more advanced fighters such as the American P–47 Thunderbolt, P–52 Merlin-engined Mustang, P–38 Lightning and the British Typhoon and Tempest revealed a tendency to 'tuck under' in a high speed dive; the thick wing Typhoon was a particularly vicious operator in this régime. E.W. 'Jock' Bonar, a Napier test pilot, put one through a series of high speed dives to investigate oil scavenging problems with its under-developed Sabre engine. On one such flight he rolled into a dive at 35,000 ft (10,668 m), the Tiffie accelerating in the vertical descent. Suddenly he had no control, elevators, rudder and ailerons were totally ineffective. Recalling the Typhoon's reputation for shedding its tail on pull-out he centralized the controls. Using elevator trimmers and a steady pull on the stick against the enormous aerodynamic forces, assisted by the fact that compressibility effects from which the aeroplane was suffering were lower as he descended to warmer and denser air the machine began to level out as Jock blacked out under G forces. When he could see again he saw that he was flying at high speed and low altitude near Royston. He was shocked to see that the wing skin was shuddering and flapping with a large number of rivets missing. The skin was buckled everywhere as a result of this unexpected encounter with compressibility effects which left the thick section of the wing at a great disadvantage.

Fortunately an automatic recorder provided details of instrument readings so the data was put to good use in the development of the Tempest with its thin wing and superior control characteristics at high, sub-sonic speed. Later, another Napier test pilot continued the high speed dive programme and died when the tail broke off in the attempted pull-out.

One of the first pilots to recognise the source of high speed instability difficulties was P.W.S. 'George' Bulman, the very able Hawker chief test pilot who served in that position from 1925 to 1945. He experienced the phenomenon when flying an American fighter during a posting to USA in the early 1940s. He immediately circulated a memo to all test pilots describing his experience and explaining that the instability was caused by shock waves and centre of pressure movement when airflow over certain parts of the aircraft disturbed the airflow pattern as sonic speed was approached. The speed of sound, known as Mach One, was at its highest in the cold, thin air of the upper atmosphere and lowest in the warmer, denser air nearer the ground. Bulman suggested that when faced with this problem pilots should not try to recover by violent action on the control column, the likely outcome being structural failure, but should ride the machine down to lower altitudes where the shock waves would decay and control could be regained. This proved to be advice which saved the lives of many test pilots in the transonic era.

In 1943 a remarkable series of test flights was initiated at the Royal Aircraft Establishment at Farnborough, now known by the miserably prosaic title of Defence

Research Agency. As well as compressibility problems it was appreciated that the onset of control surface flutter was likely to be catastrophic at high speeds. It was known that the limiting Mach Number of the Spitfire was very high, probably above 0.80, so it was decided to follow up wind tunnel tests with one of the most dangerous series of test flights ever carried out, with a Spitfire Mk IX photographic reconnaissance aircraft, the cleanest of the breed. It was to be dived from 40,000 ft (12,192 m) at full throttle to reach its maximum Mach No. at about 25,000 ft (7,620 m).

At the end of 1943 Sqn Ldr J.R. Tobin achieved Mach 0.92 and in 1944 Sqn Ldr A.F. Martindale reached Mach 0.89, a true airspeed of 606 mph (976 km/hr). At 27,000 ft (8,230 m) there was an explosion with white smoke and oil pouring over his windscreen and canopy, he could see nothing. Slowly he eased the control column back, speed dropping to a point where he might consider baling out. He then realised that he had marginal control so elected to attempt a landing to preserve the valuable data recorded automatically. The slipstream cleared some of the oil, he could not see the propeller but bits of engine were protruding through the cowling. Skilfully he glided the 20 miles (32 km) back to Farnborough, landed safely and found, to his astonishment, that the whole of the propeller and reduction gearing had broken away.

In the following month he was very unlucky when the supercharger of his Spitfire blew up at 600 mph (966 km/hr), the engine catching fire. Farnborough airfield was enveloped in cloud so he was forced to attempt a landing in a field. At the last minute he was forced by high tension cables ahead to swerve, the aircraft hurtling into a wood. In spite of spinal injuries the pilot returned to the blazing wreck to rescue the flight recorder. He was awarded a well merited AFC.

A series of high Mach No. tests with various British and American machines led to a conference in 1946 which reported that, of fifteen tested, the Spitfire, designed in 1934, was the best. Some showed violent pitching characteristics whilst the US aircraft had experienced aileron buzz, a very high frequency vibration, often the precursor of structural failure.

The limiting Mach No. of the Spitfire Mk IX, at 0.90, was superior to the 1946 Vampire jet fighter at 0.80 which showed longitudinal instability. The Meteor 1 was prevented by buffeting from exceeding 0.80. Later versions with lengthened nacelles lifted the figure to 0.84.

Apart from limitations created by airframe drag the propeller was seen as a major factor in critical Mach No. problems; the twin-engined de Havilland Hornet, with a top speed of 472 mph (760 km/hr) – the prototype achieved 485 mph (781 km/hr) and the Dornier Do 335 twin tandem-engined fighter with a top speed of 474 mph (763 km/hr) were seen as the ultimate. By this time, of course, the gas turbine had released designers from the piston engine/propeller straitjacket. Britain led the world in terms of gas turbine power and reliability although, with the Junkers Jumo 004B, Germany had an advanced axial-flow unit of high performance but with a time between overhauls (TBO) of 30 hours compared with the contemporary Rolls-Royce Welland and Derwent centrifugal-flow turbines which ran for 500 hours on type test and had a service TBO of 150 hours.

It became clear as early as 1943 that airframe design had to be radically changed to take advantage of the power and performance potential of the new engines. It was officially decided to issue a specification for the construction of an aircraft to reach the speed of sound powered by a special Whittle gas turbine with reheat and a form of thrust augmentor. Miles Aircraft designed the M52, a remarkable project with a very thin bi-convex wing section and a barrel-shaped fuselage with the pilot sitting in the transparent nose cone, he, of necessity being of very small stature. The wing was flown successfully on a Miles

'e Havilland DH 100 'ampire.
3ritish Aerospace, Hatfield)

Falcon light aircraft and construction proceeded until the summer of 1946 when a timorous Government abandoned the project on the pretext that it was not considered right that British pilots should be called upon to take such fearful risks. This attitude, of course, attracted the contempt of every test pilot but the ban remained. Britain's great chance of leadership in high speed flight, of crucial importance to the commercial and military development of aviation, had been cast away; the first of many such blows to a fine industry. Later, another specious excuse was offered that it had been calculated that with the engine power available and data on swept wing research obtained in Germany after their defeat, it was clear that the M52, with its un-swept wing could not achieve Mach One. Many years later, a design study was carried out by Rolls-Royce which confirmed that there appeared to be no reason why Mach 1 could not have been reached. The limited research carried out in UK was in the form of radio controlled models from which little information was obtained at considerable expense.

Wind tunnel tests at transonic speeds were impracticable as the confined space of the working section was prone to 'choking'. A study of German technology by the technical teams from UK, USA and Russian after the war established the base of their highly advanced technology manifest in the Me 163 rocket fighter and the twin-jet Me 262 with even more advanced missiles based upon the V 1 and V 2 bombs. The work carried out by Dr Alexander Lippisch and the Horten brothers proved beyond doubt that the swept wing was the way ahead, although it must be noted that the first aircraft to exceed the speed of sound, in October 1947, the Bell XS–1, had an unswept wing. The Germans also solved the problem of wind tunnel choking. The Me 163 was one of the most revolutionary aircraft of the Second World War, and was the first tail-less aircraft to become operational. Lippisch, having proved the feasibility of the configuration which had been used in a number of the Horten gliders, decided to power the new interceptor fighter with a Walter rocket engine using two highly dangerous chemical fuels known as T-Stoff and C-Stoff. Test flying at the Peenemunde Research Centre led to many serious accidents and deaths; even a leak of propellant into the cockpit could be fatal, the unfortunate pilot being dissolved in his seat; a crash with fuel in the tanks almost invariably led to a violent explosion. It is almost a certainty that more pilots were killed in accidents than in combat. The 163 took off on a detachable two-wheeled trolley which was immediately jettisoned; power duration was a mere eight minutes so, as an answer to the fleets of Allied four-engined bombers raiding Germany in daylight it was ineffective but alarming to crews. It reached its service ceiling of 39,000 ft (11,887 m) in 3.35 minutes. Its limiting Mach No. was 0.82; at 0.84 it would become unstable in pitch and nose down into what became known as 'graveyard dive' with little chance of recovery.

The more orthodox but still revolutionary Me 262 was a twin axial-flow Junkers Jumo turbine-engined fighter. Fortunately for the Allies many months of precious development time were wasted at the behest of that great strategist Herr Hitler, who demanded that it be turned into a bomber. It was a superb aircraft both technically and visually. Captain Eric Brown, at the time chief Naval test pilot, flew all the German types after the war and it is his opinion that the 262 was the outstanding aircraft of the war. With 18.5° sweepback on the leading edge it had a limiting Mach No of 0.86. The later de Havilland Vampire had a limiting Mach No of 0.80 and the Gloster Meteor with long nacelles 0.84.

From all of these pioneering aircraft the message came across, loud and clear, that flutter was one of the most formidable risks in transonic flight. It had been a familiar problem for many years in company with aero-elasticity, the outcome of which is the twisting of a wing or tailplane when ailerons or elevators are moved. The necessity for thin wings accentuated this problem and the high altitudes open to jet aircraft introduced further problems with cable control runs. The second Gloster E28/39, flown by Sqn Ldr W.D.B.S. Davie, was being climbed to 37,000 ft (11,278 m) when the control column seized solidly and the

Gloster GA 5 Javelin. (Gloster Aircraft Co. Ltd.)

de Havilland DH 108 research aircraft with Geoffrey de Havilland at the controls. Soon after this photograph was taken he was killed when it disintegrated at high speed.
(British Aerospace, Hatfield)

aircraft became totally uncontrollable, hurling Davie out through the canopy at 33,000 ft (10,058 m) without oxygen mask or goggles and with only one glove. The full story of this flight is told in Chapter 6.

In 1945 de Havillands were carrying out design studies for a jet-propelled airliner to fly at high altitude and high sub-sonic speed. A swept wing tail-less design was envisaged and a flying scale model was built which consisted of a Goblin-engined Vampire nacelle with a new wing and highly swept rudder. This was the DH 108, known as the Swallow. The leading edge of the wing was swept 43° and the area was 15 per cent more than the Vampire. Three prototypes were built. On May 15 1946 Geoffrey de Havilland, the son of the founder, first flew TG283 from the 3,500 yard (3,200 m) runway at RAF Woodbridge in Suffolk.

The results, in terms of speed were encouraging but it soon became clear that an airliner based upon the tail-less configuration was not feasible at that time. Work commenced upon the more orthodox design which became the DH 106 Comet I. Data acquired by the first DH 108 in exploring the sub-sonic régime indicated that a cleaner version of it with a boosted Goblin engine was likely to achieve Mach 1 and could set up a new world air speed record which, at the time, was held by Gp Capt. H.J. 'Willie' Wilson flying a special Meteor at an average speed of 606.2 mph (975.98 km/hr) set up in November 1945. By the time the second 108, TG306 was flown, Gp Capt. E.M. Donaldson had set up another record of 616 mph (991.76 km/hr). Geoffrey de Havilland, being a prudent and highly skilled test pilot had no intention of going headlong for the record and, on 27 September 1946 took off for a final test flight before flying down to the south coast record course on the following day. His colleagues at Hatfield became concerned when the 108 failed to return at the expected time. A report came in that an aircraft had been seen falling in pieces into the Thames Estuary. Next day the wreckage, and the body of the pilot were found on the mudflats at Egypt Bay, near Gravesend.

Captain de Havilland had already lost his son John at the controls of a Mosquito in a war-time collision; now his eldest son had gone. The test flight programme required a dive from 10,000 ft (3,048 m) at high Mach No. to investigate controllability and, if there was no problem, to carry out a high speed run. It became clear that the 108 disintegrated during the second test and that Geoffrey died of a broken neck before his body hit the mudflats. Part of a recorder trace found in the wreckage proved that violent instability in pitch had occurred before the aeroplane broke up. Later, flown by John Derry, the DH 108 became the first British aircraft to fly faster than sound, albeit almost out of control.

Derry's initiation into jet flying came soon after he had joined Jeffrey Quill's Supermarine test team in 1947. He had learned from the master the meticulous attention to detail required of the good test pilot and had proved his worth in testing later marks of Spitfire and Seafire, the Spiteful and Seafang. During the course of his work he became extremely interested in the problems of compressibility and the serious deterioration of control caused by the phenomenon. His particular mount for these research activities was the Seafire 47.

Group Captain John Cunningham, who succeeded Geoffrey de Havilland as chief test pilot, was deeply involved in the new Comet and had little time to continue the high speed research programme of the 108. He had seen John Derry fly at air shows and was impressed with what he saw. He offered him a post at Hatfield so, after ten months with Supermarine, he moved to Hertfordshire. His work commenced with flights in the Dove small airliner, the Hornet piston-engined fighter and the Vampire jet fighter. He began diving tests with the Hornet and Vampire to measure the limiting Mach numbers of both airframes.

Within a few weeks he commenced a test programme with the 108 directed towards an investigation of the cause of the instability believed to have led to the death of Geoffrey de Havilland. The aircraft was fitted with small tubes over the wings and nacelle connected to instruments which would record the pressures at these points at all speeds and attitudes. This second prototype, VW120, had been strengthened and fitted with a more powerful engine, a Goblin 4 rated at 3,750 lb (1,703 kg) thrust, a powered boost system for the elevon control and a more pointed nose. This was first flown by Cunningham in July 1947 and the high speed programme began with considerable circumspection. In January 1948 Derry took over responsibility and it soon became clear that an attempt on the International 100 km Closed Circuit record had considerable prospect of success. A special five-leg course was set up near Hatfield and, on 12 April he established a new World Record of 605.23 mph (974 km/hr).

Gp Capt. John Cunningham boarding the DH 100 Vampire with DH Ghost engine. In it he set up a new world altitude record of 59,446 ft (18,119m) on 3 March 1948.
(British Aerospace, Hatfield)

It had already become evident that the results of the wind tunnel tests at Farnborough were being confirmed on each flight and that the safety factor at high sub-sonic speed was perilously small. A severe nose-down pitch was likely to develop into a catastrophic disintegration of the aircraft whilst control effectiveness as the pitch-down developed was minimal. At that time it was impossible to achieve high Mach numbers in level flight so Derry commenced a series of high speed dives from about 40,000 ft (12,192 m). They confirmed that up to a high Mach number the 108 was a pleasant aeroplane to fly but Derry realised that trouble could arise without warning.

After ten of these dives, the pressure plots of which gave the aerodynamicists a heavy work load in analysis, John decided to have a break and go for the Closed Circuit record. After his success the dives continued; his reports were masterly and greatly admired by the technical people and by RAE at Farnborough. On one of these flights he almost repeated de Havilland's fatal accident. The aircraft suddenly began to pitch so he closed the throttle; subsequent evaluation of the traces showed that, in under 1½ seconds, loads of ± 3.5 G had been experienced by the airframe – another second or so would have seen the wings torn off. This was a clear replay of the circumstances of the accident, but Geoffrey would have been entirely unaware of the implications of the pitching phenomenon.

John Cunningham generated further useful prestige for de Havilland when he flew a Ghost-engined Vampire to a height of 59,492 ft (18,133 m) and broke the World Record of 56,492 ft (17,220 m) held by Italy.

Derry continued his dive test programme, slowly increasing his speed and re-checking the results of every one of the sorties until, on 6 September he had a devastating experience. It was a fine morning when he took-off to carry out a climb to 48,000 ft (14,630 m). At this altitude he accelerated to Mach 0.85 and entered a 30° dive. At 0.91 he recorded a nose-down pitch which changed at 0.93 to a wallowing motion. At 0.94 a phugoid up and down pitch developed which was slightly difficult to control. At 0.95 the nose heavy trim re-appeared and he opened the throttle from 10,600 rpm to a maximum of 10,750. No increase in speed was observed but he sensed that the drag level had increased, so he steepened the angle of dive until 0.96 appeared on the Machmeter. Suddenly the nose went down and a feeling of instability was sensed. As the dive became steeper the pitch became more violent and unstable with G forces of -2. He still felt that he had control of the situation so continued with the dive.

At 38,000 ft (11,582 m) the aircraft was almost out of control and the dive steepened to an angle beyond the vertical generating -3 G, a level which caused him to feel that his eyes were likely to come out of their sockets. Airflow was so disturbed that the elevons were useless, only a violent pull on the control column could produce sufficient effort to reduce the dive angle to around 70°. Still speed increased to 0.98 and the 108 returned to its over the vertical attitude.

By this time he was perilously near the ground with probably only a minute between him and oblivion. The column was immoveable with speed still rising. Suddenly Mach 1.0 appeared on the Machmeter. As the needle showed 1.04 he closed the throttle, this had no effect whatsoever so, in desperation, he actuated the trim flaps to their full-up position. By this time he was entering much denser air at which the Mach number was lower, the 108 slowly pulled out and at 23,500 ft (7,164 m) and a speed of 0.94 he could use the control column again. Just as he was beginning to congratulate himself on what was, by any standards, a miraculous escape the phugoid pitching began again. He retracted the trim flaps and all was well. This dive into high drama had taken little more than one minute and he flew back to Hatfield wondering how accurate the Machmeter readings were. When all the plots had been analysed he was told that the true figure was 1.02 and that he was, indeed, the first pilot to exceed the speed of sound in a British aircraft.

His high speed dives continued and, in March 1949 he had another experience similar to his 6 September sortie. This time he climbed to 40,000 ft (12,192 m). At 0.98 the familiar nose-down pitch occurred. At 0.99 he decided to set the trim flaps to pull out – nothing happened. He closed the throttle but the dive steepened and the speed increased. He was helpless, the aircraft began to roll to port and the dive steepened; with maximum pull on the column he applied full opposite aileron in the hope of correcting the roll, suddenly the aircraft rolled the other way through 90° with considerable negative G and entered a vertical dive. He had no control whatever at this time; he noted Mach 1.0 on the meter and the dive went beyond the vertical, carried out a bunt to a level attitude, rolled out and continued in a shallow dive from which he quickly recovered control.

This exceptionally dangerous and informative research programme terminated in the summer of 1949 when VW120 was flown to Farnborough for a further series of tests by Service test pilots.

John Derry had already been awarded the Segrave Trophy for the greatest performance on land, air or sea in 1947. In 1948 he was invested by Prince Bernhardt of the Netherlands with the Bronze Lion of the Netherlands for his contribution as a serving officer to the liberation of the Netherlands. The year 1949 brought him one of the highest honours which can be earned in the world of aviation, the Gold Medal of the Royal Aero Club.

It had become apparent that powered, irreversible controls were essential on very fast aircraft and Derry had emphasised this in a lecture to the Royal Aeronautical Society in 1950. The new DH 110 retained the old cable control system but, following DH 108 practice, the elevators and ailerons had powered boosters. On 22 January 1952 Derry flew the prototype WG236; he was enthusiastic about it and flew it solo for two months when Tony Richards joined him as flight observer. On 9 April Mach 1.0 was achieved and the first of many sonic booms hit the surrounding countryside. The DH 110 was the first two-seat and twin-engine operational type to go supersonic. Compared to the 108 the new fighter was almost without vice although it revealed a wing drop and a nose down pitch at high Mach numbers; it also snaked at high speed due, it was thought, to flexibility of the tail booms. Steel reinforcing beams were bolted to the booms as a stop-gap solution pending increased gauge skins to be fitted to the second machine. Later, as John suspected was likely, cable stretch proved a serious problem giving inadequate travel to the ailerons and elevators. He and Richards continued their meticulously conducted tests throughout the flight envelope of the big fighter. It was exhausting work and the pressure was beginning to tell on them. John soon realised that he could progress no further with de Havilland and, in common with most test pilots of this period, was inadequately paid for the demanding work he was doing. Gloster were in competition with de Havilland with their large twin-engined all-weather fighter, the Javelin. Bill Waterton, the Gloster chief test pilot, discussed the possibility of Derry joining his team with the likelihood of taking over as chief after a relatively short time. John decided to consider it further but to make no move until he had flown the 110 at the forthcoming Farnborough SBAC Show in September.

To revert to the ill-fated 108, the two remaining aircraft, TG306, the high speed version and TG283 were delivered to Farnborough for further trials by RAE pilots. The CO of the Aerodynamics Flight was Lt-Cdr Eric Brown. He was very suspicious of tail-less aeroplanes having flown the General Aircraft GAL 65 glider, a very dangerous aircraft which killed the famous glider pilot, Robert Kronfeld, immediately after Lt-Cdr Brown had briefed him upon its propensity to rear up at the stall and go completely out of control. He had also carried out most of the UK handling tests in glide mode of the Me 163 rocket fighter after the war so was well qualified to test the 108.

de Havilland DH 110, second prototype, WG 240.
(British Aerospace, Hatfield, via R.E.Clear)

New instrumentation was installed in TG283 and low speed trials continued for several months. Brown soon confirmed that the 108 was an extremely temperamental aeroplane with considerable potential for serious trouble at high Mach numbers. The RAE issued a report on spinning trials with a model which indicated that recovery from a spin was problematical unless action was taken immediately the spin commenced. TG283 had already been fitted with an anti-spin parachute at each wing tip so he was well prepared. An innovation for the test series was a trailing static head for stalling tests to ensure an accurate air speed recording unaffected by position error. This was a streamlined weight with a perforated spike at the nose; it was suspended on 100 ft (30.5 m) of rubber tube to ensure that it was clear of all airflow disturbances.

Eric Brown found, as did Derry, that the 108 was unstable in all three axes and, as might be expected, confirmed his reports. He found the stall to be particularly vicious in spite of the fixed slots fitted to the wing at Farnborough. After a series of such stalls he tried one 'clean' with the trailing static head deployed to see if a little opposite aileron combined with slight rudder application would delay the wing drop. It did not and the aircraft viciously adopted the inverted position. Before the rudder could be centralized an inverted spin to the right had developed. Fortunately he had studied carefully the RAE model spinning test reports and, having been applying left rudder at the stall, put on full opposite rudder with no effect whatsoever. He soon realised that the rudder had jammed, probably by the trailing static line becoming entangled with it in the spin. He pushed harder on the rudder and cleared the jam, the 108 ceasing rotating so he was able to recover at 3,000 ft (915 m).

The test programme continued and, in July 1949 VW120 was delivered to Farnborough. Eric Brown achieved Mach 0.985 in a 30° dive from 45,000 ft (13,716 m). The column was held fully back to hold the nose-down trim initiated at Mach 0.85. After a close study of the recorded data it was decided to continue the trials to investigate the inadequate damping in pitch. On 8 July he dived to Mach 0.88 at 25,000 ft (7,620 m) and to 0.86 at 10,000 ft (3,048 m) deliberately inducing a pitch oscillation to simulate turbulent air. The machine felt twitchy but he decided to go to 0.88 at 4,000 ft (1,220 m). A touch on the column to induce the pitch oscillation instantly let hell loose in the form of runaway divergent oscillation at a frequency of about three cycles per second. This vicious motion threw his head backwards and forwards at high speed, hitting the ejection seat headrest and then forwards to his chest. Fortunately he was wearing a hard helmet but in spite of this everything was a blur as he became disorientated towards loss of consciousness. He just managed to pull back the column and the throttle; the oscillation suddenly stopped.

It was clear that he too had simulated exactly the conditions which killed Geoffrey de Havilland. This flight resulted in the application of a speed restriction for future sorties. John Derry had concluded that the limiting Mach Number of the 108 was 0.97, the RAE played safe and specified an indicated M 0.87 at 25,000 ft (7,620 m) and 0.85 at 10,000 ft (3,048 m).

By the end of his six-year posting at RAE Lt-Cdr Brown had brought into the test programme Flt/Lt Stewart Muller-Rowland and Flt/Lt George 'Jumbo' Genders, the former to handle the high speed element and Genders the low speed tests. Stalling and spinning tests were to be carried out but, in the case of VW120, no actual stalls were to be initiated as anti-spin parachutes were not fitted. When Eric Brown departed Farnborough he noted in his log book:

> 'DH 108, a killer, Nasty stall, Vicious undamped longitudinal oscillation at speed in bumps'.

This verdict was, all too soon, to be justified. Muller-Rowland, promoted to S/Ldr, continued the longitudinal stability programme in VW120; on 15 February 1950 the machine broke up at Birkhall in Buckinghamshire, the pilot dying in the crash. In the absence of ascertainable defects in the aircraft it was concluded that he had exhausted his oxygen supply and lost consciousness.

The slow speed DH 108, TG283, was to be flown by 'Jumbo' Genders, also promoted to S/Ldr, who investigated its spinning characteristics; as a safeguard anti-spin parachutes were fitted at the wing tips. On 1 May 1950 Genders took off to record by automatic observer the behaviour of the aircraft while approaching the stall, at the stall and during recovery from the stall. Two stalls were to be carried out with the turbine idling at between 12 and 15,000 ft (3,658 and 4,572 m), one with flaps and undercarriage up and the other with them down. After the stalls five straight slideslips were to be made at 10,000 ft (3,048 m) if time permitted.

Fifteen minutes after take-off the 108 was reported to have crashed near Blackbushe airfield. The pilot had managed to leave the aircraft but was seen to be coming down with it, being killed in the crash. The recorder showed that the aircraft carried out the first stall in the 'clean' condition and became uncontrollable during the next stall with flaps down. It is considered that it then entered an inverted spin, the pilot deploying the anti-spin parachutes at 8,500 ft; (2,590 m) only the port one operated as the housing of the starboard one jammed. Control could not be regained so the pilot jettisoned the port parachute. A partial recovery was initiated at about 2,000 ft (610 m), but the 108 entered another spin, this time, right way up. At this point S/Ldr Genders is believed to have tried to abandon the machine, part of which struck him and incapacitated him sufficiently to prevent him pulling the rip cord. He died as he hit the ground alongside the aircraft.

There can be no doubt that the DH 108 flights constituted what was probably the most cost effective research programme ever mounted in the aircraft industry measured in terms of hardware; the shocking loss of life put a rather different complexion on it. Although no actual aircraft was developed from it, much of the data was valuable in the design of the DH 110 which followed it.

CHAPTER 10

The Transonic Years - II

For many years aircraft designers have tried to achieve control of the boundary layer of air passing over the wings with the object of reducing drag by delaying the point on the upper surface at which the flow becomes turbulent. Essentially a considerable suction must be developed over the skin by means of small holes or slots in the surface. The introduction of the gas turbine was seen by Armstrong Whitworth as a possible answer to the suction problem so, after the war, they decided to develop a swept wing tail-less design, first as a glider to prove the aerodynamics of the scheme and later in the form of a twin-jet aircraft, AW 52, the first to be powered with two Rolls-Royce Nene engines of 5,000 lb (2,270 kg) thrust, the second to have Derwents of 3,500 lb (1,598 kg) thrust each. Chief test pilot Eric Franklin carried out taxying trials at Baginton near Coventry and later at Boscombe Down in October 1947. Longitudinal stability soon showed as a major problem and it was difficult to return the nosewheel to the runway. Satisfactory modifications were made before the first flight on 13 November 1947. On approach and flare-out, movement of the control column initiated a rapid fore and aft oscillation at 2 cps. Turbulent air accentuated this instability.

W.H. 'Bill' Else joined Franklin and reported that the controls left much to be desired with far too much sensitivity in pitch. They were not harmonised and were spongy. The introduction of the second prototype with less power only compounded the problems. Both were flown at the 1947 SBAC Show and the test programme continued until March 1949 when Else had an alarming experience when making a low pass over the factory for the benefit of the workforce. A violent shuddering and banging occurred as the 2 cps pitching occurred for the first time with the Derwent-engined aircraft. An alarming +12 G to -4 G registered on the accelerometer so the machine was grounded for a full structural check.

John Lancaster joined the flight test team in May 1949 and on his third familiarisation flight descended into turbulence at 5,000 ft (1,524 m) at an IAS of 320 kt (593 km/hr). A violent oscillation, hitherto not experienced, racked the aircraft at a frequency which totally disorientated Franklin; he feared that he was about to lose consciousness and, for the first time 'in anger' the Martin Baker ejector seat shot him out to a safe parachute landing. The aircraft flew on to make a heavy landing in open country to be written-off after 65 flights in 36 hours. A speed restriction was applied to the second prototype and it was used by AW and RAE for trials to determine the boundary layer transition point. These, and other tests, continued until 1953.

This very intensive and comprehensive programme proved the impractical nature of boundary layer control in other than research aeroplanes; the slightest surface undulation has an effect upon efficiency and even dead insects on the leading edge of the wing can divert the flow. To overcome this particular difficulty the AW 52 was taxied to the end of the runway with large sheets of paper over the wings.

Armstrong-Whitworth AW 52 with Nene engines flying at the 1948 Farnborough Air Show.
(Ken Ellis Collection)

Armstrong Whitworth had hoped, as did de Havilland, that their research aircraft would lead to airliners without tails but both programmes proved beyond doubt that the configuration was not satisfactory for large passenger aircraft. Perhaps, if the active control systems of the 1980s had been available – systems which allow control of completely unstable aircraft – the story of the DH 108 and the AW 52 might have been quite different.

De Havilland proceeded to the DH 106 Comet, the career of which was so sadly blighted whilst AW continued with the Apollo four-Mamba prop-turbine aircraft. Handicapped by its undeveloped engines it was soon abandoned as a result of the startling success of the Dart-engined Vickers Viscount.

Whilst these various tail-less aircraft projects have no direct association with transonic research, there can be no doubt that the drag reduction, which could have been achieved if adequate control had been feasible would have led to major developments in this direction.

The Americans were also involved in similar experiments with, ultimately, more success than in the UK. The Northrop XP–79B was one of the most innovative fighters ever built; it originated in the fertile brains of John K. Northrop and his design team as an all-magnesium single seater to be powered by a 2,000 lb (908 kg) thrust rocket engine fuelled by the extremely dangerous combination of foaming nitric acid and aniline. The least of the problems was that nitric acid decomposes magnesium. Three wooden scale model gliders were built in 1943 and were flown by Harry Crosby and John Myers with good results. One of them was fitted with a small nitric acid/aniline rocket of 200 lb (91 kg) thrust. Harry Crosby flew it, towed into the air behind a P–38 in July 1944. He fired the rocket and, before the fuel was exhausted, reached a speed of 270 mph (434.7 km/hr). He was the first pilot in the USA to fly a rocket propelled aeroplane.

The Air Force decided that the power plant was too dangerous for Service use so concentrated upon orthodox jet propulsion. This became the XP–79B with two jet engines in the wings. In September 1945 Crosby took off for the first time, flew easily for a quarter of an hour when it began a slow roll which developed into a spin. Unable to recover, Crosby baled out at 2,000 ft (610 m) only to collide with the spinning machine; he became unconscious and, unable to deploy his parachute, he died as he hit the ground. The XP–79 programme led to a variant of the basic design powered by two jet engines, which became known as the 'Flying Ram' and was to be used, quite literally as such. The wing was built of heavy magnesium plate to withstand the impact as the pilot, lying prone in the cockpit, flew the machine to cut off the wing or tail of his adversary. After fifteen minutes flying time, in September 1945, it went out of control and was destroyed in the ensuing crash, which killed the pilot.

Prototype of Northrop XP–79B in which Harry Crosby was killed on 12 September 1945. In the background are: left, a Cessna UC–78 Bobcat, and, right, a Fairchild AT–14A crew trainer. (U.S.A.F. Edwards Air Force Base)

These military projects were the outcome of a lifelong interest of John Northrop in aeroplanes without tails which he saw as an unnecessary complication and source of unnecessary weight and drag. His first tentative venture was a pusher flying wing built in 1928. This had two slender tailbooms carrying a tailplane and twin rudders; he hoped that, at a future date these appendages might be removed. It flew well but the amputations did not take place.

Northrop was continually lobbying the Air Force to order a tail-less bomber and, as some interest was manifest, he built several scale models about one third full size; these, known as type N–9M, were flown by Service pilots and the validity of the concept was established by the excellent results obtained. The first one was flown in December 1942 but after thirty hours in the air it crashed, killing the pilot. There was no evidence of the cause of the accident. Northrop concluded that he had entered a spin from which he was unable to recover. The Americans were into the era of the giant bomber. Convair with its huge six-engined B–36 were deadly rivals to Northrop who had received an order for the tail-less bomber, the XB–35, with a span of 192 ft (52.52 m) and four Pratt & Whitney R–4360 four-row radial engines developing, initially, 3,000 hp and driving eight-bladed pusher contra-rotating propellers. In June 1946 Max Stanley made the first flight from Northrop's Hawthorne plant to Muroc Air Force Base where flight testing was to be carried out.

Edwards Air Force Base Test Center. On the flight line in the foreground is a Consolidated B–36, behind it a B–29 and to the right a B–52.
(U.S.A.F. photograph, Warren M. Bodie Archive, via Ken Ellis Collection)

No problems were experienced with its aerodynamics or the control of this unique aeroplane but the power plant was a nightmare. The huge propellers were the main area of pain and grief. Stripped reduction gear teeth; unsatisfactory operation of the translation units; blade pitch runaways and even fires were the order of the day. On one of the first test sorties the pilot had to close down two engines on one side due to propeller failure. This was a drastic test of the directional control of the aircraft but a safe landing was made. The eight-blade units were changed for six-blade ones with huge paddle blades to absorb the power; there was interference between adjacent blades and vibration and it took two years to smooth out all the problems of the aircraft, generally because of the unserviceability of the prop installation.

From the XB–35 was developed the YB–49, a jet version, handicapped initially by the fact that in 1945 the most powerful jet engine was the GE TG–180 with a thrust of only 3,750 lb (1,700 kg). Eight were used in two groupings of four in the area between the original piston engines.

The first flight was made to Muroc AFB in October 1947 and the bomber showed a sparkling performance. The reliability of the engines and services was high so the test programme proceeded at a gratifying pace. Then came a devastating blow; in June 1948 the second prototype crashed killing the crew of five including USAF Capt. Glen Edwards. It was believed that the machine had been flown in a dive beyond its designed structural limits. Muroc AFB was renamed Edwards AFB in memory of the pilot. For probably political reasons the Convair B–36 won the Air Force contract but plans were prepared to convert ten of the remaining XB–35s to jet power; after one conversion the Air Force cancelled the programme and the flying wings were relegated to history.

A British fighter of the 1950s which could be said to have had a chequered test flying career was the Gloster Javelin. Competitive with the de Havilland DH 110 it was a radical design following the aerodynamic principles for delta wing established in Germany by Dr Alexander Lippisch and analysed by the RAE after the war. Part of the RAE research programme was the Boulton Paul P 111, the predecessor of the P 120 in which Ben Gunn nearly lost his life.

The need for the Javelin originated in December 1946 with Air Staff Operational Requirement OR227 for a two-seat night fighter. Not until 1948 was the Requirement finalized as Spec. F4348 which caused Gloster to abandon their original design, similar to a swept-wing Meteor, for one with a delta wing and delta tailplane mounted on a swept back fin. It was designed to achieve Mach 0.94 with two 12,000 lb (5,443 kg) thrust jet engines.

The tail-less Boulton Paul P 111 did not fly until October 1950 by which time the design of the Javelin was reaching finality; nevertheless it provided confirmation of the validity of some of the more unusual design features of the new fighter. Further proof was afforded when the P 120 flew in August 1952; this had a tailplane but Gunn's crash took place before much data could be obtained from it.

Other contemporary aircraft of comparable configuration were the Avro 707 tail-less deltas built to confirm the aerodynamics of the projected Avro 698 bomber, to be named Vulcan. The first of these 707s also confirmed the validity of the Javelin concept. This aircraft soon crashed at Blackbushe killing the pilot, Eric Esler. It was not possible to explain the crash but it seemed that the configuration was not a contributory factor. The next 707 did not fly until September 1950 as Gloster learned little of value to the Javelin programme. It did, however, give chief test pilot, S/Ldr W.A. Waterton, flight experience in a delta; he concentrated upon evaluation of the tricky low speed area of the flight envelope.

Four prototypes of the Gloster GA5, as it became known, were ordered. They were to be fitted with two 9,000 lb (4,082 kg) thrust Armstrong Siddeley Sapphire engines. They were to have all-moving tailplanes with orthodox elevators and power boosted ailerons. Ability to trim the tailplane incidence was helpful in the transonic region and it also permitted the use of landing flaps. Waterton was shocked by the design of the flying controls with only limited hydraulic assistance. He was convinced that, like its predecessor the Meteor, it would become heavy at speed. Protests to the design department met with little response. The first flight of the prototype, WD804, now named Javelin, proved his doubts to be well founded; even on taxying trials in October 1951, lowering the flaps caused the nose to rear up. Modifications were made, reluctantly, to the tailplane incidence range and, at the end of October, Waterton flew the Javelin for the first time.

Northrop XB–35 flying wing bomber. Initially powered by piston engines driving contra-rotating propellers; this one, the second prototype, 42–38323, had single propellers. Two aircraft were converted to be powered by six J–35 turbojets. This first flew in May 1950.
(U.S.A.F. Edwards Air Force Base)

Almost as soon as he was airborne vibration developed at the tail and, at 200 mph (322 km/hr) it shook the whole airframe. After 30 minutes at 150 mph (241 km/hr) he landed without difficulty. The machine flew well and showed considerable promise but there were many niggling problems in which, according to Waterton, the design staff showed little interest. In some respects there were dangerous characteristics in the area of control. Near the stall the elevator controls reversed, the column having to be operated in the opposite direction to normal. The machine tightened up in a turn and pitched up when the flaps were deployed. Again the design staff resented any suggestion that their swan was a bit of a lame duck.

As the tests progressed Bill found that it was extremely hard work to carry out aerobatics – a highly undesirable state of affairs in a fighter. He would not carry out a loop, believing that the physical effort involved in pulling out of a fast dive would be beyond him. At this time the profit motive tended to persuade certain people in the industry that aircraft must be put into production as soon as possible and that test pilots must not let their quest for perfection stand in the way. Many did not realise that the objective of the test pilot was to ensure that the aeroplane was safe for the average squadron pilot to fly and did not require the skill of a test pilot as safeguard against disaster. It was unfortunate that George Carter had retired at an early stage in the test programme, as he would certainly have listened to his chief test pilot, as Michael Daunt found when he criticised both the Typhoon and the Meteor.

By June 1952 WD804 had made 98 flights, 84 of them in the hands of Waterton; some alterations had been made to the controls, still heaviness was apparent on take-off and there was pitch instability at low speeds. Competition with the DH110 was hotting up and both aircraft were to be demonstrated to Fighter Command top brass. In June 1952, on a hot summer day, Bill took off for a prolonged flight at high speed; he decided to show the aircraft to the USAF at Fairford to indicate that they were not unique in producing innovative aeroplanes. He opened the throttles and the big fighter roared on at 3,000 ft (915 m). He circled Fairford and, on his return to base, increased power to 90 per cent and then on to full throttle reaching a speed about 30 mph (48 km/hr) lower than his previous maximum. Suddenly smooth flight was transformed into a crazy blur of vibration – flutter! The dreaded condition had happened. Before the throttles could be closed or the air brakes deployed there were two violent bangs and then silence as the nose began to drop towards the ground only a few seconds away. He quickly realised that closing the throttle had induced the nose-down pitch so he increased power to bring the aircraft into level flight again.

With the machine likely to be in an weakened condition he dare not subject it to further stress by lowering the powerful air brakes, so he was in a serious dilemma. All his instincts, as a test pilot, were directed to bringing the crippled Javelin home so that the problem could be identified; in any case the risk of ejecting from it at such a high air speed was a severe one. He wondered if the tailplane trimmer could be used to control pitch, if so it might be possible to juggle the airbrake and throttles to make a safe landing. On the other hand total de-stabilisation might be the outcome, with fatal results.

With the control column gripped firmly between his knees and his right hand on the canopy jettison lever he slowly wound the trim wheel right back and was relieved to find the nose rising into a climb. At 10,000 ft (3048 m) he throttled back and levelled out at an indicated airspeed of 345 mph (555 km/hr). At least he could now bale out if the machine could not be landed with a reasonable chance of survival. Waterton reported to Control that he was heading for the Bristol Channel where, if he had to leave it, the Javelin could fall into the water, avoiding a disaster on the ground. He simulated all the actions necessary for landing and was agreeably surprised when he realised that he had a fighting chance of a successful outcome, so, with fuel levels falling fast he radioed Control asking them to warn Boscombe Down that he would attempt a landing on their long runway, other nearby airfields were also alerted.

The approach to the runway seemed interminable as Bill battled with his emotions; reason demanded the saving of a valuable prototype whilst he saw vividly the images of the burned bodies of pilots who he had tried to save from wrecked and burning aircraft which had come to grief on landing. As soon as he was committed to the landing he had no time for introspection – wheels down, flaps to be partly lowered at 1,500 ft (457 m) with an airspeed of 230 mph (370 km/hr). He made a wide circuit to align the Javelin with the main runway which ran from East to West.

Column between the knees, left hand on the trimmer with his right arm across his chest to control the throttles he descended through 1,000 ft (305 m) to 500 ft (153 m) at a speed of about 63 mph (101 km/hr) faster than normal as control was seriously degraded; so he crossed the boundary praying that a gust would not ruin his approach. He eased the throttles back as the wheels touched in a perfect landing. Suddenly all was lost, the aircraft bumped into the air again to fall back upon the undercarriage, the oleo legs compressed and hurled it back into the air again. The heavy machine bounded along the runway until a near stall dropped it heavily upon the port undercarriage leg which went through the wing rupturing the fuel tank, the contents of which immediately caught fire as the wing hit the runway slewing the machine on to the grass and slowing it down. Once more it bounced into the air to land, this time, heavily upon the starboard leg which also went through the wing to start another fire on the other side, the Javelin swung round to subside, a blazing wreck with the pilot surrounded by smoke and flame and marvelling that he was still alive.

Fortunately, to improve airflow on the approach he had left the canopy in the closed position and it had, so far, protected him from burns, now, however it seemed likely that it was only a temporary reprieve as the button which moved it aft was totally ineffective. By this time he was in dire peril with the canopy immoveable and the perspex melting in the suffocating heat. Bill had the presence of mind to switch on his neat oxygen supply and fumbled for the axe stowed in the cockpit for use in such an emergency. It could not be found as the bumping had dislodged it from its fixings. More fuel tanks exploded as, in a frenzy of activity, he hammered on the perspex and on the button; miraculously it began to move, in sheer desperation he forced it two thirds open and leapt out of the wreck. As the fire tender arrived he rushed back to the nose to recover the flight recorders to which foam had been directed. They were unharmed and provided valuable evidence of the cause of the accident. It proved to be due to flutter which tore the elevators away; for his skill and courage in bringing the aircraft back and saving the recorders Bill Waterton was awarded the George Medal.

Fortunately the second prototype was almost ready for the first flight which was made by Waterton on 7 July 1952. Severe limitations were placed upon its flight envelope until all the lessons from the disaster had been learned. It was the first British aircraft to be fitted with a flight resonance system which enabled a thorough check to be made on the natural resonant frequencies of the whole of the airframe components. The system was devised by Geoff Longford of the Gloster Research Department and consisted of electrically rotated eccentric weights in the structure; these could be operated at different speeds by the pilot and any sympathetic resonance of the airframe identified by recorders.

Having mastered the technique of the flight resonance system Waterton flew the new machine at the Farnborough Show and it soon became clear that the thick wing was a serious handicap to achieving the performance required so modifications were made to the wing to improve its aerodynamic form and to reduce the tendency to tip stalling which caused the tightening up in turns. The second prototype WD808 was fitted with the new wing and first flew on 28 May 1953. Two weeks later Peter Lawrence, who had joined Gloster from Blackburn in 1952 was asked by Bill to give a second opinion on the elevator control at low speed which appeared to be sluggish. Lawrence had flown WD808 with the earlier wing and was familiar with it. He studied the test reports of his chief's flight in it and took off for a preliminary sortie prior to a more intensive study later in the day after a conference with Waterton. Half an hour after his afternoon take-off a radio message was received by Control from Lawrence 'I am in trouble', then a few garbled words and silence. He was believed to be just south of Bristol at the time. Then came a message from the police that an aircraft had crashed near Bristol; it was the Javelin. Peter Lawrence had entered an irrecoverable deep stall and, realising that he was descending towards a school playing field tried to steer the machine away from it leaving his departure too late for the ejection seat and parachute to operate effectively. His body was alongside the wreck. Once again a chief test pilot had the harrowing task of visiting a young widow to inform her of the death of her husband.

The flight recorder showed all the detail of the reasons for the accident; the use of the large flaps at too slow speed and an excessive angle of attack which caused the wing to blanket the elevators, thus preventing recovery from the stall. The trace indicated that the Javelin descended with virtually no forward speed. This tragedy was the second recorded occurrence of this type of stall which was to kill a number of fine pilots later, although in 1937 George Errington of Airspeed had experienced what must have been a super stall when flying the Queen Wasp biplane target aircraft, he found that by throttling back and increasing the angle of attack the machine would descend under perfect lateral control with no forward speed. With a propeller in front it was easy to blow air over the elevators and pull out without difficulty. It is sadly ironic that George lost his life, with Peter Barlow and his crew in June 1966 when a de Havilland Trident developed a deep stall near Felthorpe, Norfolk; recovery proved impossible and the machine hit the ground in a horizontal attitude with no forward speed. In 1963 Mike Lithgow, with a test crew, took off from Wisley in a BAC 111 to measure stability at approaches to the stall with the centre of gravity as far aft as possible. Forty-two previous flights had explored this régime up to CG aft, with varying flap angles. On this flight the approach to the stall had been checked 'clean' with no flap. Then 8° was selected which caused a high angle of incidence but no pitch down as might be expected. The machine was in a classic deep stall; all on board died as it hit the ground.

As a further indication of the seriousness of this phenomenon 'Spud' Murphy, of Handley Page, had the dubious distinction of being only the second pilot to enter a deep stall in a jet aircraft when his Victor bomber succumbed in 1962. He and his co-pilot were able to bale out at 500 ft (152 m); the story of this sortie is told in Chapter 15. The outcome of these tragedies was the incorporation of various aerodynamic devices to make the identification of approach to the stall more positive and, in some cases, stick pushers were incorporated to dive the aircraft out of dangerous attitudes.

In March 1954 W/Cdr R.F. 'Dickie' Martin succeeded Bill Waterton as chief test pilot. He had been in command of Aerodynamics Flight at RAE since the death of S/Ldr Muller Rowland in the DH 108 and had achieved a degree of notoriety in the press when he was named as the pilot who had aimed a sonic boom at London causing questions to be asked in the House of Commons. Newspapers had reported that the new Javelin fighter was unable to fly at supersonic speed. Gloster, as befits a reputable company apologised but the point had been made! Yet another tragic accident marred the development programme of the Javelin. On 21 October 1954 an RAE pilot, F/Lt R.J. Ross crashed into the Bristol

Channel. It was presumed that he entered a spin at too low an altitude and did not realise how rapidly the type descended in a spin. He hit the water before recovery; neither the aircraft nor the body of the pilot was recovered.

Many hours of test flying and the introduction of an all-moving slab tailplane without elevators, one of the first to be fitted to a British aeroplane, overcame many of Bill Waterton's frustrations and enabled the Javelin to be delivered to squadrons in February 1956. Generally the type was popular with its pilots. There was a plan to develop another version with a thin wing to improve performance substantially so that Mach 1.0 plus could be achieved in level flight. The notorious Duncan Sandys White Paper of 1957 with its absurd conclusion that guided missiles would soon replace manned fighters caused the contract to be cancelled and hastened the demise of the Gloster company.

The entry into service of the Javelin and experience with the DH 110 convinced the Air Staff that a single-seat fighter was also needed. Hawker had not followed up their success with the Tempest into the jet era except for several prototypes, the first of which, the P 1040 which first flew in September 1947, this had an unswept wing and was ultimately developed into the Sea Hawk naval fighter; in view of the state of the Hawker works at that time Sydney Camm, the famous chief designer, commented with asperity, 'Thank God for the Royal Navy' and put the design office into top gear to the ultimate development of the elegant Hawker monoplanes to go into production, the P 1067 Hunter.

Chapter 8 tells of the disagreement between W.E.W. 'Teddy' Petter and the board of the Westland Aircraft Company which led to his resignation to join the English Electric Company at Warton, Lancs. He took with him outline proposals for a new jet bomber which became the remarkable Canberra, first flown by W/Cdr Roland 'Bee' Beamont on Friday 13 May 1949. At last a high altitude high speed jet bomber was in the air. With two 6,000 lb (2,724 kg) thrust Rolls-Royce Avon engines and a relatively low wing loading it proved to be a lively performer and showed few problems; one was a sharp variation in rudder response due to overbalance, which was easily corrected before the second flight by

English Electric Canberra bomber. A prototype. (Ken Ellis Collection)

modifying the horn balance. The whole of the test programme was completed with virtually no drama which might have been expected with such a new design. It had a performance superior to contemporary fighters and the test flight team began to consider aerobatics as a feature at air displays and demonstrations to potential foreign customers.

'Bee' Beamont flew the prototype some distance from Warton to avoid alarming the 'doubting Thomases' at senior management level and developed a series of manoeuvres based upon loops and rolls which showed to perfection what a superb aircraft the new bomber was. They were first performed publicly at the 1949 SBAC Show at Farnborough by 'Bee' and were demonstrated throughout the world, surprising the onlookers who could hardly imagine that a bomber could be capable of such manoeuvres almost within the area of the airfield.

By 1950 the Canberra was in volume production, ultimately being built at four factories and entering service with No. 101 Squadron at Binbrook in May 1951. It was the first British jet bomber and the first to serve in the RAF. The ultimate accolade was its production by Martin at Baltimore as the B–57 for operation in the USAF.

Having successfully launched the outstanding Camberra bomber Teddy Petter turned his attention to a fighter design which became a classic, a quantum leap to Britain's first and only supersonic fighter to go into series production. He envisaged two engines, one on top of the other in a deep fuselage with 60° of wing sweep-back. It would have powered controls, a highly advanced avionics pack and weapons system. The Ministry of Supply and RAE were doubtful if such a young design team were capable of such a project but, in 1947, issued a study contract followed by an order in 1949 for two prototypes and a static test airframe.

Because of the doubts felt by the RAE scientists that 60° sweepback was a serious step into the unknown and that a reduced angle would be safer the Short Company was instructed to build an experimental aircraft, the SB 5, which could be fitted with wings of varying sweep angle and tailplanes in positions from the low point of the fuselage to the top of the fin.

English Electric had decided that the right place for the tailplane was low down on the fuselage out of the wing wash, realising that a higher tail had been largely responsible for pitch-up problems with various contemporary fighters and that the high position on top of the fin was an invitation to the near-fatal deep stall which had killed, and would continue to kill, pilots of aircraft which entered this régime.

Short SB–5 research aircraft.
(Aeroplane Monthly)

English Electric P1 prototype WG760. (British Aerospace, Warton)

At the request of RAE the first flight by Tom Brooke-Smith, chief test pilot of Short Brothers, was made in 1953 with the wing swept 50° and the tail in what the English Electric designers thought was the most dangerous location at the top of the fin. Brooke-Smith found that provided he avoided flight near the stall the aeroplane flew reasonably well albeit with coarse controls and no climb ability above 8,000 ft (2,438 m) where thrust equalled drag. An interesting aspect of the test sorties was the first experience of a phenomenon suspected from the wind tunnel tests that a highly swept wing generated a strong leading edge vortex which had a stabilising effect upon lateral control at high angles of attack – a factor which was of vital importance in the design of Concorde.

With the imminence of the first flight of the new P 1 aircraft, Beamont was invited to fly the SB-5 at Boscombe Down. His first flight in it was on 11 August 1953 and he was, initially, somewhat unimpressed by the rather agricultural nature of the beast. His 23 flights in it revealed much of value in handling swept wing aircraft at low speed and from it was developed the chordwise slot to control the vortex pattern near the aileron, a feature which appeared on the P 1 and all subsequent Lightnings. The major contribution to the P 1 programme was to prove that the basic design was absolutely right and that the reservations at Ministry of Supply and RAE were entirely without foundation. In other words, the SB-5 was a waste of money. It was, however, used later, with 70° wing sweep to join the HP 115 in Concorde research at RAE Bedford.

The first flight of the P 1, WG760, was made by Beamont on 4 August 1954; it was remarkably successful and M 1.0 was exceeded on the third flight without re-heat which had not been fitted at that stage. A few minor modifications were necessary to aileron gearing and in the static balance of the rudder and aileron circuits, later the Aden guns and re-heat were installed in the second prototype, WG763. This enabled the performance to be checked between M 1.1 and M 1.5. These tests revealed that the fin area was marginal and would be inadequate when long range tanks and missiles were carried. Several increases in area were incorporated and one of them led to a serious accident which nearly cost the life of test pilot John Squier; a second one seriously injured Jimmy Dell and his flight test engineer, Graham Elkington. Both failures occurred with the trainer version of the Lightning.

In his book *Testing Years* 'Bee' Beamont recalls some of the less dramatic episodes of the P 1 development programme. A firing range had been set up on the coast near Warton, to the consternation of the local residents. One, a senior citizen, was considerably affronted when Desmond de Villiers managed to place a number of 30 mm spent Aden shell cases in his garden! The location was quickly changed. 'Bee' himself, had an alarming experience when extending the flutter envelope to the maximum subsonic IAS. At 800 ft (243.8 m) over Morecambe Bay he was increasing the test speed from 575 kts to 585 kts. Vibration was created by 'bonkers' fired explosively by pressing the gun firing button. As he did so a violent explosion occurred, the aircraft bucked and he could see nothing; his first thought was that he had blown a wing or the tail off, but as the 'explosion' continued and he began to see again he realised that either the windscreen or the canopy – or both – had disappeared and he was sitting in a 550 kt draught, his helmet and visor had also disappeared so his eyes had to remain closed as he pulled back power and the stick to gain height for a bale-out if this drastic step became necessary. At 400 kts at an altitude of 4,000 ft (1220 m) he was able to see again and realised that the screen was still in place but the canopy had gone. A difficult landing was safely made with the pilot suffering severely from an injection of glass fibre from the cockpit lining into his eyes. Two other canopy failures occurred before a satisfactory modification to the locks was made; in both cases the pilot was Desmond de Villiers and in one of them he became the world's first open-cockpit supersonic pilot – a dubious distinction, indeed!

The prototype Lightning was, of course, different to the P 1 although it shared the major handicap of inadequate fuel capacity, average test sorties being around 30-40 min duration. XA847 cleared its first Service release point of M 1.5 by a handsome margin, achieving M 1.8 in its first 30 flights and M 2.0, for the first time in the case of a British aircraft, one year later. It proved to be a superb aeroplane with good handling qualities. By 1957 its success was assured but only if the fuel capacity could be increased, as, indeed it was. Surprisingly no autostabilisation was required to ensure stability in all axes up to a speed beyond Mach 2.0. Beamont later cleared it to M 2.14. For the purpose of achieving a high degree of weapon aiming accuracy an autostabilising system was installed.

The rate of climb was a breathtaking 30,000 ft (9,144 m) in 2½ min. whilst low level acceleration to 700 kt/M 1.1 from brakes off was 2 min.

The development programme involved no fewer than 21 prototypes and pre-production aircraft to clear the very advanced weapon systems carried by the Lightning. There were few dramas during the intensive testing period, Desmond de Villiers' open cockpit experience has been mentioned; in the next chapter two miraculous escapes by other test pilots will be recorded.

The Lightning proved to be superior in combat manoeuvrability to all its contemporaries, including the Mirage, Phantom and Starfighter. It gave superb service in the Squadrons.

Lightning Mk 2A with ventral fuel tank and Firestreak missiles. (British Aerospace, Warton)

CHAPTER 11

Transonic and Subsonic Experiences

John W.C. Squier, one of the Warton test pilots, must be one of the luckiest pilots to survive an exceptionally hazardous incident. He was briefed to fly the prototype, XL628, Mk IV Lightning with widened cockpit to take pilot and instructor side-by-side. He was briefed during the morning of 1 October 1959 to climb to 35,000 ft (10,668 m) and accelerate to M 1.7 noting engine data at every 0.1 Mach above M 1.0 to M 1.7 at which speed he was to climb to 40,000 ft (12,192 m) stabilise and make a 360° roll to starboard using maximum aileron with feet off rudder. Taking off at 1115 hours local time he accelerated to 450 kt (834 km/hr) climbing at M 0.9 to 35,000 ft (10,668 m) as briefed. As speed stabilised at M 1.7 John Squier called for a fix from Ulster radar and was informed that he was 20 miles (32.2 km) due west of St Bee's Head; at that point he switched on the instrumentation and applied maximum starboard aileron with both feet off the rudder pedals; a high speed roll developed and when he centralised the controls to stop it the aircraft yawed violently to starboard to a degree which was considerably greater than had been previously experienced in maximum aileron rolls when flying single-seat Lightnings. He realised that a structural failure must have occurred and, as the aircraft was yawing violently in both directions and also pitching, totally uncontrollably, an ejection was essential. On reaching up to grasp the seat blind he noticed that the pitot probe was bent right across the air intake.

The blind was pulled and, after what appeared to be minutes, the canopy detached; after what appeared to be an even longer period the seat fired. As he left the aircraft he was not really conscious of the air blast but was trying to hold firmly to the face blind with a powerful force being applied to his arms. Eventually they were pulled away from the blind and were spreadeagled with John experiencing intense pain in the shoulder joints as if the arms were being pulled out of their sockets with the impression of violent rotation. Suddenly there was the feeling of a quiet descent in the seat, then there was a clang as the seat locks detached to part company with its occupant. It was not immediately apparent that the parachute had not opened; only when passing through cloud and emerging at the bottom did Squier realise that the sea looked very close, at which point he pulled the manual override, suddenly the parachute deployed. He hit the water almost immediately but the life jacket was not inflated. As he went down to the extent of the shroud lines he triggered off the inflation bottle and immediately returned to the surface, mixed up with the shroud lines from which he disentangled himself to release the 'chute. The dinghy in the survival pack was inflated, fortunately, right way up but full of water. With some difficulty he climbed into it; the baler had disappeared so a shoe had to suffice. Having found the baler the job continued with it until most of the water had gone. It was then time to rig the SARAH (search and rescue and homing) beacon and its aerial. The earpiece was entirely dead instead of emitting the low pitch hum to indicate that it was operating. It remained dead.

John Squier's Vampire. If it had hit the tree the outcome might have been very different.
(John Squier)

After a tidy-up of the dinghy and extending its cover to keep warm he was violently sick, bringing up sea-water. No more nausea was experienced. When he abandoned the bonedome he could not find the oxygen mask which appeared to have been blown off when ejection took place, this would account for the complete absence of any recollection of events from the shoulder pain to recovery of consciousness shortly before hitting the sea. Two hours later an amphibian flew over from the north without spotting the dinghy; as it approached Squier grabbed a two star signal rocket and pulled the pin, this, too, failed to operate; an hour later the aircraft returned; another two star red was actuated; it began to hiss and then went out; the final rocket worked perfectly but, by this time, the amphibian had passed overhead.

For the rest of the day he did nothing but sit in the dinghy until dark when he erected the sea light which was a slight comfort during an endless night. When dawn broke he pulled back the dinghy covers to find rain and poor visibility which did, at least, reveal a coast line. He thought that it was the east coast of somewhere – probably Ireland; if so he was concerned at the prospect of being carried out into the Atlantic through the Giant's Causeway, but, at least, it offered a hope and a place to aim for, so he began to paddle with his hands; this was not very effective and the use of a knee-pad sent the dinghy round in circles; he found a piece of driftwood alongside and was able to break it into two reasonable paddles; some progress was then made to about 200 yards (183 m) from the shore, the current preventing a closer approach and moving the dinghy out again. This went on for hours with ships passing as he blew the whistle in an attempt to attract attention.

Later he saw a large house with a garden but could not approach it. Some hours later the wind and tide changed, moving the dinghy towards a small bay with a tower in it; he eventually reached the tower and moored to it to rest and attempt to produce some water from the solar still which he had erected as soon as he boarded the dinghy. When, after his rest, he decided to make another attempt to reach the shore he discovered, to his dismay, that the tide had gone down so that the knot of the mooring line was out of reach; not having a knife he managed to sever the line with the sharpe edge of a tin containing some pastilles. Seaweed covered the edge of the sea so he pulled himself to the rocks by the seaweed and dropped into about four feet of water. On reaching dry land his balance was so bad that walking was impossible; crawling on all fours he found a path leading to trees and a house. He was able, at that stage, to walk with difficulty into the garden of a house where a woman, the matron of the school, as it proved to be, was picking flowers. She told John that the story of his loss was in all the papers. He was put to bed and the police and a doctor were summoned. Sadly, the dour Scottish constable could not understand Squier's accent and he could not understand the broad Scottish accent of the policeman who decided that he had better send for the sergeant! The doctor soon arrived but was not familiar with the problems of patients subjected to supersonic ejection from an aeroplane at high altitude. He inspected the ears which were painful and decided that both drums had been burst; happily, he was in error in this diagnosis but John's eyes were in a very bad state, like raw liver. John was then transferred by ambulance to Stranraer Cottage Hospital – his point of arrival was Scotland not Ireland. On the following day four doctors from the Institute of Aviation Medicine appeared and diagnosed two compressed vertebrae resulting from the ejection. After two weeks he was transferred by air from West Freugh to Warton and then to Preston Royal Infirmary where he spent another month.

During the ensuing investigation of the event which led to John Squier spending 36 hours in the sea the failure of the survival gear was a matter of considerable concern; the oxygen mask torn off by the blast was replaced by a different design now used by all RAF pilots; the SARAH beacon was found to have a completely useless high tension battery. It was found to be one week outside its inspection time and the battery was flat; the air pressure top-up pump for the dinghy could not be used as the hard plastic connector on the dinghy itself had been broken during ejection. The investigation into the actual accident led to the conclusion that although all the single-seat Lightnings had carried out the identical 360° roll at M 1.7 it was the first time that it had been carried out on a two-seat aircraft. It was concluded that the thickening of the forward part of the fuselage to contain the second seat had detracted from the stability of it, particularly with two Firestreak missiles fitted as well.

John Squier's dreadful experience gave him the dubious accolade of being an almost unique 'guinea pig' and the Institute of Aviation Medicine must have obtained valuable information about survival equipment and techniques which would be of great benefit in the design of equipment, including the ejector seat itself. His injuries resulting from the ejection at M 1.7 included haemorrhaging of his eyes and middle ears, he became totally deaf after a week, fortunately this was a temporary handicap; both legs were black with bruises from the knee downwards with his right elbow being badly bruised over an area one foot long, presumably due to his arm being knocked on to the SARAH battery which was stowed on the right side of the survival pack. Apart from the vertebra injury these injuries were superficial.

A totally unnecessary ordeal after such an experience was the attention of the Press representatives who harried and harassed John and his wife for eight months; their opinion of what he politely calls the 'gentlemen of the Press' is a very low one.

Ultimately, eight months later, he returned to flying, initially in the Company Dove but moving to Canberras before he retired from flying in December 1966.

Ill-informed speculation attributed the Lightning T5 mishap to the low operating loads on the selector button facilitating easy operation of the gear. Although it was considered unlikely to be the primary cause, temporary guards were fitted over the buttons until the system could be reconsidered.

Six years later Jimmy Dell, a very experienced Lightning test pilot, was investigating with George Elkington, his observer, roll/inertia coupling characteristics in XM966, the Mk V trainer prototype. Squier's experience was repeated, Dell and Elkington ejecting at 35,000 ft (10,668 m) and 3 G. After a 90° roll it became obvious through the rapidly reducing rate of roll and swift diversion that catastrophic structural failure had occurred. Fortunately the crew were safe and most of the wreckage was recovered.

Exhaustive tests revealed that directional stability at small angles of side-slip was inadequate and the non-linearity led to a yawing action and ultimate fin failure. The problem was easily solved.

On 3 November 1947 John Squier had experienced a serious accident in a DH Vampire which was being built at the Samlesbury factory of English Electric, one of the Mk 3 aircraft on order from the Royal Canadian Air Force. It was a routine test, the second one flown. He began his take-off on Runway 26 which had a farmhouse only 200 yards (183 m) from the end and almost in line with it. At ten feet (3 m) the engine cut. The runway was only 1200 yards (1097 m) long so a landing back on the runway was impossible; he missed the aerodrome fence and headed for a hedge with the farmhouse slightly to the right of the line of flight and a tree slightly to the left, the distance between the two being less than thirty yards (27 m) the Vampire hurtled between the two obstacles and struck the ground in a shallow, dried up, pond which hurled the aircraft back into the air. Squier went through the bottom of the seat and the canopy shattered; he was then airborne again towards a row of trees and very conscious of the fact that half a ton (508 kg) of Goblin engine was behind him and a light wood shell in front. He decided that to avoid total disaster he must put one wing down by applying full aileron to starboard; the tip hit the ground and the aircraft spun round to slide backwards, stopping with the tailplane six inches (15 cm) from the nearest tree. He was fortunate to escape with minor injuries and a slightly strained back.

Lightning test pilot, George Aird also had a miraculous escape in an incident which occurred near Hatfield on 13 September 1962 – the superstitious may note the frequency of these events. On that date he was flying from the DH runway on a bright clear day with a north-east wind which required the use of Runway 06. Whilst the Lightning was airborne an arrester barrier was deployed at the eastern end. George completed a re-heat test up to M 1.7 which, after the Squier's episode was the limit set by fin restrictions. This sortie was flown off the south coast at 36,000 ft (10,973 m).

During the return flight the test engine was shut down and two unsuccessful attempts made to re-light. The third attempt was successful but fuel which should have been vented was retained by a blocked drain and, later, ignited via a small crack in the tail-pipe. A double 're-heat' warning appeared on the panel as he descended through 15,000 ft (4,572 m) NE of Hatfield runway which he could clearly see ahead. Descent speed was 400 kts (739.6 km/hr) with air brakes out and engines to Idle/Fast Idle. A quick check over the instruments and weaving the aircraft from side to side failed to corroborate the fire warning. Aird decided to attempt a landing in the hope that the fire warning was spurious as was frequently reported in air safety magazines of the period. He decided not to jettison the big ventral fuel tank to avoid injury to people on the ground. If Runway 24 had been in use he would have made a safe landing but the circuit to approach 06 was just too long. Ten seconds from touch-down the Lightning pitched violently upwards; George quickly pushed the stick forward instinctively and then waggled it in disbelief as it appeared to be disconnected. Realising that he had no control he pulled the ejection seat face blind and came to in the middle of a large greenhouse alongside the St Albans Road at Smallford. He recognised an agreeable sensation of being sprayed with warm water and concluded that he was in Heaven! Describing the arrival he said,

'My legs spoiled the greenhouse and vice-versa but I suffered no back injury from the ejection'.

From experience with the early bang seats he had pulled the face blind handle as a reflex action which saved his back and his life at that very low altitude, also saving his face from injury as he went through the glass – the top handle does not exist on modern seats. It happened that a photographer, Jim Meade, was in the vicinity and photographed the episode, producing one of the most remarkable aviation photographs of all time. The pitch-up was due to the tailplane actuator anchorage being weakened by the fire.

George Aird experienced two subsequent fire warnings, one in a DH Comet IA due to a leak of hot gas and one in a heavily laden DH Sea Vixen in which he carried out an overweight single-engine landing at RAE Bedford, Hatfield runway being too short for a Sea Vixen at 41,000 lb (18,600 kg). This warning proved to be spurious and remained on after the fire drills had been carried out and the suspect engine had been shut down. On the Comet sortie a double hydraulic failure led to a 30 mph (48 km/hr) trundle off the end of the runway with all four engines shut down; there was no pressure for the brakes or the nose-wheel steering and the flaps were half-way down. There was just enough pressure in the flying control circuits to enable Aird to rudder away from the old ILS blockhouse at the end of the runway before stopping on the grass.

This was an example of the manner in which test pilots make a substantial improvement in air safety. The problem was due to a defective hydraulic hose in one of the systems and a faulty non-return valve which permitted a leak from the sound system to the defective one. The shelf life of the hose was reduced.

Flypast at Hatfield on 8 April 1968. Comet 1A, XM823, en-route to R.A.F. Shawbury prior to permanent display at Cosford Aerospace Museum as G-APAS in B.O.A.C. colours.
(British Aerospace, Hatfield, via George Aird)

George Aird in the cockpit of Sea Vixen XJ476.
(British Aerospace, Hatfield, via George Aird)

Another example of the manner in which deterioration can cause serious problems was the experience of S/Ldr David Masters who was chief test pilot at the Fairey factory at Ringway, Manchester. A rather elderly Vickers Viking had been allocated to Ringway for removal of a de-icing spray rig fitted during its time at RAE. The aircraft, VL229, was not accompanied by any information about its flying characteristics and maintenance information was sketchy in the extreme. David worked out a test schedule which, he felt, was likely to offer a future owner a safe and well-behaved flying machine. On 23 July 1958 he was to make the first flight, indeed, it was his first flight in a Viking, so accompanied by a colleague, John Ford, he took off and climbed to a suitable height to commence the test schedule. Towards the end of the flight, as he was about to hand over control to John Ford, he noticed that the fuel pressure gauge for the starboard engine was reading less than the port gauge and was flickering. Checks proved that the starboard fuel pressure was more sensitive to throttle opening than to rpm, suggesting the pump was OK but there was no restriction between the pump and the gauge pick-up point near the carburettor, so it was assumed that there was trouble in the fuel filter. A radio call was made for clearance to make an immediate landing. John Ford wanted to feather the propeller for the obvious reason that less asymmetric drag would be caused but David Masters had an instinctive feeling that this was wrong. A test pilot must, under such conditions, quickly establish a set of options and decide upon the one most likely to be successful. David's 'parade of concepts', as he called it, was:

1. The runway was out of wind to port.
2. There would be a weathercock swing to starboard.
3. I had little idea how well I'd be able to hold it without a bit of help from the starboard engine.
4. If I could'nt control the swing without help from the starboard engine, we would almost certainly 'ground loop'.
5. The likely outcome of a ground loop would be collapse of port undercarriage and penetration of port integral fuel tank causing a nasty fire.

As David summarised:

> 'It all added up to "keep that engine running if you possibly can". There was of course, the alternative of landing on runway 28 instead of 24. We would then be landing out of wind to port instead of to starboard and a weathercock would then be to port – against the live engine which could be used to help control it. But runway 28 was only 1,000 yards (914.4 m) long. For a single-engine landing, well out of wind, on one's first flight on the type? I don't think so, thank you...'

A safe landing was made and, as the Viking cleared the runway, the starboard engine failed completely. Later, the hangar engine fitter showed David a copper gauze fuel filter. It was 75 per cent clogged with a suede-like material in an attractive shade of lilac. Further investigation showed that the Viking integral fuel tanks had been sealed originally with an asbestos-based sealing compound which, over a period, broke down and contaminated the fuel with microscopic particles. When this was discovered an immediate Technical Service Instruction was despatched to all operators. Fairey Aviation was presumably not on the list, so it remained for David Masters and John Ford to find out the problem for themselves – fortunately they survived the experience. David was shaken when Harry Spencer, the fitter, said 'I have news for you, that is the filter from the *port* engine!'

Contrasting styles I. David Masters with Sperry engineer Oliver preparing to fly the prototype Fairey Gannet on an autopilot check sortie.
(David Masters)

Contrasting Styles II. Designed by Marcelle Lobelle, formerly chief designer of Fairey, this inflatable fabric delta wing flying machine was intended to be stowed in a valise to enable secret agents to enter and leave enemy territory. First flown in 1935 by S/Ldr 'Jock' Harvey it was known as the flying mattress, later, as the Durex delta. David Masters, seen in the 'cockpit', demonstrated it at White Waltham when it was inflated and flying within 20 minutes. Peter Twiss also flew it without much enthusiasm – the use of a tyre pressure gauge for a structural check did not, somehow, seem quite convincing! (David Masters)

From 1925 there has never been a period when the Royal Air Force was not equipped with Hawker designed aircraft; this proud record must be associated with the very high quality of the Hawker test pilots and the rapport which they enjoyed with Sydney Camm and his senior designers. As the prototype P 1067 approached the date of its first flight the Company suffered a shocking blow when the chief test pilot, S/Ldr T.S. 'Wimpy' Wade was killed in the P 1082, as the all-swept P 1052 was known. The reason for this accident on 3 April 1951 was never established. Wade's assistant, S/Ldr Neville Duke, a highly decorated fighter pilot, was appointed to succeed him. Duke had been posted to Hawkers at Langley as a break from operations and the experience gave him a taste for experimental flying. He was accepted for the No 4 Course at the Empire Test Pilots School and experienced the problems of compressibility at high Mach numbers in the Meteor used at the School. At the end of the Course he was posted to the High Speed Flight being formed at Tangmere to make an attempt upon the World Speed Record. In command was Gp Capt. E.M. Donaldson with S/Ldr Bill Waterton as the other member of the team. In very poor weather conditions along the South Coast Donaldson achieved a speed of 616 mph (991.76 km/hr), only 10 mph (16 km/hr) faster than the previous record.

On completion of his ETPS Course, Duke was posted to the Fighter Test Squadron at Boscombe Down, becoming involved in research flying at high altitudes and high Mach numbers in Meteors, studying compressibility effects. By the end of his posting he would have completed three and a half of his eight-year flying career in test flying which he had decided that he must continue when he left the Service. In August 1948 he joined the Hawker test team under Bill Humble who was chief at that time; Wimpy Wade was due to succeed Humble in the near future so Neville would be in line for the job.

One of his test flights was in the P 1040 fitted with a Snarler rocket engine; in this guise it was known as the P 1072 and had a most spectacular climb performance. During his last flight in it he was re-lighting the rocket when it exploded setting fire to the tail. He shut down and made a hasty landing.

The death of Wade meant that the test programme of the P 1067 fighter was the responsibility of Neville Duke so he flew an Avon-engined Canberra to practise re-lights in the air, and an American F–86A Sabre.

The prototype, WB188, was painted a pale duck egg green colour with RAF roundels and looked very attractive. In June 1951 it was at Boscombe Down ready for taxying trials. A short hop to check the feel of the controls led to burned-out brakes due to the thrust developed by the high idling speed of the Avon. On 20 July 1951 WB188 was flown for the first time, Duke being delighted with its performance and handling. It was named Hunter and was demonstrated at the SBAC Show in September, Duke flying it at 700 mph (1,127 km/hr) over the crowd. In January 1952 M 1.0 was reached in a 40° dive and, in April, signs of airflow breakaway and tail buffeting were noticed at M 1.03. Various remedies were unsuccessful until the joint between the elevators and the rudder were faired in with a streamlined bullet. By June M 1.06 was achieved without buffet and, on 10 July Neville flew it to Brussels in 25 minutes to give the first supersonic demonstration of the aircraft before the public.

Two major problems arose during the course of the test programme. The aircraft was so clean that it was very difficult to decelerate it in combat simulation. For some extraordinary reason such a requirement had not been included in the general fighter Specification and it provided a serious challenge to the Hawker design office. Sydney Camm is quoted as saying 'The Hurricane did not need airbrakes so why should this aeroplane?', but in practice, to decelerate such a clean design a large braking area was needed and its location was critical to avoid a sharp pitching moment when deployed. Finally one was designed to fit under the rear fuselage, spoiling the clean lines of it and ensuring that the brake could not be used during the last stages of the flare-out due to inadequate ground clearance. Months of delay elapsed before the braking problem was solved.

When the gun firing trials of the Hunter were carried out on the ground in February 1953 no problems were experienced, however, when flight testing began with the Aden guns of the production aircraft based at Boscombe Down it was found that the engine flamed-out as soon as the guns fired. Fighter Command was also in dire trouble with the Supermarine Swift which had entered service only a few weeks before the Hunter; both showed signs of engine surge when the guns were fired. A hasty rectification programme was initiated, the flame-out problem was overcome by Rolls-Royce who devised a 'fuel dip' system, as soon as the gun button was pressed the flow rate of fuel was reduced. This was quite satisfactory. For obviously different reasons the scheme was also employed on the BAC 111 airliner. The Mk 2 Hunter was fitted with the Sapphire engine which was not subject to surging problems and the guns were cleared for firing up to 47,000 ft (14,326 m). During the course of development one of the aircraft was modified to include area ruling of the fuselage. This was a formula developed in 1953 by Richard Whitcomb at NACA to achieve minimum transonic drag by ensuring that the cross section of the fuselage from nose to tail should be constant and conform to the cross section of the ideal shape for a specific Mach number. In an attempt to make use of this formula a Mk 1, WT571 was fitted with bulges aft of the wing but little improvement in performance was achieved, indeed, the effect was adverse as flow separation around the empennage caused deterioration of control characteristics. Another Mk 1, WT656, was fitted with blown flaps, for which air was trapped from the compressor and ducted to the leading edge to be blown over the flaps to reduce the stalling speed and consequently the landing speed. The advantages were not considered to be worth the complexity and cost involved.

A much more valuable modification was the provision of drop tanks to increase the wholly inadequate duration of around 40 minutes, highly unsatisfactory in a fighter aircraft. Initially two 100gal tanks were fitted to wing pylons fairly close to the fuselage whilst, later, two more were attached to outboard pylons. Together with an increase in internal capacity from 337 gal to 414 gal the Hunter could, in the Mk 4 version, carry 814 gal of fuel. The addition of a follow-up tailplane whereby the incidence of the tailplane followed the movement of the elevators, restricted stick loads and consequent excessive structural stress at high Mach Numbers and altitude, together with the installation of the Rolls-Royce Avon Series 200 engine, transformed the Hunter into a highly efficient transonic fighter and a real 'pilot's aeroplane'. Frank Murphy flew the first Mk 4 in October 1954 and, in the next one, was involved in a horrifying accident. Flying near Chichester he was carrying out fuel system tests which involved turning the booster pumps off, an action likely to stop the engine. This occurred and he was unable to re-light it. With cloud from 1,000 ft (305 m) to 6,000 ft (1,829 m) he had to rely upon guidance from the control tower at Ford, near the cathedral city. He had already made four emergency landings here in various aircraft. He carefully planned his approach with a possible diversion to Tangmere. Suddenly radio contact ceased as power from the batteries had been drained by the attempts to re-light. As he broke cloud his alignment with the airfield was good but he could not lower the flaps. Determined to save the machine, he remained with it and landed at 230 mph (370 km/hr) with the undercarriage retracted. The Hunter developed a violent bounce and Murphy almost lost consciousness. Eyewitnesses counted fifteen bounces and then the aircraft slewed sideways through a caravan park where two people were killed. It hurtled on over the Clymping road where it broke into three pieces. The cockpit went on rolling for another 100 yards (91.4 m) and, because of the weight of the gunpack underneath came to rest in an upright position. Marks of all the bolt ends in the canopy frame were found in the top and sides of Frank Murphy's helmet which was split from front to back. This was the first time that the new British 'bone dome' had been tested in an emergency and the Institute of Aviation Medicine, to say nothing of Frank himself, was well satisfied with the outcome. The pilot spent many months in hospital recovering from his injuries.

In August 1955 Neville Duke was carrying out gun firing trials in a Hunter off Littlehampton when a turbine disc failed. He coaxed the machine to Ford and received the Queen's Commendation for saving it. The engine was changed and Neville returned to Ford to collect the aircraft. At 1,000 ft (305 m) over Chichester the engine slowed to idling thrust. His options were strictly limited. Thorney Island, an RAF Station near Portsmouth was the nearest aerodrome but he arrived at too high a speed for a normal landing on the runway so touched down on the rough grass surface at 200 mph (322 km/hr), the Hunter immediately developing a series of galloping bounces characteristic of tricycle undercarriage aeroplanes with the centre of gravity well aft. The machine was almost out of control when Duke decided to select 'undercarriage up'. Only one main leg retracted, but, at least, it saved a fatal stall at the top of one of the rapidly increasing bounces. The Hunter careered on in a series of arcs with the pilot sitting in it utterly incapable of exercising any control. At the aerodrome boundary it hurtled over a ridge and crashed nose first into a hollow.

From the disintegrated wreckage Neville Duke emerged, cut, bruised and aching. When he looked at the scene of devastation around him he marvelled at his good fortune to survive such a crash and he realised, at that moment, the serial number of his Hunter, 562, added up to 13 as did the number of the Tomahawk, AN337, in which he crashed in the

Neville Duke boarding the prototype Hawker P1067 for its first flight at Boscombe Down, July 1951.
(Hawker Aircraft Ltd., via Neville Duke)

Western Desert in 1941.

In the crash his spine had been fractured. The reason for the power loss was a small piece of fluff in a fuel vent valve. After a protracted period on his back whilst the spine healed he returned to test flying but he was in pain when G forces were experienced. He felt that this was a most unsatisfactory state of affairs so, in October 1956 he relinquished his post in favour of A.W. 'Bill' Bedford who is chiefly remembered for the memorable work he carried out in developing the Hawker P 1127 into the remarkable Harrier.

The Supermarine Swift was developed almost in parallel with the Hawker Hunter; it embodied design features inherited from the up-dated post-war Spitfire, with a laminar flow wing, named Spiteful which, in turn, became the Seafang in naval service. From it was developed the Nene-engined Attacker. As Supermarine's initiation in the art of jet propulsion it presented many problems which were discovered by Jeffrey Quill and his test team at Chilbolton airfield near Salisbury. Air intake design is a critical factor in the case of jet aircraft and errors in this area can cause considerable drag as was discovered with the Attacker. Fuel tank control and the design of the spring tabs on the elevator and ailerons were other areas of difficulty whilst, at the speed of this aircraft – 550 mph plus, (885.5 km/hr +) flutter became a particularly hazardous phenomenon requiring a major programme of resonance testing. When Lt-Cdr Mike Lithgow flew the prototype for the first time on 17 June 1947, he had the benefit of one of the first Martin Baker ejection seats, a vital safety aid in testing jet fighters. Directional instability was immediately apparent at all speeds; it could be generated by the pilot or would occur naturally when flying through turbulent air. The trailing edge of the rudder was corded to make a considerable improvement. As the aircraft was intended for carrier operation much of the test programme concentrated upon the effect of lift spoilers and the general slow speed handling characteristics, followed by ADDLs (airfield dummy deck landings). In October 1947 carrier landings by Lithgow, Lt-Cdr E.M. Brown of RAE and Lt S. Orr of A&AEE were made. The absence of a large propeller ensures that a jet aircraft will tend to float on landing although the somewhat old-fashioned 'tail-dragger' undercarriage was a definite asset in carrier landings.

A serious problem emerged during flight test, this was the tendency of the rudder to lock over in particular conditions of side-slip, particularly when fitted with long-range tanks. Two aircraft were believed to have been lost through this defect which was cured by fitting a dorsal strake.

There were many other serious problems and many modifications included a tricycle undercarriage; manoeuvrability at altitude was poor and instability was inherent in the design. The outbreak of the Korean War in 1950 increased pressure to put it into service as quickly as possible; the production prototype was flown by Mike Lithgow and he experienced serious control problems and severe vibration which caused a fuel cock link to fail and cut off the fuel supply. He pulled off a brilliant dead-stick landing at Chilbolton with no damage to the aeroplane.

The Mk 2 with four 30 mm Aden guns had an extended leading edge to contain the ammunition packs. This created a totally unacceptable pitch-up on the application of G at M 0.85, the aircraft going over onto its back: many 'fixes' were tried but with little success. The only mark of the Swift which adequately fulfilled its role was the Mk 5 which became a high speed low altitude tactical reconnaissance aircraft to replace the Meteor 9. The Swift represented a sorry saga for the magnificent firm of Supermarine with a poor return for vast expenditure.

The Fairey Aviation Company embarked on a programme designed to achieve supersonic flight soon after the war. Their first design, the FD 1, was originally envisaged as a VTOL project but as no suitable engines were available, it was then looked at as a guided missile and scale models were launched at the Australian Woomera range – an interesting aspect of this 19.5 ft (9.5 m) span aircraft with a Rolls-Royce Derwent engine was that it was the first aircraft to fit a primary surface – the wing, built of a composite material, Durestos. Its flight duration was only 20 minutes so its value as a test aircraft was limited. It had very large control surfaces and was extremely sensitive, 'A dicey little box' as test pilot Peter Twiss described it to the author. Gordon Slade, the chief test pilot, flew it on its first flight and seemed to be profoundly relieved to return to earth safely!

The FD 1 provided useful data for the FD 2 and reached M 0.82 in 1953. The superb FD 2 design was held up by pressure of the Korean war and on 6 October 1954 Twiss, who had succeeded Gordon Slade as chief test pilot, flew WG774 from Boscombe Down. The first twelve flights were entirely successful with all systems working perfectly and handling qualities beyond reproach. Number Thirteen, was however, a rather different sortie. Forty miles (64.4 km) north of Boscombe Down at 20,000 ft (6,096 m) the engine stopped as the fuel warning light came on and the contents gauge needle returned to zero five seconds after reading 'full'. The FD 2 had no reversion to manual control in the event of engine or hydraulic failure, although a reservoir provided capacity for limited control actuation. So, following the philosophy of 'Hands off, feet off, move nothing unless you must' Peter Twiss radioed Boscombe Down tower for a vector to bring him straight in with the minimum of control movement. The directions were so good that as he broke cloud at 350 mph (563.5 km/hr) and 3,000 ft (914.4 m) the aeroplane was directly in line with the runway. Twiss selected undercarriage down to reduce speed and found that there was only sufficient hydraulic power to lower the nose-wheel, and, at 170 mph (273.7 km/hr), raise the nose to land on the rear fuselage and the nose-wheel. The arrival caused serious damage to the rear fuselage but none to the wings. The cause of the incident was the failure of a rubber seal in the air intake; it had blown out to allow high pressure air to enter the wing and collapse the bag fuel tanks. As they distorted, the fuel valves were jammed so that the fuel load as unusable.

Peter Twiss was awarded the Queen's Commendation for Valuable Service in the Air for saving the prototype under exceptionally difficult circumstances. The programme was delayed six months but, on 10 March 1956 he established a World Air Speed Record of 1,132 mph (1,822.52 km/hr), 310 mph (499.1 km/hr) faster than the previous record held by an American F-100C Super Sabre.

Fairey FD 2 research aircraft. Holder of the world's air speed record of 1,132 mph (1,823 km/hr) set up by Peter Twiss on 10 March 1956. (Ken Ellis Collection)

For such an early venture into supersonics the FD 2 was an outstanding technical achievement; during the record flight the pilot noted only a slight change in trim at M 0.95 and a flick of the ASI needle at M 1.0 as the shock wave passed the static vent. Great credit is due to Charles Chaplin the chief designer and his team and to Peter Twiss who was awarded the OBE.

It is an indictment of the British Government at that time to recall that the record breaking flight was made in a climate of complete indifference in Whitehall who did not believe that the FD 2 could achieve speeds in excess of 1000 mph (1610 km/hr); the Ministry of Supply refusing to participate in such a venture. Ultimately they agreed to lend the aeroplane to Fairey on condition that the Company paid for its insurance and a fee for the services of the recording team from RAE Farnborough. This must be the most parsimonious example of official inertia since the 1931 Schneider Trophy race which had to be financed by Lady Lucy Houston. Immensely encouraged by their success, Fairey proposed the construction of a supersonic fighter and comprehensive specifications were submitted based upon the FD 2. There was little interest and discussions dragged on until early 1957 and when success appeared to be within reach, suddenly, on 4 April, the notorious Duncan Sandys delivered his White Paper ordering the cessation of orders for all manned fighters for the RAF. The British Aircraft Industry, which had served the nation so well, was set back ten years and the perpetrator of this outrage was ultimately rewarded with a peerage.

A new regulation which prohibited supersonic flying at heights below 30,000 ft (9,144 m) over populated areas of Britain severely handicapped Fairey's trials of the FD 2 so, in collaboration with the French Air Force and the Dassault Company, flight trials were moved to Cazeau near Bordeaux. Forty-seven supersonic flights were made from there giving the Dassault team a valuable insight of what could be done with delta wing fighters, as indeed, they had themselves found out with the Mirage range, the first version of which had first flown in June 1955. It is an interesting coincidence that the superimposition of a plan of the Mirage upon a plan of the FD 2 reveals almost identical lines. The success of the Mirage range of fighters reveals yet again the utter folly of the decision to abandon the Fairey fighter project which would undoubtedly have been a serious competitor to the French aircraft in world markets.

Later the FD 2 was modified at Filton to have an ogival delta wing as a test aircraft for the Concorde project investigating the high speed area of the flight envelope; in this form it was known as the British Aircraft Corporation BAC 221. Together with the Handley Page 115 delta wing low speed research aircraft, the 221 was flown extensively at RAE Bedford to provide invaluable data which led to the brilliant technical success of Concorde: both research aircraft may now be seen with one of the Concorde prototypes at the Fleet Air Arm Museum at Yeovilton.

BAC 221 research aircraft. Converted from Peter Twiss's record-breaking Fairey FD 2 to carry out research work on the ogival delta wing design for Concorde. (British Aircraft Corporation, via Ken Ellis Collection)

Bristol 188 stainless steel research aircraft.
(Bristol Aircraft Ltd., via Ken Ellis Collection)

An interesting, if abortive, supersonic programme was developed by the Bristol Aeroplane Company resulting from a 1946 submission of a design for a four-jet long range bomber. By the late 1940s the Britannia airliner took up so much development effort that no further work was carried out upon the bomber project. However, in 1953 Bristol submitted proposals and a tender for an aircraft capable of sustaining Mach 2.75 for a period long enough to record steady-state kinetic heating effects at a stagnation temperature of 250° C. As the temperatures locally might rise considerably higher than this it was necessary to build the airframe of stainless steel with its formidable problems of stiffness, strength, weldability and corrosion resistance. From these proposals emerged the Bristol 188 research aircraft. Coincidentally with its number it had a landing approach speed of 188 knots and a maximum flying speed of M 2.88. Designed for minimum drag at M 1.4 the aircraft was a mid-wing monoplane with a slightly waisted fuselage and two 14,000 lb (6,356 kg) thrust de Havilland Gyron Junior engines in long nacelles mounted at the half-span position on a straight centre section. The outer panels were swept sharply back at the leading edge. The all-moving tailplane was mounted on top of the fin, the leading edge of which was sharply swept. Materials capable of meeting the high temperature requirement presented immense difficulty and the welding of thin stainless steel was only overcome by using a new technique known as 'puddle welding' in an argon arc. Powered controls were fitted and the on-board telemetry and recording equipment was undoubtedly the most comprehensive to have been installed to date; it was contained in a special bay forward of the wing which also housed the cockpit refrigeration equipment. The fuel tanks were also contained in the fuselage which was only wide enough to accommodate a pilot in an ejection seat. The instrumentation pack could measure continuously changes in temperature, pressure, acceleration, strain and vibration and could transmit the readings, where necessary, to a ground control room where a pilot and an engineer monitored the data and alerted the pilot to any information which affected his sortie. He was, in this way, able to concentrate wholly upon the requirements of the sortie without distraction. Two flying prototypes were built, XF923 and XF926, a third airframe was delivered to RAE Farnborough for test in the Structures Rig.

On 14 April 1961 the Bristol chief test pilot Godfrey L. Auty, took off from Filton for the first flight which served as a delivery flight to A&AEE, Boscombe Down. In preparation for his work with this very advanced aeroplane Auty had flown a number of aircraft at RAE Bedford, including the Avro 707A and the Fairey FD 2 in which Peter Twiss had established the World Air Speed Record in 1956. At Edwards Air Force Base in California he was invited to fly the Lockheed F–104 and at Wright-Patterson Field he flew the Convair F–102. He even experienced the sensation of weightlessness by joining the astronauts in their training Boeing. In Britain he flew the Lightning at Warton and the Gyron-powered Javelin at Hatfield. As the 188 climbed out of Filton on its maiden flight the undercarriage lowered again as a hydraulic pipe failed. Auty had a tape recorder strapped to his thigh, to complicate his problems a control button on it came adrift and jammed all communication with the chase aircraft and with ground control. Fortunately the emergency undercarriage actuator operated satisfactorily when he arrived at Boscombe Down. The predicted wind direction had changed through 180° so the safety barrier was at the wrong end of the runway; fortunately the landing was perfect. In September 1962 the 188 was demonstrated at the Farnborough SBAC Show and returned to Filton on 15 November on completion of its initial test programme of 19 flights with an average sortie time of just under 30 minutes. The handling qualities of the aeroplane were extremely satisfactory with no longitudinal stability problems at M 1.0; Godfrey Auty enjoyed flying it. The major problem was engine surge with the Gyron which had not been developed for use at such speeds – no high speed wind tunnel work could be carried out upon the installation as no such tunnel existed in UK. As the surge developed it reached a peak at supersonic speeds, and the aircraft pitched and yawed to a point where it was almost impossible to identify which engine was surging. Auty flew the second prototype XF926 from Filton on 29 April 1963 and 52 subsequent sorties were made before the test programme, severely handicapped by the engine surge problem, came to a conclusion in January 1964.

It became obvious that the wing plan of the 188 was totally outmoded and that the ogival delta had been proved by the BAC 221 (ex FD 2) was the right approach for the new supersonic airliner under consideration. Godfrey Auty flew the 221 on its maiden flight on 1 May 1964. The data obtained from this aircraft and its companion the HP 115, was immeasurably more valuable to the Concorde project than the flights of the 188 which, apart from the surging difficulty, were handicapped by the limited fuel available in the aircraft.

CHAPTER 12

Post-War Transonic and Supersonic Achievements

Earlier chapters reveal the problems of compressibility which pilots experienced in the 1930s and 1940s but with no recognition of the reasons for them. Highly streamlined fighters were approaching in a dive the transonic region which exists between Mach 0.7 and 1.3 and is the régime in which airflow over the aeroplane varies in velocity in different places from the subsonic to the supersonic.

As Mach 1.0 is approached airflow over the wings becomes turbulent and shock waves form, the centre of pressure moves and instability results with a turbulent wake which impinges upon the tail of the aircraft. At this time wind tunnel design was not capable of simulating these speeds and conditions as the throat of the tunnel would choke at high speeds. When the American National Advisory Committee for Aeronautics (NACA) developed the slotted throat tunnel this particular problem was overcome but this did not occur until the Second World War was over. Test pilots and, indeed, military pilots remained in a 'suck it and see' situation.

Chapter 9 contains an account of the tests carried out at RAE Farnborough to establish the limiting Mach No. of a Spitfire IX. These were an advanced form of the hazards faced by pilots until the advent of the slotted throat tunnel, hazards which led to the deaths of many test and military pilots. The de Havilland 108 Swallow was the primary transonic research aircraft of the immediate post-war period; it killed three pilots.

The United States, with its vast financial and technical resources and its access to German data and personnel was quick to establish a programme to study transonic flight. The US Air Force and Navy were sufficiently powerful to sponsor their own projects whilst NACA had an equal interest but inadequate funding to sponsor its own projects, although its highly qualified staff offered a valuable design input to private contractors and to the two Service projects. The prime contractors were Bell and Douglas who both prepared designs taking advantage of the latest technologies in gas turbine and rocket propulsion.

To ensure security and continuously good flying weather a base was established at a desert site in the Antelope Valley of California where there were few inhabitants, almost perfect weather and Muroc Dry Lake, the bed of which formed a natural airfield with almost limitless length runways in all directions. NACA established its High Speed Flight Station at this lonely spot which had been a bombing and gunnery range since 1933 and, in 1941 became a training station; after Pearl Harbor it became a coastal patrol aircraft base. In 1949 it was renamed Edwards Air Force base in honour of Capt. Glen W. Edwards, a test pilot killed when a Northrop YB–49 tail-less bomber crashed in June 1948.

In 1945 the Programme was established, the Air Force sponsoring the rocket propelled Bell XS–1 and the Navy the jet propelled Douglas D–558. There were two versions of the Douglas aircraft, the D–558–1 Skystreak and the D–558–2 Skyrocket. Skystreak had an unswept wing whilst the Skyrocket had a swept wing and a mixed power plant, a gas turbine which permitted take-off and cruise at M 0.80 for thirty minutes with a rocket motor for high speed dash. The Navy claimed that it was the first supersonic aircraft as it had the ability to make a normal take-off from the ground – the XS–1 was launched from a bomber at altitude. NACA soon launched a collaborative programme with the USAF and, within three years a stable of nine separate research aircraft was in service (*see* table).

X Series Research Aircraft

Bell XS–1 (X–1)	Unswept wing	Rocket engine	USAAF	1st Flight 1946	Air drop
Bell X–1 (advanced)	Unswept wing	Rocket engine	USAF	1st Flight 1953	Air drop
Bell XS–2 (X–2)	Swept wing	Rocket engine	USAF	1st Flight 1955	Air drop
Douglas XS–3 (X–3)	Unswept wing	2 turbo-jets	USAF	1st Flight 1952	Ground T/O
Northrop XS–4 (X–4)	Swept, semi-tail-less	2 turbo-jets	USAF	1st Flight 1948	Ground "
Bell X–5	Variable swept wing	1 turbo-jet	USAF	1st Flight 1951	Ground "
Convair XF–92A	Delta wing	1 turbo-jet	USAF	1st Flight 1948	Ground "
Douglas D–558–1	Unswept wing	1 turbo-jet	USN	1st Flight 1947	Ground "
Douglas D–558–2	Swept wing	1 rocket + 1 turbo-jet.	USN	1st Flight 1948	Air and Ground T/O

A total of twenty aircraft was built, during the course of the programme six were lost costing the lives of four pilots and one crewman of the launch bomber.

A radar tracking system was set up at Muroc and also a telemetry system installed to record data from sensors in the aircraft and transmit it directly to recorders at the ground base. The XS–1 had a six-channel system to transmit airspeed, position of control surfaces, altitude and acceleration. If the aircraft was lost, data recorded on the flight might provide an explanation of the circumstances.

In October 1946 the second of the two XS–1s arrived at Muroc, this was to make the first powered flight. During the deep study of the DH 108 disaster the designers of the XS–1 concluded that their aircraft must have an orthodox tail unit mounted high on the fin to avoid the wing wake and, proportionally, thinner than the wing to retain control if the wing suffered compressibility problems. To conserve fuel and eliminate the weight of a retractable undercarriage the aircraft was launched at altitude from a suitably modified Boeing B–29 bomber; it landed upon a retractable skid.

All data processing was handled by NACA who were highly skilled in this art. During contractor's trials at Bell's Orlando plant, test pilot Jack Woolams reported that the aircraft flew satisfactorily but showed a degree of instability before touch-down, a feature which persisted throughout the programme of both aircraft, the second of which had a slightly thicker wing. Tests at Muroc began at the end of August 1947 just as the US Army Air Force was given independence of the Army to become an autonomous organization as the US Air Force. The rocket engine of the XS–1 was a four-barrel unit fuelled with liquid oxygen and alcohol. Each barrel developed a thrust of 1500 lb (681 kg) and could be fired independently. The thin wing was unswept. The US Navy D–558 programme was, in parallel, also under development at the Douglas plant at El Segundo and there was, of course, keen rivalry to be the first to achieve Mach 1.0.

The Bell team at Muroc had recruited Chalmers 'Slick' Goodlin to replace Jack Woolams who had been killed in the crash of a racing aircraft. On 11 October 1946 a glide flight of seven minutes duration was made following launch from the B–29. Powered flights followed; on 9 October Goodlin reached M 0.79 at 30,600 ft (9,327 m) – the Bell target was M 0.80, at speeds beyond this the aeroplane was an unknown quantity. Wind tunnel data

Bell XS–1 under Boeing B–29 launch aircraft. (General Osmond J. Ritland, via U.S.A.F. Edwards Air Force Base)

was non-existent above M 0.85 so some tests had been carried out with a small section of wing mounted perpendicularly upon the wing of a P–51 Mustang; these had revealed some data at a diving speed around M 0.93 but beyond this the performance of the aeroplane was highly problematical and great care would need to be taken in approaching M 1.0. By the end of May both XS–1s had completed two powered flights and proved that the Specification requirements had been met. The Company was disappointed to learn that the main test programme would be carried out by USAF and NACA test pilots.

A two-phase programme was agreed between NACA and the Air Force Materiel Command. The first XS–1 which had a thin wing of 8 per cent thickness to chord (T/C) ratio would be flown to M 1.1 as quickly as prudence permitted. The NACA team would concentrate upon transonic research with particular emphasis upon stability, control and flight loads using the second XS–1 with the thicker wing which had a T/C ratio of 10 per cent. The project pilot would be Capt. Charles 'Chuck' Yeager who would have as his alternative or chase pilot Lt Bob Hoover, the other member of the team being Jack L. Ridley.

Yeager flew a glide flight on 6 August 1947 and shocked the fairly staid NACA team by carrying out two rolls immediately after launch. During the third flight he carried out a two turn spin. By the end of August he had reached M 0.85 in powered flight and, having been fully approved to fly the XS–1, he began the sorties designed to culminate in the so-called 'sound barrier' being broken.

During each flight Yeager edged nearer and nearer to his goal and after landing all the telemetry data was studied and compared with the on-board recordings.

In October he reached M 0.94 at 40,000 ft (12,192 m), carried out a roll and found out that he had no control in pitch, the control column being entirely inoperative. Power was cut and a landing made at base where an inquest was held with the aerodynamicists who were concerned that such a problem should arise so early in the programme. It was concluded that the shock wave generated by the tailplane had moved aft as speed increased and was located right on the hinge line to negate the effect of the control surface. A major and very important modification was made, the tailplane mounting was altered so that its incidence could be adjusted by a button on the control column. This proved to be an entirely satisfactory solution and, in due course, led to the all-moving tailplane used now on most aircraft.

Yeager's next flight, the eighth, was bedevilled with frost on the inside of the canopy so that he had to be guided in for a landing by another pilot flying alongside. A speed of M 0.994 was recorded on that sortie. The high tech solution to the frost problem proved to be a precautionary spray of the interior of the transparencies with *Drene*, a well-known ladies' hair shampoo.

On 14 October supersonic flight was achieved. Yeager had fallen from a horse and had broken two ribs which had to be strapped up by a private doctor so that the military authorities were unaware of his condition. An important tool which he had to take with him was a length of broomstick to help him lock the entry hatch.

The orange coloured aircraft, named *Glamorous Glennis* after Yeager's wife, was loaded into the bomb bay of the B–29, fuelled with liquid oxygen and ethyl alcohol ready for take-off at 10.02. At 5,000 ft (1524 m) Yeager, in acute pain, squeezed himself into the XS–1 and carried out his pre-launch drill. Two P–80 Shooting Stars acted as chase planes and, at 10.26, at 19,700 ft (6,004 m) the aircraft was released from the B–29. Yeager checked his rocket engine by a test firing of all four chambers, he shut down two of them and climbed to altitude when he opened up the other two. With a total thrust of 6,000 lb (2,724 kg) and trailing a long flame punctuated with yellow shock diamonds *Glamorous Glennis* roared upwards to reach M 0.90, continuing to 0.93. The moving stabiliser was checked and found to be entirely satisfactory.

As fuel was consumed the XS–1 became lighter and continued to accelerate, at M 0.98 indicated air speed the needle of the machmeter fluctuated and went off the scale indicating that the shock wave on the nose was supersonic and moved aft across the pitot orifice. At the same time ground observers heard the characteristic double bang generated for the first time by an aeroplane but familiar to the unfortunate Londoners and residents of European cities who endured attack by the V–2 supersonic rocket bomb in the closing stages of the Second World War.

The data recording equipment proved that Chuck Yeager had indeed achieved supersonic speed – the mythical 'sound barrier' had been breached at a speed of M 1.06 at 43,000 ft (13,106 m) – a true air speed of 699 mph (1125 km/hr).

This milestone in aviation history which, but for the craven attitude of British officialdom, might have been achieved by the Miles M–52, gave immense impetus to the United States programme; by the end of 1947 the XS–1 had flown at M 1.35, 926 mph (1490 km/hr). The ultimate speed of this aeroplane with its unswept wing was reached by Yeager on 26 March 1948, it proved to be M 1.45, 957 mph (1540 km/hr).

In parallel with the Air Force programme NACA was flying its own XS–1, the thicker wing version. On 21 October 1947 Herb Hoover carried out the first gliding flight. To his considerable embarrassment he landed heavily and collapsed the nose wheel assembly, this grounded the aircraft until December. This particular problem plagued all the XS–1s due to their unusual landing flare and touch-down characteristics.

During the first powered flight on 16 December Hoover cautiously approached M 1.0 and on 10 March 1948 achieved M 1.065 to become the first NACA pilot and the first civilian to do so. On 30 November Howard Lilly also exceeded M 1.0.

These flights and those of two other pilots who joined the programme, Robert Champion and John Griffith, produced immensely valuable aerodynamic data. NACA was mainly concerned with flight characteristics near the speed of sound rather than ultimate speed obtainable. It was then possible to correlate the data with wind tunnel results and derive the correction factors to bring model data into line with flight data. A major step forward was the development of the adjustable horizontal stabiliser and the realisation of its effect upon controllability throughout the transonic speed range, an effect which led to its use on all supersonic fighters.

The effect of the thicker wing at transonic speeds was a surprise to the scientists who found that the 10% T/C ratio wing developed 30% more drag at transonic speeds than the 8% ratio wing on the Air Force XS–1. As a by-product of these flights great progress was made in advancing the development of speed measuring systems for high speed flight.

At last the deep fears and doubts surrounding supersonic flight had been dispelled; it could be achieved in relative safety but much research flying remained to be carried out to discover all the 'gremlin' activity suspected of being endemic to it. Many, many sonic booms were to resound over the Mojave desert and, for a long time, there were no protests from the environmental industry which was in its infancy.

Yeager's Mach 1 flight almost coincided with an important event which actually took place two weeks earlier, on 1 October 1947. This was the first flight, by George Welch, North American's test pilot, of the new NA XP–86 fighter prototype. The XP–86 was an elegent aeroplane embodying lessons learned from German technology during Allied technical missions to their research facilities after the war. To improve performance and reduce drag at transonic speeds a fully swept plan form for the wing was decided upon. The first flight almost ended in disaster; on the landing approach it became clear that the nosewheel would not lock down. With fuel for a flight time of only about forty minutes Welch tried every trick to avoid landing on the main wheels and the nose, finally, with the nose as high as possible, he bounced the main wheels hard on the runway, the shock locked the nosewheel down so that a normal landing could be made. The machine was an instant success. By May 1948 Welch had dived it at over M 1.00.

Six months after the first flight of the XP–86 the eminent British test pilot W/Cdr Roland 'Bee' Beamont made an Air Ministry sponsored visit to the USA to fly various new aircraft preparatory to his forthcoming test programme of the English Electric Canberra for which, as chief test pilot, he was responsible. He was extremely fortunate to be permitted to fly the XP–86 and decided to go beyond the briefed sub-sonic speed range and go for Mach 1+.

A shallow dive at 27,000 ft (8,230 m) achieved Mach 0.95 when mild buffeting and lateral trim problems heralded the onset of compressibility effects. An increase in dive angle showed no comparable increase in speed so he assumed that the expected drag rise was taking place. He climbed back to 33,000 ft (10,058 m) and dived at 30°, after a 3,000 ft (914 m) loss of altitude Mach 0.98 showed on the meter, again buffeting and trim changes occurred so he trimmed them out and dived more steeply. At 0.99 the starboard wing tended to drop with nose heaviness. The buffeting suddenly reduced and the machmeter showed 1.01. There were mixed feelings among the Americans about this British pilot doing what so many American pilots had not had a chance to do. When he was introduced to Chuck Yeager at the Officer's Club the American looked rather sourly at him with the comment 'Is this the Limey that's been flying the XP–86?' He had not yet flown it!

'Bee' was very impressed with the aircraft which as the F–86 Sabre, reached a build total

Douglas D–558–1 Skystreak. Note the superb surface finish.
(Douglas Aircraft Company, via Donald N. Hanson)

of 2000. They served with distinction in Korea.

During the course of the test programme Chuck Yeager had a number of very dangerous experiences which only his skill enabled him to survive without injury. In January 1948 he was flying the X–1 at M 1.10 when a high frequency vibration affected the cockpit and smoke became apparent although no fire warning light was on. Fuel was dumped with some trepidation as the pilot was aware of the risk that this highly volatile fuel might be ejected into a fire somewhere aft. After several minutes he decided that he was not likely to be blown to pieces and made a safe landing. It was found that a small fire had burned insulation in the engine compartment.

This phenomenon became a regular occurrence for the next few flights and Yeager confessed to fear every time he launched. Finally one of the Bell engineers discovered that an incorrect gasket had been fitted in a vital situation during an engine overhaul. After two more flights Chuck was relieved for a well earned rest. The last one, his 23rd, was unsatisfactory as the rocket motors failed to fire due to short circuit in a switch. A number of other pilots reached Mach 1.0 in the X–1, Jack Ridley reaching Mach 1.23.

There was, of course, intense rivalry between the test pilots of the manufacturers, the Army, the Navy and NACA. The Douglas rival to the X–1, the D–558–1 Skystreak was proclaimed by the Navy to be the world's first supersonic aircraft as it could take off from the ground. (Later it followed the X–1 in being air launched from a bomber).

Larry Bell asked Yeager if he could take-off loaded from a runway on the admittedly weak undercarriage designed only for the landing of the aircraft with no fuel on board. Chuck agreed to try with a 50 per cent fuel load. He fired all four rockets simultaneously and hurtled down the runway; at a speed of 200 mph (322 km/hr) he lifted off and selected gear up, as it went up the actuating rod failed and the wing flaps departed the aircraft. Eighty seconds after the start he was at 23,000 ft (7,100 m) at M 1.03. After a total flight time of 2½ min he landed safely having disproved the Navy's claim!

A new version of the X–1, the X–1A, was longer and had a bubble type canopy, it also had an improved fuel system to sustain more power. Yeager piloted the chase aircraft as Bell's pilot 'Skip' Zeigler flew it to M 0.93. He saw the shock waves rippling across the wing as Zeigler reported heavy buffeting and aileron buzz. Chuck had, himself, experienced this and told Skip to continue until the trouble abated. Zeigler chose not to do so and, after three more similar flights, reported to Bell that the machine was unstable; it was returned to the Buffalo Works where Zeigler was asked to carry out tests upon another research aircraft, the Bell X–2.

He was about to be launched from a B–50 bomber when, at 20,000 ft (6096 m) the liquid oxygen tank exploded. Zeigler had no chance of survival as the X–2 was blown out of the bomber to fall into Lake Ontario. Yeager was persuaded to take over the X–1A programme and was first launched from a B–50 on 21 November 1953. The Bell designers considered that the small tail of the aircraft would lead to loss of stability at M 2.3 which was his target to beat M 2.0 claimed by NACA's Scott Crossfield in the Douglas Skyrocket.

On 12 December he made the fourth powered flight, being released from the bomber at 30,000 ft (9,144 m). His flight plan was to climb to 70,000 ft (21,336 m) to nose over in a curve to commence the Mach 2 run. At 40,000 ft (12,192 m) he was climbing too steeply at M 0.8 and soon reached 80,000 ft (24,384 m). The engine flamed-out at M 2.0 and he dived for his maximum speed. At M 2.4 the nose yawed to the left, opposite rudder had no effect, a wing rose but applied aileron had no effect either; suddenly the aircraft was totally out of control, it diverged in all axes, as a test pilot would describe it. Effectively aerodynamics was no longer part of the equation, it was just a lump of metal tumbling uncontrollably from the sky with Yeager being hurled about inside it hoping fervently that his harness straps would continue to hold him in the cockpit.

Totally disoriented Chuck retained a vestige of memory which told him that the setting of the horizontal stabiliser was 'leading edge down'. He fought against the G forces to find the trimmer switch and retrimmed the stabiliser. His windscreen had misted up, suddenly it cleared and he saw that he was in a spin heading for a crash into the Sierras. He recovered at 25,000 ft (7,620 m) and set course for base so battered, bruised and bewildered that he did not know whether the aircraft would hold together or, indeed, whether he was capable of landing it. Suddenly, at 5,000 ft (1,524 m) he was lined up with the runway where he touched down safely at 270 mph (435 km/hr). He had spun 51,000 ft (15,545 m) in 51 seconds. This was the end of Chuck Yeager's involvement in the X series test programme.

In 1955 a USAF test pilot, Pete Everest, achieved M 2.5 in the X–2 and finally made 2.87 before leaving the programme. As had been predicted by the aerodynamicists, stability was on a knife edge as he approached the high Mach number. A graduate from the British Empire Test Pilots School, Iven Kincheloe, took over the task. On 7 September 1956 he flew the X–2 to 126,000 ft (38,405 m). The low density of air at that height left the control surfaces virtually useless, the machine banked to port as it reached the top of the arc but the pilot dared not risk trying to correct it.

It is sad to record that this brilliant pilot, whose name graces the principal award at ETPS, the Kincheloe Award for the best pupil, was killed at Edwards AFB when the engine of a Lockheed F–104 failed on take-off.

Another Air Force pilot, Mel Apt, was briefed to carry out the last flights of the X–2; he was warned that control movements should be very gentle above Mach 2.7 as violent divergence might result. Launched from a B–50 he reached Mach 3.2, 2,094 mph (3,370 km/hr) at 65,500 ft (19,964 m) with the aircraft behaving perfectly. He turned to return to base, suddenly the X–2 went totally out of control knocking Apt unconscious and entering an inverted spin. He revived and attempted to regain control; deciding that he could not do so he operated the emergency release of the escape capsule which formed the nose and cockpit section, preparatory to ejecting from it and using his own parachute. Tragically he was too late, the capsule hurtled into the desert killing him instantly. He was awarded, posthumously, the Distinguished Flying Cross.

The other contender in the supersonic arena, Douglas, had already built up a considerable reputation in the civil aircraft field with the DC–1, DC–2 and DC–3 transports in the 1930s and with the larger four-engine DC–4 during the war. During the early days of the formulation of the supersonic programme, John Stack, a leading NACA scientist, had expressed reservations about the radical Bell rocket aircraft programme and believed that a more orthodox jet propelled aircraft capable of being ground launched should be built. The US Navy were interested and considered that such a design would be capable of development into an operational type. Proposals were sought from the Douglas Company for such an aeroplane which would not be expected to exceed the speed of sound; it was, therefore, to be radically different to the Bell design.

NACA research engineers at Langley Field would take an active interest in both projects but would be primarily interested in the Douglas D–558 as the design came to be known.

It was a subsidiary programme to the XS–1s' and took a fairly low priority, the first aircraft named Skystreak was underpowered with a General Electric TG–180 engine with 4,000 lb (1814 kg) thrust. This had an unswept wing and was flown initially by veteran Douglas test pilot, Gene May. The second D–558–1, Skystreak set a world air speed record of 650.3 mph (1047 km/hr) but there were technical problems with the undercarriage locks in the retracted position whilst, on one flight, a hurried landing had to be made by Howard Lilly as smoke from an electrical fire filled the cockpit.

On 3 May 1948 Howard Lilly, after an aborted take-off due to lock trouble, took off again after adjustments and, as he climbed out, a failure in the compressor section of the engine hurled debris through the fuselage cutting into fuel lines to start a major fire and severing the tail control links. Lilly had no chance, the aircraft rolled and dived into the lakebed.

It soon became clear that Skystreak did not have the development potential to turn it into a Navy fighter. As it approached Mach 1.0 its controllability deteriorated markedly, stick forces became intolerably high and the aircraft wallowed through the sky. John Stack suggested that the attachment of small metal vanes to the wing in a spanwise location would create vortices over the wing and improve controllability; this was tried out by gluing them in position, they made a considerable improvement. Many aircraft of all types have had vortex generators fitted since that original experiment. With them, the Skystreak finally reached Mach 0.99.

The Skystreak was followed by the D–558–2 Skyrocket which was a very different aeroplane. This too, was flown by Gene May in its early test programme. It was a very elegant design with slightly swept wings and a mixed power plant. A Westinghouse J–34 jet engine was used for take-off and cruise aided by some of the power from four rocket reaction tubes built by Reaction Motors which took over completely for the very high speed element of the test sorties. The only payload was 625 lb of telemetry equipment.

As with the X–1s, two of which had blown up during the launch, the propellant was the very dangerous combination of hydrogen peroxide and liquid oxygen. The slightest speck of dust in the system was enough to create a disastrous explosion. Perhaps not surprisingly the engineering test pilots at the El Segundo plant were not falling over themselves for the privilege of flying this hot ship, which seemed to have a strong similarity to a time bomb likely to blow them into small pieces across the desert.

Ultimately responsibility for the project fell upon William Bridgeman, a pilot who had

Douglas D–558–2 Skyrocket at roll-out, November 1947. Note the flush cockpit canopy which was altered before the first flight.
(Douglas Aircraft Company, via Donald N. Hanson)

served his apprenticeship flying Catalinas and Liberators for the US Army Air Force during the war and DC–3s after it. His first assignment with Douglas was to test the AD Skylark single-engined military aircraft. When he took over responsibility for the Skyrocket the only pilots in USA who had flown at Mach 1 were Chuck Yeager and Pete Everest of Bell and Gene May in his own company. Also in this select group was, of course, 'Bee' Beamont and John Derry. Derry by that time, had achieved sonic speed in a DH 108, although the aircraft was virtually out of control at the time. These five pilots were the repository of the whole world's experience of transonic flight in a very dangerous régime. Admittedly design departments had been working on the problems for about a decade but their theories were largely unproven so, for the pilots, it was a step into the hazardous unknown.

The Douglas aircraft were also based at Muroc with data analysis being carried out at the Douglas Air Development Center at Dayton, Ohio. As with the Bell projects, once the company's test pilots had completed their test programme the Service and NACA pilots would carry out their own schedules and verify the results.

In the event of serious trouble the Skyrocket pilot could eject in the whole of the cockpit capsule. When a safe speed and altitude had been reached the rear bulkhead could be jettisoned to allow the occupant to leave the capsule and deploy his parachute. It was a useful concept if the trouble arose at altitude but of little value low down.

In his book *The Lonely Sky* Bridgeman gave a vivid account of his training flights in an F–80 fighter, the hours he spent studying the one inch thick data manual for the Skyrocket and many hours with the engineers and Gene May to ensure that he was absolutely familiar with the complicated procedures necessary to prime the rocket motor – all the actions had to be completed in ten seconds.

An alarming flight in an F–80 brought him face to face with the reality of compressibility in a dive to determine the limiting Mach Number. Suddenly a violent hammering vibration shook the aircraft which, as he put it 'Stripped him of ego and reduced him to a startled child'. Fortunately he did not apply force to the stick to pull out but just tried to remember what had been said about another F–80 pilot who had bored a deep hole in the Mojave Desert under similar circumstances. As the machine descended to warmer and denser air the speed of sound moved away from his own speed and, with the Mach No at 0.75, the controls became effective again after a mere thirty seconds of drama which felt like an eternity. He realised that he had been told that the limiting Mach No was 0.80, but had rashly exceeded it. To the question 'Well how did you like it?' from a ground crew sergeant he replied 'It's different.'

Once again George Bulman's theory on control under compressibility conditions had been proved correct and yet another pilot's life saved.

Bridgeman continued with his F–80 familiarisation flights and sessions with Gene May accompanied, on occasions by the eerie whistle as the liquid oxygen being pumped into the Skyrocket's tanks at a temperature of minus 297° C vented from the relief valve. As the aircraft moved to its take-off point on a special trailer another vehicle accompanied it to feed liquid oxygen into the tanks to replace that vented off.

After take-off using the jet engine, assisted by two of the rocket tubes, a climb to 40,000 ft (12,192 m) was made, the turbine being closed down and the other two rockets being fired to give the one and a half minute fuel burn at the rate of one and a half tons per minute to accelerate towards M 1.0. After a dead stick landing had been made at the end of the test sortie a month was spent in the hangar where the Skyrocket and its power plant was stripped right down and meticulously inspected before the next one and a half minutes of data gathering.

The ill-fated X–2, in which Mel Apt lost his life, about to be launched from a B–29 bomber.
(U.S.A.F. Edwards Air Force Base)

After four weeks at Muroc during which he witnessed five flights with May at the controls, Bridgeman was briefed for the 60th research flight of the aircraft. He put on the G suit, bone dome, boots and oxygen mask as Gene May repeated his warning of the Skyrocket's propensity to develop a dutch roll at 250 kts, (455 km/hr) the machine weaving from side to side and rolling at the same time. For a nerve racking six weeks his assignment was postponed as the Navy required urgent data which only May could obtain. At last the moment arrived. At dawn the procession made its way to the take-off point, Col. Pete Everest, the senior Air Force test pilot flew the F–86 chase aircraft over the group and the starting litany began.

The turbine spooled up to full power, the Skyrocket rolled, underpowered without rocket assistance, slowly it built up speed took off and handled like a truck, according to Bridgeman. He commented after the flight, 'It scares me a little but not too much.' A reaction of the true test pilot. With May at the controls Mach 1.05 had been achieved, the Bell X–1, air launched beat the Douglas team with Mach 1.4. Bridgeman continued with his further five familiarisation flights without using the rocket motor and soon became accustomed to the unusual characteristics of this unusual aeroplane. On the sixth sortie, with Chuck Yeager as chase pilot, the rockets made a faultless start at 30,000 ft (9144 m) and their 7,500 lb (3,402 kg) of thrust moved the Machmeter needle swiftly to 0.85. At 0.90 a tremor ran through the airframe and then disappeared. A 3 G turn into the buffet zone created vibration as the fuel was used up. As he slowed, Yeager caught up and radioed,

'D'you hold with rocket flying, boy?'

'It's mighty sudden ain't it, captain' responded Bridgeman.

An important objective of the test series was to establish the buffet boundaries in the transonic flight régime; on his first flight Bill had experienced the slight tremor at Mach 0.9

This photograph indicates the magnitude of the operation of NACA's High Speed Flight. In the foreground is the Douglas D–558–2 Skyrocket with its ground crew. Test pilot Scott Crossfield is seen in front of the aircraft. Behind is the Boeing B–29 launch aircraft with its air and ground crews. The two Sabres are chase aircraft whilst the motor vehicles provide ground support including tracking, communications, re-fuelling, maintenance and rescue services. (U.S.A.F. Edwards Air Force Base)

which was so transient that it defied analysis, at least he now knew that the Skyrocket showed no evidence of serious compressibility problems at high Mach numbers so, by January 1950, it had been decided to press on to attempt Mach 1.0 in level flight but in a 1 G turn.

On his next flight with Yeager as chase, he noticed buffeting between 0.91 and 0.95 and a distinct tendency for the port wing to drop, as the aerodynamicists had predicted. Fairly hard aileron deflection was needed to resist this tendency and the Machmeter recorded 1.02 just as the rocket fuel was exhausted. An unexpectedly violent deceleration hurled the pilot to the limit of his harness as the buffet boundary was crossed in the reverse direction.

Future flights extended the envelope and Bridgeman's own expertise with the Skyrocket. On one sortie, at an altitude of 33,000 ft (10,058 m) at M 0.85 the fire warning light came on and the siren sounded. This was one of the danger scenarios which he had studied for so many hours so his response was automatic. He turned back to base and waited for the fuel to run out; to jettison it could have led to a fire and a catastrophic explosion if the chemicals had found the fire in an unknown location. In any case consumption at the rate of one ton a minute was faster than the jettison rate. The 23 interminable seconds to fuel cut were spent sitting tensely in the cockpit awaiting the violent deceleration to which he was now accustomed. Chuck Yeager caught up and reported that the Skyrocket appeared to have lost its tail pipe fairing and black smoke was pouring out. It became clear that the fire was in the gas turbine so he shut it down and pressed the extinguisher button, whereupon the warning light went out and a safe landing made after a very tense flight.

As the aerodynamicists developed the drag charts it became apparent that the prediction that it would rise to prohibitive levels at and above Mach 1.0 were not sustainable but it was equally clear that the fuel load was insufficient to achieve climb to the altitude necessary to go beyond Mach 1.05. The only alternative seemed to be to follow the Bell practice and launch the Skyrocket from a bomber. Two new research aircraft were built with only rocket propulsion and a B–29 was modified to launch them. As the tests were to be carried out at around 70,000 ft (21,336 m), a height already achieved by the X–1, custom-fitted pressure suits were required by the pilots. A series of 'indoctrination' exercises and tests were carried out; after sessions with the medical officers when Bill Bridgeman flew back to Muroc in a DC–6, he was amused by the remarks of a fellow passenger, 'God, we're high, 23,000 ft, do you think that we will ever go higher than this?'

CHAPTER 13

Post-War Transonic and Supersonic Achievements – II

For the new air launches a new series of emergency procedures was devised. The B–29 had, at the time, an unenviable reputation for in-flight fires. Pete Everest had also experienced an in-flight fire in the X–1 itself. The B–29 pilot released it seconds after Everest had leapt from the cockpit to the ladder linking it to the bomber. The X–1 fell away to blast a 40 ft deep crater in the Mojave desert.

Some doubt was expressed whether the Skyrocket would drop cleanly away with the hydraulic latches being relied upon to act in unison. A foul-up in this mode was too awful to contemplate. However, when the first launch was made from a familiarisation flight at 40,000 ft (12,192 m) without a pressure suit being worn by the pilot a copy-book exercise took place. The machine was one of the turbine powered versions and, as the engine flamed out at Mach 0.95 and the rockets consumed all their fuel a glide at Mach 0.8 began back at base. En route the windscreen frosted over and Chuck Yeager moved alongside to direct him in to a safe landing. The generator had stopped with the engine and the relay which connected the radio to the battery also failed so Bridgewater was isolated. Recalling his emergency procedures he operated the manual switch and regained contact with Yeager. He managed to air-start the turbine to help his approach and, with no forward vision, made a faultless landing.

The next flight would be directed towards extending the boundaries of the flight envelope to a degree never achieved before. The objective was Mach 1.5, 1,000 mph (1,610 km/hr), 76 mph (122 km/hr) faster than Yeager in the X–1. Hitherto performance had increased by small increments as the handling of the aircraft was explored but this would be a quantum leap with, probably, many more imponderables – were there any more barriers to penetrate beyond what was called the sound barrier?, what were the chances of deadly flutter of the control surfaces or, indeed the wings themselves? There would be no warning, just instantaneous disaster as disintegration of the aeroplane took place. It was not exactly encouraging to sit in the climbing B–29 and listen to the conversation of the ground crew:

'She's carrying 5,486 lb (2,488 kg) of explosive, this trip, enough to blow the whole base up!'

At 40,000 ft (12,192 m) the ex-airline pilot searched his soul:

'One false move and I'll blow myself all over the sky, why aren't I on some warm beach with my ass planted in the sand?'

A few seconds later one of the rockets showed a pressure drop, an agonised discussion with the technicians led to the mission being aborted, three tons of fuel was jettisoned and the B–29 returned to base for the bugs to be worked out of the system. The air temperature of -50° C had caused moist air to freeze in the fuel line and blocked vital orifices. Five flights were aborted in three months; caution was the vital consideration, particularly in the context that in the preceding nine months the US Air Force had lost 62 pilots testing aircraft destined for the Korean war.

On the sixth mission one of the two chase aircraft developed engine trouble, a replacement took off, he reported an engine surge and returned to base. That flight also was aborted. Fifty seconds from launch on the seventh mission pressure on the No 3 rocket dropped. Bridgewater ordered that the launch be abandoned partway through the count-down, he began his closure drill. To his dismay he realised that the B–29 pilot had not heard him and was proceeding to launch. He worked furiously to reinstate the systems as the aircraft dropped from the belly of the bomber. The performance of the rocket engine was now problematical but, fortunately, a perfect start was made.

At Mach 1.25 the Skyrocket began a gentle rocking motion and an oscillation from side to side. She steadied and the Machmeter moved swiftly to 1.4 as the rockets consumed all their fuel. A 175 mph (281.75 km/hr) deadstick landing was made on the 7-mile-long runway. After all these troubles Bridgeman embarked upon the next flight with a sense of foreboding, the launch was perfect and he commenced the arced flight path which would reach 45,000 ft (13,716 m) at its upper point. As he entered the supersonic region the mysterious roll began again, becoming more pronounced at 800 mph (1,288 km/hr), the rudder pedals began to jerk with a force he was unable to overcome. Burn-off of the fuel seemed to take an eternity as the aircraft became increasingly uncontrollable at 1000 mph (1,610 km/hr). At 45,500 ft (13,868 m) he cut the rockets and reduced speed for a fairly uneventful return to base. The aerodynamicists were puzzled, they could only suggest that in some mysterious way the rudder was affected by shock waves from the rocket tubes below it. To lock the control surface for the high speed runs a plunger was fitted under the control of the pilot. On the third air-launched flight M 1.72 was achieved, 200 mph (322 km/hr) faster than the best speed recorded by the X–1s and the Skyrocket became the world's fastest aeroplane.

The target speed for the programme was raised to Mach 2.00. Flight No 4 achieved M 1.79 at 64,500 ft (19,660 m) with trouble being experienced with frost forming upon the cockpit glazing. The fifth, and penultimate, flight was extremely unpleasant, the roll developed in a menacing fashion which the pilot was unable to control with the ailerons. At M 1.85 he decided to cut power and try to pull out of the steep dive which had developed. Frost impaired his vision and the aircraft was virtually uncontrollable, he managed to initiate a slow pull-out and entered a gentle climb which, he had decided was his only safe option. Speed decayed as the Skyrocket flew silently upwards.

In an attempt to overcome the lateral and horizontal stability problems it was decided to change the flight plan from a rapid push-over from the powered climb to the diving course into a much more gentle trajectory. On the last flight the lateral instability occurred at 63,000 ft (19,202 m), at 80,000 ft (24,384 m) Bridgeman curved over into his high speed run, M 1.988 was reached without much trouble, setting another world record before the Skyrocket was transferred to NASA for their test programme.

Ed Heinemann, the Douglas designer, and Bill Bridgeman were honoured for their work in the Skyrocket programme; Heinemann received the Sylvanus Albert Reed Award of the American Institute of Aeronautical Sciences in 1951; the AIAS gave Bridgeman the Octave Chanute Award in 1953.

The Douglas X–3 was flown from August 1953 to May 1956 by NACA test pilot Joe Walker, later tragically killed in a mid-air collision between his F–104N and the giant North American XB–70A Valkyrie Mach 3.0 research bomber. On 8 June 1966 the two aircraft took off for a test sortie which was to be initiated after a photographic session with several other new aircraft. Closely formating near the Valkyrie's starboard wing Walker's F–104 entered the powerful vortex zone off the delta wing and was hurled across the tail

The North American XB–70A Valkyrie six-engined experimental bomber, of which two were built, was designed for speeds of Mach 3+. It was expected to provide data for a large supersonic jet transport and was first flown on 21 September 1964. Telemetry provided data on 36 separate functions with a further 900 measurements recorded on magnetic tape at 20,000 samples per second. The aircraft were valuable tools in evaluating the problems of large aircraft in supersonic flight particularly in checking sonic boom levels and compatibility with normal traffic. The second aircraft included modifications to improve the poor stability characteristics above Mach 2.5. After the catastrophic collision with an F/104 which destroyed both aircraft and killed most of the crew members most of the remaining sorties of the survivor involved boom tests until it was retired in February 1969 to be displayed in the Air Force Museum at Wright-Patterson AFB, Ohio. Together the two aircraft completed 129 sorties in 252 hours, 38 minutes. Twenty-two hours were flown at M2.5+. Note the adjustable wing tips deflected downwards and the F-104 chase 'plane. (U.S.A.F. Edwards Air Force Base)

fins breaking them off; it then crashed into the port wing exploding in flames. The bomber was fatally damaged; slowly it went out of control and then violently yawed and rolled to the right tumbling as it fell. The crew ejection devices did not work as planned and most of the crew, including test pilot Carl Cross, lost their lives. In Joe Walker America lost a man who was generally considered the finest research pilot of his day.

Peripherally, the Bell X–3 made a useful contribution to tyre research. Its landing and take-off speed were so high that tyre failure was a regular occurrence. Lessons were learned which are embodied in current tyre designs.

The X–5 was the world's first high performance aircraft with a variable geometry wing capable of actuation during flight. The Bell test pilot 'Skip' Zeigler first flew it from Edwards AFB, as Muroc had become known, on 20 June 1951. It had vicious spinning characteristics, the second aircraft killed Maj. Ray Popsen, a USAF pilot, in October 1953. Nevertheless it was a valuable research aircraft which was one of the first to meet all the requirements of the USAF and NACA.

By 1954 it was clear that the original batch of supersonic research aircraft had been developed to the limit – indeed, in some cases far beyond original requirements. A new Project 1226 was formulated and the North American submission was accepted and became the X–15. Three aircraft were ordered in 1955. By this time the famous Century series fighters were in development and flight research was carried out with some of them to the benefit of the X–15 programme. One of the most significant was the Lockheed F–104 Starfighter. First flown by Lockheed test pilot, Tony Le Vier, on 7 February 1954, it became the first operational interceptor fighter to be able to sustain Mach 2.00. It held the world's air speed and altitude records. To call the Starfighter a 'hot rod' would be an understatement, it was once described with some accuracy as having 'no visible means of support ', its wings were of 21 ft 11" (7.0 m) span machined from a solid billet with a very sharp leading and trailing edge. It was powered by a Wright XJ65 10,000 lb (4,536 kg) thrust turbojet with re-heat and had a 'T' tail.

Plagued by stability problems, NACA's underpowered, but elegant, Douglas X–3 first flew in August 1952. The very long fuselage and short wing created high inertia in yaw and pitch, being one of the first examples of the dangers of inertial coupling which nearly killed Joe Walker when flying it in October 1954. Thereafter it became a 'hangar queen' an expensive lesson to later designers, although exploratory flights into the phenomenon carried out until 1956 provided valuable data.
(Douglas Aircraft Company, via Donald N. Hanson)

In 1963 three F–104s were fitted with a 6,000 lb (2,722 kg) thrust Rocketdyne AR–2 rocket engine above the jet pipe, they also had extended wing tips, an enlarged fin and rudder and reaction 'puff-pipes' at the nose, tail and at the wing tips. They were capable of reaching an altitude of 130,000 ft (39,624 m) and were later used in the space exploration programme for astronaut training.

In October 1958 NACA became NASA, National Aeronautics and Space Administration, its dedication to space exploration gave added impetus to the X–15 which was seen to be of considerable value to Project Mercury – manned space flight. The targer speed and altitude for the X–15 was established as Mach 6.6 plus and 250,000 ft (76,200 m). The final Specification demanded 76,000 m and a speed of 2,000 m per sec – Mach 6.0.

A complex associated project was the development of a high altitude continuous tracking radar range to cover a distance of 484 miles (780 km), the system being served by three radar stations which would provide precise data on the position of the aircraft, its altitude and speed over the ground. The route was from Wendover, Utah to Edwards AFB. By July 1959 it was completed, the three stations having radar tracking telemetry facilities and data collection by oscillograph and magnetic tape.

On each sortie 87 channels from the X–15 sampled data ten times per second and relayed it to the ground station. The cost was very high, $3.3 m was spent on the range by the USAF but it was of immense value to the later high speed programme. Two Boeing B–52s were modified to carry the X–15 under the wing and North American test pilot Scott Crossfield was named as the project pilot. On 10 March 1959 the first flight took place with the two aircraft joined together but without a launch; several similar ones followed and, on 8 June the X–15 was released to glide back to base. On the approach to land it began a violent pitching motion. The control system was modified to give extra authority at low speeds. On 17 September the first powered flight was made with two Thiokol XLR–11 rocket engines from the X–1 series which had to be used until the 57,000 lb (25,855 kg) thrust XLR–99 was available. This flight was made by the second aircraft, M 2.11 was reached at an altitude of 52,340 ft (15,953 m). This aircraft was damaged on 5 November when an explosion and fire in the engine necessitated a landing at one of the emergency sites, Rosamund Dry Lake. There was insufficient time to jettison the whole of the propellant load so, at overload, the landing impact was sufficient to buckle the long fuselage. By February 1960 it was operational again.

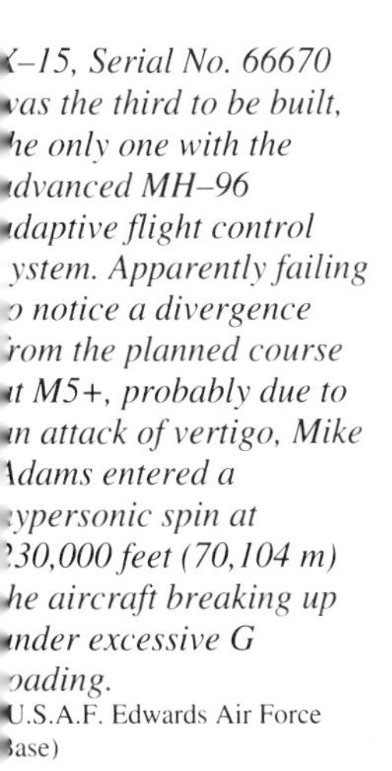

–15, Serial No. 66670 vas the third to be built, he only one with the dvanced MH–96 daptive flight control ystem. Apparently failing o notice a divergence rom the planned course t M5+, probably due to n attack of vertigo, Mike dams entered a ypersonic spin at 30,000 feet (70,104 m) he aircraft breaking up nder excessive G oading. U.S.A.F. Edwards Air Force ase)

The X–15 below the starboard wing of the Boeing B–52 launch aircraft.
(U.S.A.F. Edwards Air Force Base)

The first aircraft was fitted with the more powerful rocket engine and, on every flight Scott Crossfield, Joe Walker, the NASA pilot and Capt. Bob White of the USAF broke record after record. Later a number of other NASA, USN and USAF test pilots joined the team – one of them was Neil Armstrong of moon exploration fame. By the autumn of 1960 Joe Walker had achieved 2,196 mph (3,535.6 km/hr) to be beaten in February 1961 by Bob White flying at 2,275 mph (3,662.8 km/hr); he had, on 12 August 1960 climbed to a record height of 136,500 ft (41,605 m). By autumn 1961 the score was 3,500 mph (5,635 km/hr) and an altitude of 215,000 ft (65,532 m).

The third X–15, fitted with the powerful XLR99 engine was undergoing ground running tests on 8 June 1960 with Scott Crossfield in the cockpit, the ground crew retired to a nearby shelter. As the throttle was opened a violent explosion occurred immediately behind the cockpit moving it forward about 24 ft (7.3 m) Crossfield, unhurt, found himself surrounded by yellow and orange flame which darkened as the fire brigade poured foam on the aircraft. He saw one of his mechanics rushing to unlock the canopy which was effectively protecting him from the fire. Scott was shocked to see Art Simone's fingers burning on the very hot metal so decided to get out himself to save him from serious injury. To avoid being burnt on the side of the fuselage he jumped upon Art's back and both fell into the pool of foam and water.

Before it was possible to make a telephone call to base to report that fifty million dollars worth of aircraft had blown up the press hounds were in full pursuit. To put them off he said that the accident had not been too serious, he was unhurt but his trousers had been soaked when he fell into the foam! He suddenly realised what a scoop he had given them; sure enough an East Coast newspaper carried the banner headline 'Test pilot wets pants!'

Generally the safety record of the X–15 programme was excellent considering the nature of it. On 9 November 1962 ill-luck struck on the 74th flight when John McKay suffered a malfunction at 54,000 ft (16,460 m). He found that fuel could not be jettisoned so another over-weight landing was inevitable. The gear collapsed, the pilot was seriously injured and the aircraft was badly damaged.

On 15 November 1967 a USAF pilot was making his seventh flight in the X–15. He reached M 5.2 and 266,000 ft (81,077 m) and rocked the aircraft to enable the ground trackers to identify its exhaust plume. It was seen to divert at 90° to its normal flight path and enter a spin, still at a speed of M 5.0. It spun from 230,000 ft (70,104 m) to 125,000 ft (38,100 m) when it began its fatal dive with the ground instruments recording loads of ± 15 G. It disintegrated and Major Michael Adams died in the wreck.

A total of 199 flights was made between 1959 and 1966. The writing was on the wall for the X–15 programme when President Kennedy made his historic vow, in 1962, that Americans would fly to the moon. Many engineers and test pilots, including Scott Crossfield, believe that the moon project was a mistake at that time. Crossfield was convinced that the further development of X–15 type aircraft to a point where they could be used to put a space station in orbit as a further stage towards planetary flight. It would certainly have offered the prospect of valuable spin-off in both military and commercial aviation which certainly was not the case with any of the later orbiters.

A valuable beneficiary of the X series programme was the remarkable Lockheed YF–12A which became the SR–71A, Blackbird. This brilliant Mach 3 design was in the forefront of development as, when it first flew in April 1962 as the YF–12A, the first M 2.0 fighters were only just entering service and the only experience of M 3.0 was with the X–2 on the last flight which killed the unfortunate Mel Apt.

The Blackbird ranged far and wide across the world with its high altitude cameras collecting photographs of almost unbelievable definition. When they were phased out of service in 1992 there was still no military aircraft to rival them or, indeed, to replace them.

Britain's only excursions into sustained supersonic flight were the Lightning interceptor fighter (*see* Chapter 10) and the Anglo-French Concorde airliner. At the time of Concorde's development, which originated in 1955, the USAF was operating the F–100 Super Sabre, the world's first combat aircraft capable of sustained supersonic flight other than in a dive. In 1956 Convair flew the prototype of its B–58 Hustler Mach Two bomber which embodied lessons learned from its XF–92A delta wing supersonic research aircraft, the F–102 Delta Dagger and the F–106 Delta Dart fighters capable of M 1.50.

The French had exceeded M 1.0 in August 1954 with the small SFACMAS Gerfault, their first jet powered delta to fly. This was followed by SO 9000 Trident 1 mixed power plant research aircraft and the SO 9000 Trident II which flew at 1242 mph (2000 km/hr) in January 1957 piloted by Jacques Guingard, later to be co-pilot of Concorde. In 1956 came the SE 212 achieving M 1.5 on its first flight and the prototypes of the delta winged Dessault Mirage III and Nord 1500 Griffon exceeded M 2.0 in level flight. The test pilot associated with the Griffon, who was the first European to exceed Mach Two, was André Turcat, later to be the chief French test pilot for Concorde.

In 1957 the Super-Mystere B–2 became the first supersonic interceptor fighter to go into squadron service in Western Europe.

It became clear that M 2.0 was entirely feasible for military aircraft so, it was felt, it was only a question of development to take advantage of the remarkable performance now capable of achievement and direct it to civil airliners.

In 1955 the Supersonic Aircraft Technical Committee (SATC) was established to represent British interests in studying the characteristics of such a project. This is not the place to record the tortuous arguments, technical, commercial and, above all, political, to say nothing of media vituperation stirred up by 'know-it-all' journalists and the BBC. Suffice to say that Concorde survived all these slings and arrows and became an outstanding technical success which conferred immense prestige upon the British and French aircraft industry and the two national airlines, although it must be said that one of the strongest 'knockers' was the national carrier, British Overseas Airways Corporation; it is now, 25 years later, the flagship of British Airways fleet. Clearly, the problems faced by the designers were immense and the development cost was far above budget; a major blow was the considerable increase in fuel prices which ensured that overall profitability was not one of Concorde's characteristics. It was a most satisfactory coincidence that the British Aircraft Corporation and Sud-Aviation, builders of the very successful and innovative twin-jet airliner, were thinking along broadly similar lines although Sud envisaged an aircraft with a much shorter range for their supersonic design. Superimposition of general arrangement drawings of the BAC Type 223 and the Sud Super Caravelle reveal an almost identical profile in plan, side elevation and front elevation.; the BAC design had a narrow delta wing with a straight leading edge whilst the Sud Aviation proposal had the ogival delta wing, a shape which became part of the Concorde design. On 29 November 1962 the historic Agreement to co-operate was signed by Britain and France to develop a supersonic airliner jointly the main contractors being BAC and SNIAS, now known as Aérospatiale, responsible for the airframe with Rolls-Royce and the French SNECMA organisation being responsible for the engines.

The fact that in so many respects the design was based upon entirely new technology with hitherto unknown problems necessitated a major programme of component and sub-assembly tests at the earliest possible stage.

The selection of the cruising speed was dependant upon the ability of the structural materials and system components to withstand the high level of kinetic heating generated by supersonic flight. Mach 2.2 was the maximum cruising speed achievable with an airframe built of well-proven aluminium alloys. A consideration was the fact that engine efficiency increased as speed rose to M 3.0. Such an airframe would have required the use of expensive titanium and stainless steel; titanium and stainless steel are difficult to work and the experience of the Bristol engineers with the Bristol 188 research aircraft built of stainless steel (*see* Chapter 11) ruled out the use of this intractable metal.

Finally Mach 2.04 was chosen as the maximum operating speed within the structural and aerodynamic parameters. At this speed the maximum skin temperature comes close to the limit of 127° C in standard atmosphere. At these levels a small reduction in temperature brings significant advantages in terms of fatigue life.

Two complete airframes were built for test purposes after a substantial number of detail tests had been carried out. One of them was used at the Aérospatiale Toulouse plant for static load testing whilst the other was subjected to fatigue tests at FAE Farnborough. This one was covered with ducting through which hot and cold air was pumped to simulate the thermal cycles of flight. At the same time about 100 hydraulic rams applied simulated flight loads to the structure.

Operations at 60,000 ft (18,288 m) required a much higher cabin pressure than hitherto; to maintain a cabin altitude of 6,000 ft (1,829 m) at that altitude the pressure had to be about 11 psi, for subsonic jets it was customary to use 8 psi. So the cabin had to be cyclically tested to an appropriate pressure above working level.

At Toulouse the static test airframe was also subject to tests under transient and steady temperatures. Kinetic heating was simulated by 35,000 infra-red lamps whilst 15,385 gallons (69,939 litres) of liquid nitrogen was used to cool the airframe. The skin could be cycled between 120° C and -10° C in fifteen minutes whilst the hydraulic rams continued to apply appropriate structural loads which were recorded from 8,000 data pick-up transducers every two seconds.

These tests were completed in 1972 permitting the aircraft to operate at 385,000 lb (174,635 kg) all-up weight. The tests continued to 400,000 lb (181,439 kg) with damage being applied to certain high stress areas to see if fatigue failure was likely to be induced.

Another major test area was the fuel system. Concorde, in common with other supersonic aircraft, experiences a centre of pressure change in the transonic régime, which results in movement aft as the speed increases thus inducing a nose-down pitch. This would normally require an upward movement of the pitch control surface whether it is an all-moving tail, elevator or elevons. The higher the speed the greater the degree of PC shift; in the case of Concorde it is about 6 ft (2 m). With normal controls this would necessitate a fairly high level of control surface deflection which would create unacceptable drag. A neat solution was found in using the fuel load to re-balance the aircraft.

Most of the 95 tons (96,526 kg) of fuel is contained in the wings but up to 33 tons (33,530 kg) can be used for trimming via tanks in the forward fuselage and the tail. A full scale rig was erected to perfect the details of the scheme which has proved to be entirely satisfactory.

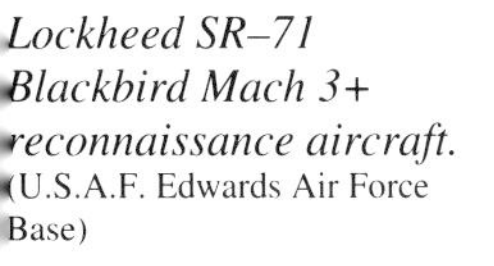
Lockheed SR–71 Blackbird Mach 3+ reconnaissance aircraft. (U.S.A.F. Edwards Air Force Base)

In parallel with the structural tests the Olympus engine was air tested in a replica of the Concorde nacelle slung under a Vulcan bomber. This test was only of limited value as the Vulcan is a sub-sonic aeroplane, so extrapolation of data had to be made to arrive at a reasonable correlation with predicted performance. The total thrust of the Olympus engines installed in Concorde is 152,000 lb (69,947 kg) for take-off, of which up to 20% can be contributed by the reheat system.

The wide speed range of the aircraft presented the designers of the engine installation with some very difficult problems; compressors will not operate in a stream of air travelling at supersonic speed, it must be at subsonic velocity so must be decelerated in the intake from M 2.01 to M 0.5. As the intake is only 11 ft (3.35 m) long, a complex system of computer controlled ramps inside the nacelle with doors on the outside was designed to achieve this and ensure a reasonable fuel consumption. To obtain the desired range it was essential to operate the engines as near to the surge point as possible. A temperature rise within the intake of 200° C was yet another variable to be considered. Cruise performance proved to be as predicted but take-off and transonic thrust was inadequate so reheat became necessary. By this means the most economical fuel consumption was achieved whilst accelerating through the drag-inducing transonic range to cruising speed.

Exit nozzle design was another area of considerable complexity, a compromise becoming necessary between lift, drag, reverse thrust and weight.

The aerodynamic design of Concorde was developed through a programme of some 5,000 hours of wind tunnel testing to refine the exceptionally complex wing shape and form. Its continuous camber and twist along the leading edge combined with camber and taper over the surfaces to achieve the desired performance required the highest degree of accuracy and quality control in manufacture.

One of the most valuable research tools was the Handley Page 115 research aircraft. The earliest Concorde model tests had clearly indicated that the narrow delta configuration would achieve adequate lift at high angles of attack by the generation of powerful vortices over the wings thus allowing the aircraft to touch down at a reasonable speed. To prove the reality of this the 115 was built as a simple aircraft powered by a 1,900 lb (862.6 kg) thrust Bristol Siddeley Viper turbojet. The leading edge of the 20 ft (9.1 m) span delta wing was swept 74.7° and was of balsa wood so that section and camber could be altered easily. S/Ldr Jack Henderson was one of the project pilots and the test sorties were carried out mainly at RAE Bedford. He had spent many hours in the simulator programmed with the results of the wind tunnel tests and model flying. There were doubts about the controllability of the 115 but Henderson was most agreeably surprised by its flight characteristics. After many ground runs the first flight took place on 17 August 1961 and lasted for 31 minutes. It proved to be a delightful aeroplane to fly and provided valuable information for the next four years. One of the most valuable series of tests was to visualise airflow at varying angles of attack. Smoke was injected into the centre of the vortices and a mixture of red ink and kaolin was injected along the wing surface to define the boundary layer flow. Occasionally it was possible to see the condensation cloud over the wing as the 115 flew through thin cloud.

The 115 proved beyond doubt that high lift devices such as flaps and slats were unnecessary for Concorde although, as speed decayed, the wing drag increased considerably resulting in the approach speed being well below minimum drag speed. This was advantageous to the extent that it obviated the need for air brakes but the pilot had to be careful in monitoring his approach speed and to apply sufficient power to overcome the increased drag. Concorde is equipped with auto-throttles which deal with the situation without any action by the pilot.

Iandley Page 115 esearch aircraft. Aeroplane Monthly)

High speed research was carried out at RAE Bedford by the Bristol 221 which had been the Fairey FD 2, WG774, in which Peter Twiss established a world speed record, as related in Chapter 11. It had been converted by the Bristol Company to have an ogival delta wing of the same configuration as Concorde. It was first flown from Filton by Godfrey Auty on 1 May 1961 and proved to be useful in providing data at the high speed end of the range when flown from RAE Bedford.

In 1965 Brian Trubshaw was appointed Director of Flight Test and Chief Test Pilot for both Bristol and Weybridge. The Air Registration Board, later to become the Civil Aviation Authority, had been extremely concerned at what they saw as the limited test pilot input to Concorde compared with that available at Aérospatiale. Trubshaw had flown for BAC since 1950 when he had left the RAF to join Jock Bryce's team on the Valiant. Since then he had tested the Viscount, Vanguard, BAC 111 and the VC 10, so had a clear appreciation of the Certification requirements for civil aircraft generally; he was also responsible for the technical back-up for Concorde as well as the purely flying aspect of the project.

Concorde had already been a reality for several years so he had to catch up with all the work already carried out at Filton and Toulouse. One aspect of the design caused him considerable concern. Due to the high angle of attack in the landing phase it was necessary to droop the whole of the nose section to give the pilots an adequate view. The technique had already been proved by drooping the cockpit section of the Fairey FD 2 but Concorde was to have a visor which could be moved to streamline the windscreens into the line of the nose and fuselage. Supposedly the high temperature over the nose section at cruising speed necessitated a metal visor with a small glazed aperture to give a view in the event of the visor jamming in the extended position. 'Trubbie' was horrified at the prospect of trying to land Concorde under such conditions; he considered that a score of 'two for a brave try' was appropriate. His objections were supported during a meeting with George Moore of the US Federal Aviation Authority who stated very firmly that under no circumstances would the FAA accept such a scheme. Faced with this uncompromising stance the present design of a toughened glass visor was devised. Sixteen airlines showed initial interest in the aircraft so many meetings were held to try to find a common formula for flight deck layout. Finally, the task was the responsibility of 'the Troika' – British Airways, Air France and Pan Am.

Another problem was the Filton runway which had been extended to accommodate the huge Brabazon airliner but still left much to be desired in terms of length and the rise in the middle of it. All flight testing was moved from Filton to an RAF airfield, Fairford, which was only an hour's drive from Filton. At the peak of the programme about 500 people were based at Fairford, a measure of the complexity of the flight test programme, which was made even more complex by the fact that the Certification Authorities in Europe and USA had virtually no experience of the technical and operational requirements of supersonic aircraft.

The two prototypes, 001 at Toulouse and 002 at Filton were, indeed, prototypes; they were slightly smaller than the production version and all the systems were quite different. A valuable technical development emerged, for example, in the design of the braking system; the prototypes were fitted with brakes on each of the eight main wheels each comprising eleven steel discs faced with sintered iron-based friction materials. In the production aircraft this design was changed to discs made of carbon-carbon composite material which was being developed for rockets. A weight saving of 1,200 lb (545 kg) per aircraft was made. One of the Dunlop engineers responsible for the design stated, in a 1988 Technical Paper, that every kilogram saved on Concorde was worth £500 per annum to the airline. There are many other examples of technical spin-off from this aeroplane.

On 31 December 1968 the Russians stole a march on Britain and France by flying for the first time their own supersonic airliner, the Tu–144, almost identical in general layout with Concorde and generally known as 'Conkordski'! On Sunday, 2 March 1969 Concorde 001, F-WFSS, was flown from Toulouse by André Turcat, Director of Flight Test at Aérospatiale. The aircraft weighed 250,000 lb (113,400 kg) and reached a speed of 250 kt (463 km/hr). The droop nose remained down but the undercarriage was raised. After 28 minutes Turcat and his crew made a perfect landing, decelerating with the use of reverse thrust and the tail parachute. Turcat was impressed with handling, saying that it was better than the computer predictions had indicated.

It was the turn of Brian Trubshaw, who had already flown 001, to fly 002, G-BSST, with John Cochrane in the right-hand seat from Filton on 9 April 1969. Apart from a malfunction in both radio altimeters the 42 minute flight to RAF Fairford was equally satisfactory and, after the inevitable media hype had died away, the test programme began in earnest.

Gilbert Defer, in 001, experienced a serious engine surge which spat ramps and debris out of the front of the nacelle, some of the parts being ingested into the adjacent nacelle. This occurred at M 2.0 with no untoward effect upon the controllability of the aircraft. The only other large four-engine supersonic aircraft in service was the American Convair B–58 Hustler bomber. An emergency of this nature would have left it barely controllable so the implications in terms of Concorde flight safety were encouraging. Nevertheless it proved that strengthening of some of the intake components was essential.

The two prototypes and two of the pre-production aircraft were used for flight test, each carrying about 12 tons (12,200 kg) of test equipment. The pre-production aircraft with longer fuselages and an all-up weight of 340,000 lb (154,233 kg) with a few minor changes to the wing shape were almost representative of the airline version. The test gear on board

Concorde 002 taking off on her maiden flight from Filton 9 April 1969.
(British Aerospace, Filton)

recorded up to 4,000 different parameters such as acceleration, attitude, temperature and pressure which were recorded on magnetic tape for subsequent evaluation on the ground. Some of the data recorded in the French aircraft were telemetered to the ground station during the sorties.

Line pilots from British Airways, Air France, Pan Am and TWA were invited to fly Concorde after experience upon the development simulator at Toulouse. They were most complimentary about the aeroplane and observed that it would present no problems to either air or ground crews.

The Type Certification requirements demanded that Concorde should be compatible in airline service with normal subsonic aircraft. For reasons of crew safety the prototype was fitted with escape hatches and parachutes whilst high altitude suits were worn on the early flights. The hatches were soon sealed off and shirt sleeves and headsets became *de rigeur*! The most urgent and vital task was to expand the flight envelope as quickly as possible to ensure that M 2.0 could be achieved within the predicted fuel consumption and all-up weight levels. This target was soon achieved and the aeroplane proved to be very easy to fly.

A series of demonstration flights overseas was carried out by both the French and British test teams. To meet Certification standards route proving flights were carried out by Aérospatiale and Air France who flew 203 over their planned North and South Atlantic routes whilst BAC and British Airways flew 204 over their planned North Atlantic, Middle East and Asian routes. 755 hours was recorded with a further 204 hours during flights with the two prototypes.

A problem which had not been experienced in the temperate European climate was encountered in tropical regions where temperature variations above the tropopause are not uncommon and were of a magnitude which led to instability in control by the autopilot as it sought to maintain a constant Mach No. The variation was found to be as much as from M 1.9 to M 2.1. Modification became necessary to eliminate this instability by combining the auto-throttle and the autopilot commands. This overcame the difficulty without any input from the pilot.

Aérospatiale, with the 001 prototype, were responsible for the handling characteristics of Concorde; stalling was, of course, high on the programme. A narrow delta wing has no defined stall as with orthodox designs, it can reach a very high angle of attack and then descend in a deep stall at a very high rate and, theoretically, cannot be pitched out. It was, therefore, important that the aircraft was not allowed to go that far. The French were determined to avoid a 'stick-pusher' but fitted a device which operated in a similar manner through the autostabilisation system and created a hydraulic pulse through the hydraulic circuit to the control column to warn the pilot of the impending instability. It even gave protection in yaw as, at high AoA, the fin is blanked to an ineffective level. A higher degree of authority by the autostabiliser was fed to the rudder so that yaw control under these conditions was immediate and positive. A 'stick wobbler' was also introduced into the circuit. The autostabilisation system is Mach Number oriented and valuable work was done by the French engineers in perfecting the whole flying control system by adjusting gearing and computer characteristics in what is a very complex arrangement giving characteristics appropriate to the Mach Number being flown.

The other very complex area of development was the engine controls; common to aircraft and engine handling was the effect of the spill doors under the nacelles. In the event of an engine failure at M 2.00 it is essential to vent the air entering the nacelles to avoid buffeting and high drag. A double engine failure creates a problem in that as the two spill doors under each of the nacelles open to allow venting the flow creates a rolling moment, an effect which is quite the opposite to the behaviour of a conventional aeroplane after engine failure.

The design of the nacelle intake system was based upon the principles of air velocity control mentioned earlier. It was realised that engine surge was a risk likely to affect the low pressure compressor at the front of the engine but very unlikely with the high pressure one behind it. Consequently, the stressing of the ramps and other control devices was predicated upon LP compressor surge. In practice, the force of the pressure wave created by the surge was under-estimated. Brian Trubshaw, explaining surging to the author, said:

'It is just like an enormous and very loud backfire, not what you want with the roast beef and champagne!'

After hundreds of hours of flight test the design of the intake system was proved to be entirely satisfactory within the commercial flight envelope of the aircraft. One of the problems associated with the programme was the level of sonic boom generated by Concorde. The areas defined for the tests were the North Sea from the north of Scotland to the coast of East Anglia or flying a race-track pattern from the Irish Sea to the Bay of Biscay. Where extended supersonic runs were necessary it was important to fly a straight course of about 800 miles (1,288 km) with radar surveillance and access to rescue services. It was not possible to find a route which was entirely over the sea but the minimum number of people were disturbed along a North/South track over the coasts of Scotland, Wales and Cornwall. Warning was given to inhabitants that these flights were to take place – only about fifty were required.

Overseas flights were a fairly early part of the programme. Brian Trubshaw told the author that 'people thought that we were mad to take Concorde overseas at such an early stage'; nevertheless it was an extremely successful venture, it showed this beautiful aircraft to those who it was hoped would be purchasers, it proved what could be achieved within the framework of European co-operation and it also proved that Concorde could be integrated with existing subsonic operations. Above all, it showed a remarkable degree of serviceability. On its 42nd flight, on 25 May 1971, the French prototype, 001 flew to Dakar. On 4 September 1971 001 flew a 15-day tour of South America. The British 002, flown by Brian Trubshaw, with 'Johnnie' Walker and Peter Baker flew to the Middle East and as far as Japan and Australia. Only one demonstration had to be postponed due to mechanical trouble.

There were few dramas during the programme apart from the surging problems; flutter tests revealed no difficulty. In August 1974 two loud bangs were heard as the undercarriage was lowered on the approach to Fairford, the port main gear did not show a green light and inspection through a floor hatch showed that the retraction ram and main side stay had detached so the leg was not effectively supported. Fuel was burned off to the minimum and a landing made with great care being taken to reduce the side load on that leg. A braking

Brian Trubshaw and co-pilot John Cochrane on the flight deck of Concorde 002. (British Aerospace, Filton)

parachute was deployed and the thrust reversers used to avoid undue braking loads and the aircraft came safely to a standstill. It was found that both legs were in a weak condition due to a pin connecting the side stay to the main leg failing through the centrifugal load applied to it as the undercarriage was lowered during a turn. Suitable mods were carried out.

A combustion chamber fault caused some difficulty in early production engines and an undercarriage leg had to be changed at Bahrain; beyond these minor faults this remarkable aircraft, an early example of fly-by-wire controls with manual reversion, met all its Specification requirements.

One of the most significant aspects of the Concorde programme was its acceptance from a noise level point of view. No noise requirements had been laid down by the Certification Authorities but individual airfields such as London Heathrow and New York Kennedy had clearly defined noise limits at specific points under the departure and arrival flight paths. At the outset it was known that Concorde could not meet those at Heathrow but the British Authority accepted that this was the case. At New York, however, the Port Authority insisted that the aircraft should meet the local standards. It was necessary to establish specific noise abatement techniques for each runway to ensure conformity. These techniques, developed over many hours of flying, sought to achieve standards acceptable at all airports whether noise levels were specified or not.

Throughout the development of this superb aeroplane considerable support was given by the National Aeronautics and Space Administration (NASA) at their Ames Dryden facility. They offered the use of their advanced flight simulator for the establishment of field performance requirements. From this programme it was established, for example, that minimum unstick speed was not the limiting factor for lift-off but rather the zero rate of climb speed.

The present Chairman of British Aerospace Airbus Division, Mr R.M. 'Bob' McKinley, was Assistant Director of Flight Test responsible for the technical side of the Flight Test Department under Brian Trubshaw. He made an extremely valuable contribution in steering this most complex aircraft through one of the most exhaustive test programmes ever undertaken.

Peter Baker gave high praise to Gordon Corps, the Civil Aviation Authority test pilot who was charged with Certification of Concorde, for which, of course, there was no technical precedent. His input was invaluable as, indeed, it proved to be later to Airbus Industrie in flight testing their new range of high performance airliners. It was a great loss to the aviation world when, in 1993, Gordon died of a heart attack when climbing a high peak near Kathmandu in Nepal to investigate the loss of an Airbus which had flown into the terrain.

On 21 January 1976, at 1140 hrs GMT, British Airways and Air France began their Concorde services with BA operating from London to Bahrain and Air France from Paris to Rio de Janeiro. The fact that, at the time of writing, the aircraft is still providing luxury travel across the Atlantic at Mach 2.00 is a tribute to those who designed, built, test flew and operate this remarkable Anglo-French airliner of unsurpassed beauty. It seems set to continue to do so well into the next century.

CHAPTER 14

The Development of Vertical Short Take-off and Landing (V/STOL) Aircraft

It has long been the ambition of the world's more enterprising aircraft designers to develop an aeroplane, other than rotary-winged, capable of vertical take-off and landing. It remained beyond the bounds of possibility until the 1950s when adequate engine power became available in the lightweight gas turbine.

As early as 1941, Dr A.A. Griffith, chief scientist of Rolls-Royce, and one of the pioneer thinkers in jet propulsion, had envisaged such aircraft in practical terms accepting that wings appropriate to high speeds were highly inefficient at low speed and would require vertical thrust to make the 'thistledown' landings which he believed were possible when engines of the right power/weight ratio could be developed. Not until the 1950/60 period did his ideas begin to take shape with the development of the RB 108 jet engine with a thrust of eight times its own weight whilst the later RB 162, a more advanced concept, offered thrust of more than sixteen times its own weight.

Griffith conceived a large supersonic airliner with banks of the small jet engines in the slim delta wing with banks of propulsion engines one above the other, in a twin-fin arrangement at the rear of the aircraft. Few engineers, even today, would consider this costly and complicated concept to have a viable future but it provided a stimulus to further effort towards V/STOL.

It was realised that the problems of control and stability during the hover would be a serious matter in any size of aircraft so, as a joint effort with RAE Farnborough and the Ministry of Supply, Rolls designed a jet-borne test rig to investigate these aspects of design.

In America various types of VTOL fighter were proposed some using a powerful turbo-prop for lift off when the aeroplane was standing on its tail; prototypes were built and flown and the immensity of the control problems soon became apparent. The Ryan Aeronautical Company was one of the leaders in this work and the author is indebted to Peter F. Girard, who was responsible for flight testing the experimental aircraft, for a description of the programme carried out on two of the designs, the jet propelled X–13 Vertijet and the VZ–3RY propeller-driven tilt-wing type.

The X–13 was capable of flight in three different régimes; conventional wing lift, vertical flight under jet lift conditions or transitional flight between the first two régimes. This, of course, had never been achieved before with a jet propelled aircraft. Bell Aircraft Corporation were strong rivals of Ryan in the vertical flight arena and had investigated various methods such as jet deflection, rockets, tilting rotor and tilting duct. The world's first tilt-rotor fixed wing aeroplane was the Bell XV–3 with rotors at the tips which acted in the helicopter mode for take-off and in the thrust mode by rotating through 90° forward. It made its first vertical take-off on 23 August 1955 but was damaged in a crash after a number of successful flights. It was rebuilt after a programme of full scale wind tunnel tests; flight trials of the resulting second prototype led to the first transition from vertical to

Rolls-Royce Thrust Measuring Rig, alias the Flying Bedstead.
(Rolls-Royce plc)

horizontal flight and back again to land which took place on 18 November 1958. By 1961 over 100 full transitions had been carried out and the speed of the aircraft had ranged from 15 mph (24 km/hr) rearwards to 181 mph (291 km/hr) in the forwards direction. It reached an altitude of 12,000 ft (3,658 m).

Development work with a series of similar aircraft led, ultimately, to collaboration with Boeing Vertol and the development of the Bell Boeing SV–22 Osprey Tilt Rotor aircraft which has proved to be a major step forward in this demanding field.

In 1947 Ryan had mounted an Allison J–33 engine on a test stand to investigate the directional control aspect of the concept by thrust variation. The next stage was to mount the engine in a vertical test rig which was later fitted with a cockpit, controls and a delta wing for actual flight trials. These were so encouraging that the USAF awarded a contract in 1953 to build the X–13.

The Rolls-Royce Thrust Measuring Rig was built to determine whether it was possible to control such a device by means of jet efflux alone rather than with orthodox controls. The maximum thrust/weight ratio had to be at least 1.25, 25% more than the total weight of the machine. It was to have a fuel capacity capable of supporting 15 minutes of flight. Control of it should feel natural to the pilot accustomed to normal aeroplanes. It was to have complete freedom of movement within a space of at least 100 ft (30.5 m) by 100 ft up to a height of 50 ft (15.25 m). It was also necessary to ensure that it could hover just above the ground without becoming excessively hot. The pilot must be safeguarded in the event of engine or control failure. The rig was built with two Nene 101 engines facing in opposite directions to overcome the powerful gyroscopic effects which would be generated. They were modified to permit 10 per cent of compressor air to be bled off for use in the attitude control system. The elbows used to direct the thrust downwards were located as near as possible to the centre of gravity to reduce pitching and rolling moments. The air bled from the compressor was directed through appropriate valves to the extended nozzles at the front and rear of the rig where they would provide pitch control and to the two nozzles extending from the sides to give stability in the rolling plane. Yaw control was achieved by an orthodox rudder bar which swivelled the engines. The control column moved the nozzles which, of course, were directed downwards.

It was decided, from the outset, that an autostabilisation system would be installed, this was to be developed by RAE to control the valves and linkages produced by Rolls-Royce. The throttle was arranged in the form of a helicopter throttle with movement up and down. In the interests of safety the rig was to be operated initially suspended from a gantry erected at the R-R Hucknall test flight base. The rate of descent of it was controlled by synchronous motors winding the suspension cables. The gantry itself was 45 ft (13.7 m) high and spanned 60 ft (18.29 m). The pilot was mounted on a platform above the engines with his instrument panel, controls and the autostabiliser.

On 3 July 1953 the 'Flying Bedstead', a name to which Lord Hives, the Chairman of Rolls-Royce strongly but vainly objected, was wheeled out for ground runs. Three days later W/Cdr Jim Heyworth, the R-R chief test pilot, began the flight test programme by opening the throttles and extending the four undercarriage oleo legs a few inches. He reduced power but the oleos did not close again on one side. A repeat of the sequence made matters worse so the throttles were closed with the rig suspended on its cable and resting against part of the gantry. Further restrictor cables were fitted and the tests continued. Control was found to be reasonably good but, with the cable restraints, a true analysis was impossible. By 9 November 20 hours of operation was recorded and the opportunity was taken to return the rig to works for various modifications to be incorporated.

When trials continued there were many problems of control and it was not until June 1954 that the pilot could transfer his thought processes from how long he could remain airborne to what manoeuvres he could make. By the end of this second series of gantry tests a duration of nine minutes had been achieved.

On 3 August the great day of the first untethered flight arrived. Capt R.T. Shepherd, who, after many years as chief test pilot, had been recruited from retirement to assist with the rig tests, was invited to make the flight. He lifted off and made a circuit of the test area, moving backwards and forwards at will using all the controls which behaved perfectly. Further tests were carried out in winds up to 20 mph and at heights up to 50 ft (15 m). The programme was now extended to include other pilots, notably from RAE.

One of the RAE pilots was S/Ldr Jock Harvey who had been invited to 'fly' it first in the gantry when another RAE man had declined the opportunity, telling Harvey that he did not want his wife to be widowed and his children orphaned! On that encouraging note, Ron borrowed a Mosquito and flew to Hucknall. After two ascents on the rig he recorded that it was remarkably stable for an apparently top-heavy machine weighing over 3 tons (3,051 kg), no uncontrolled movement could be detected in pitch or roll. He considered the autostabiliser a magnificent achievement. He flew it at night and said that, with floodlights illuminating the scene it was an impressive affair with some engine parts glowing red hot and the whole thing making a fiendish noise and, in rain, the drops falling on the hot metal produced enormous clouds of steam. He decided that the safety aspect of the 'Bedstead' depended entirely upon the autostabiliser reliability and that failure in free flight would be catastrophic. He, therefore, explored flight by manual control only; he found that it was sensitive in pitch but sluggish in roll and likened the sensation to flying a fighter in pitch and a bomber in roll.

Flight in the open arena was commenced and great care was needed to avoid landing with drift of more than 5 mph (8 km/hr) otherwise the rig would capsize and kill the pilot, as, indeed happened to one of them. He was flying the second 'Bedstead' which was being prepared for delivery to RAE Bedford. On 28 November 1957 whilst being flown on the gantry for the last time he lost control and crashed. This was the end of the Thrust Measuring Rig programme as the Rolls-Royce RB 108 lift engine and the Short SC–1 'flat-riser', in which five of them were installed, had flown. The 'Bedstead' project was entirely successful and had proved the concept of jet powered VTOL aircraft in UK.

Across the Atlantic the USAF sponsored the jet propelled Ryan X–13, built for research into the transition stage of flight, and the USN sponsored two other designs which, it was hoped would prove to be successful fighters for service aboard merchant ships and small naval vessels. Both were prop-turbine tail-sitters with contra-rotating propellers. These were the Convair XFY–1 'Pogo' and the Lockheed XFV–1 Salmon. Only the Convair aircraft achieved vertical flight when, on 1 August 1954, James 'Skeets' Coleman made the first free hover at a height of 150 ft (45.7 m) on 2 November during which he achieved transition, flew for some minutes in wing-borne mode, made the transition back to vertical landing mode and a smooth touch-down. The Lockheed aeroplane did not make a vertical take-off, relying upon a launching trolley to lift off horizontally. Its pilot observed that 'it was awfully difficult to land looking over one's shoulder.'

Ryan X–13 undergoing rig tests.
(Ryan Aeronautical Co., via Peter F. Girard)

Ryan X–13 taking off on its tricycle undercarriage.
(Ryan Aeronautical Co., via Peter F. Girard)

Ryan X–13 with vertical take-off and touch-down undercarriage.
(Ryan Aeronautical Co., via Peter F. Girard)

Ryan X–13 approaching 'hook-on' platform.
(Ryan Aeronautical Co., via Peter F. Girard)

To the Navy it became increasingly clear that the inevitable lag in the engine and aircraft control systems combined with the often violent rise and fall of the ship in a seaway, combined with its pitching ensured that such operations would be extremely hazardous. Nevertheless Ryan proceeded with the X–13 Vertijet as it became known. Two were built powered by the 10,000 lb (4,536 kg) thrust Rolls-Royce Avon engine without afterburner. This was the most powerful gas turbine available at the time and had a favourable thrust/weight ratio.

To avoid the weight of a tail-sitter landing gear appropriate to the 4 G load of a touch-down it was decided to build a large hook under the cockpit which would engage from the hover with a short horizontal cable on the raised bed of a ground support and landing trailer. The short-coupled, high wing tail-less configuration was not conducive to a high level of directional stability so a large fin was used with endplate stabilisers at the wing tips. Good visibility in the hover was difficult to achieve; with particular attention to cockpit fenestration and the ability to rotate the pilot's seat forward a reasonable compromise was achieved.

After the successful completion of initial wing-borne trials with a temporary tricycle landing gear a temporary tail-sitter tubular undercarriage permitted testing in the vertical mode. The first flight in this form was on 28 May to be followed by simulated hook-on trials and, on 28 November 1956 the second X–13 flew and achieved successful transition from vertical to horizontal flight and a reversion to vertical mode for landing. W.L. Everitt was back-up pilot, as Pete Girard continued with the test programme which provided valuable data.

Although the test site was 2,350 ft (716 m) above sea level the powerful Avon engine gave a thrust/weight ratio at take-off in excess of 1.11 even though ambient temperatures were high. Hovering presented no control difficulties due to the excellent response of the engine and jet reaction control system whilst the effect of ground winds was less than had been predicted. The estimation of altitude and velocity when in the vertical attitude required considerable concentration on the part of the pilot, 150 ft (45.7 m) appeared to be the maximum at which the pilot could, with accuracy and confidence, judge velocity and position, above this much checking and double checking was required. Above 300 ft (91.4 m) the vertical velocity meter was a necessary aid although it was still possible to let down safely from 700 ft (213.4 m) to 1,000 ft (305 m) without instruments but with a high level of concentration.

Seat position control was a particularly important matter. As the cockpit work-load during transition was so high it was essential that the seat could be controlled by a button on the throttle. Should a malfunction occur in vertical flight the pilot would be in serious difficulty; not only would visibility be impaired but his inner ear and visual sense references would be displaced to a level which could induce disorientation, no other flight circumstances caused either disorientation or vertigo.

The powerful engine developed high gyroscopic moments when the aircraft moved in pitch or yaw in the vertical flight mode, a factor exacerbated by the light airframe. The original test vehicle revealed a form of non-linear cross-coupling which varied in direction as well as magnitude of control input due to the differences between lateral and longitudinal moments of inertia, this proved to be unacceptably confusing to the pilot and the control system was modified to overcome it.

Flight simulator investigations indicated that in wing-borne flight, the aircraft would have a serious inadequately damped oscillation in all planes which could diverge under certain low load factor and rate of roll conditions. Early flight tests proved the simulator predictions of the oscillations to be so serious that the flights were terminated until roll dampers could be installed. Even with these the first flight ended in a semi-emergency landing. Yaw dampers were then fitted which improved stability to a point where free flight trials could continue although some fairly alarming characteristics were manifest.

A major difficulty was the limited fuel load which permitted virtually no margin for error when operating off the hook – approximately nine and a half minutes duration was the limit; hook demonstration flights were usually of seven and a half minutes duration. Another potential hazard was reliability of the fly-by-wire control system which was an amalgam of electrical, hydraulic and mechanical sub-systems, some of the latter operating at very high temperatures. The brakes of the conventional landing gear fitted for tests in the conventional flight mode caused problems as, to save weight, they were of marginal capacity. As landing speed was high a runway length of 9,000 ft (2,743 m) was required, the brakes tended to burn out and a wheel and brake change was often needed after a single landing. An anti-spin parachute was used later as a landing aid but it was really too large for the job causing violent decelerations which left weals from the pilot's harness on his shoulders during the last part of the deceleration.

During one landing at Andrews AFB on a 7,200 ft (2195 m) runway, prior to the flight to demonstrate the X–13 at the Pentagon, it failed to deploy and the brakes were inadequate to stop the aircraft from running into the barrier at the end of the runway; being of unusual configuration it tore away from the barrier asymmetrically and almost overturned.

As may be expected the transition phase of flight offered the greatest difficulty to the pilot and the problems were greatest in the landing transition from wing-borne to vertical flight. This manoeuvre was carried out at low altitude to minimise the rate of fuel consumption. It was found most satisfactory to make the transition at approximately constant altitude as the stall effect upon the wing was not excessive whilst the aircraft rotated into the high angle of attack and then into the vertical lift mode. In a descending flight path followed by rotation a high degree of airframe buffet made the control of vertical velocity much more difficult. Throughout the manoeuvre the aerodynamic parameters were constantly changing as the wing approached and passed through the stall state. As the thrust vector inclination changed and kinetic energy was dissipated the dynamic situation became most complex. The problems diminished in intensity as the experience of Pete Girard grew. There were also difficulties when the pilot's input and that of the automatic control diverged as they did under certain flight conditions.

Nevertheless the Ryan X–13 programme was an extremely valuable one creating a mass of data which was of benefit in the design of autostabilisers for all types of aircraft, not just V/STOL types.

It must be appreciated that Girard was entering upon an area of flight research hitherto unexplored and fraught with potential for catastrophe. Some of his personal recollections indicate the level of risk involved. The Jet Reaction Control System had been developed over many years by Ryan and the Stability Augmentation System (SAS) was a single channel unit with a more elementary back-up; as it used magnetic amplification it was extremely vulnerable to the vibration inherent in the aeroplane. Fortunately a surprising degree of reliability was experienced.

During the flight tests at Edwards AFB the realisation that the simulator predictions were accurate developed at 50 ft (15.2 m) above the lake bed. As soon as the nose was lowered to land the X–13 entered a violent dutch roll, directly coupled in phase with the longitudinal oscillation due to the gyroscopic inputs of the rotating stage of the engine. The nose would describe a large figure eight with its axis approximately 30° to the horizontal. The period of the oscillation was about one second and in attempting to oppose it he tended to get into phase with it to make matters worse. The gyroscopic effect from the engine accentuated the problem and added a degree of 'sharpness' to the motion leading, on the first flights, to the feeling that the oscillation would accelerate and diverge with disastrous consequences at this low altitude. It was found that a higher degree of damping of the oscillation took place in the flare with higher lift coefficients, a factor which probably saved the aeroplane from tumbling on several occasions. At this stage it was decided to fit the roll dampers and later, the yaw dampers.

In the 'Pogo' mode, take-off was complicated by the fact that, due to the interaction of the ground reaction force vectors, the pitch and yaw control became reversed in their effect, additionally it was not possible to align the engine thrust vector to the true vertical plane. On take-off it skittered along the ground until it rose clear of it. It was necessary to 'jump' it into the air before horizontal velocity built up, thereafter it was a delight to fly. Girard found it impossible to make a gentle take-off, it was 'all-or-nothing'. On one occasion after the replacement of some components of the SAS, it leapt into the air in an unstable condition due to the components having been wired up in the reverse sense. He was able to return to the ground without damage.

On one hovering flight at higher altitude saturation of the SAS, due to a transient, occurred and the aeroplane descended like a wobbling top, rotating in pitch and yaw at rates up to 60° per second. Peter Girard was able to return to horizontal flight and extricate him and the X–13 from a very ugly situation.

The VZ–3RY aeroplane was built to investigate the tilt-wing concept and the value of applying deflected slipstream over the wing. This principle was first applied by Crouch/Bolas before the war and was used by both Airspeed Ltd and the General Aircraft Ltd in two fleet spotter aircraft built in 1940. Both had four small Pobjoy Niagara 130 h.p. engines to spread the slipstream across the wing; neither was particularly successful as they were under-powered and the wing incidence was fixed.

The VZ–3RY used two large diameter propellers driven from a fuselage-mounted gear box connected to a Lycoming T–53 gas turbine. Massive flaps at the rear of the wing could deflect the slipstream downwards and endplates at the tips restrained the airflow to the span of the wing. In hovering and low speed flight, control in the pitch plane was achieved by a vectored nozzle at the end of the fuselage mechanically linked to the control stick. Lateral control was achieved by special slot-lip ailerons mounted at the 38% chord point of the wing and the ability to change the pitch of the propeller blades differently. This pitch change could only be effected when the flaps were down in the hover or slow speed mode; for normal flight there was no differential pitch.

Initial trials at Lindberg Field, San Diego, with the tail-wheel undercarriage revealed that on take-off the high 'T' tail was stalled due to the high ground angle of the fuselage. The front of it would lift off with the tail still firmly grounded! The aeroplane could be pitched nose down by braking sharply so that the tail then became 'un-stalled' and take-off achieved. The slot-lip ailerons were found to be too small for adequate lateral control even with flaps up whilst wing lift was found to be extremely sensitive to power level due to the slipstream effect. On the first landing, on 29 December 1958, a rapid closure of the throttle led to a large loss of lift and a rather rough arrival. The ailerons were increased in size and a tricycle undercarriage fitted. This improved matters considerably.

Pete Girard is not a superstitious man but, on the 13th flight on Friday the 13th he had serious problems. The aircraft was inadequately provided with emergency escape facilities for the pilot, the only route being through a hatch under the fuselage behind his seat. Later an ejection seat was fitted in an open cockpit. There had been a failure of one of the high-speed drive shafts from the engine to the propeller gearboxes, due to a malfunction of the hydraulic damper. Hitherto the propellers in the fixed pitch mode had operated with medium blade angle; on this flight the blade pitch control system had been activated but one of the propellers would not change from low pitch. Girard adjusted the other one for symmetry and returned to base at slow speed and low pitch noting that oil was leaking from the port gearbox. Concerned by the possibility of a shaft failure he decided to make an idling power landing, gaining speed for the round-out during the final approach at an angle of approximately 40°. The flare was abrupt and critical and until this moment he did not realise that the drag of the governed turbo-shaft engine-driven windmilling propeller was very much higher than on previous flights. At the high drag levels the aircraft could not be flared-out in time as the speed built up too slowly. It slammed into the runway causing serious damage to the aeroplane and injury to Pete Girard who was taken to hospital.

Ryan VZ–3RY deflected slipstream V/STOL aircraft.
(Ryan Aeronautical Co., via Peter F. Girard)

After the VZ–3RY had been rebuilt W.L. Everitt continued the test programme until he was, sadly, killed in another V/STOL aircraft, the Ryan XV–5A, in October 1966.

A milestone in the development of jet propelled V/STOL aircraft was the Bell X–14, a simple design powered by two Armstrong Siddeley Viper turbo jets. Deflectors behind the tail pipes directed the jet efflux towards the ground during take-off and landing with compressed air nozzles at the wingtips and tail providing control at hover and during low speed flying. The first hovering flight was made on 19 Februrary 1957 and the first transition was made on 24 May 1958.

It became clear from these various programmes that the tail sitter concept was not the answer but the Bell X–14 and the Ryan VZ–3RY showed the way ahead which was followed with various success throughout the world.

In Britain the success of the Rolls-Royce Flying Bedstead had encouraged the Company to develop a lightweight turbo-jet which could be used as a lifting engine. The 2,000 lb static thrust RB 108 had a thrust/weight ratio of 8:1. The Ministry of Supply, in addition to sponsoring this engine, issued a Specification for a research aircraft able to take-off by lift engines alone and accelerate into wing-borne flight, returning to earth vertically. Short Brothers received a Contract for two prototypes of the design which they submitted to the MoS. Construction began in 1955 and the first one, XG900 was ready for engine runs on 7 December 1956 with only the propulsion engine installed, the bay to house the four lift engines being faired over.

Tom Brooke-Smith had been appointed chief test pilot in 1948 and had flown a number of unusual research aeroplanes, including the Short SB 5, part of the Lightning fighter development programme and the Sperrin four-jet bomber built as a safeguard against failure of the much more radical 'V' bombers being designed (*See* Chapter 15). In 1951 he had experienced a serious accident in the SB 1 glider built to test the effect of a new so-called aero-isoclinic wing designed to eliminate the tendency of a high aspect ratio wing to twist under aileron loads. He was being towed into the air by a twin-engined Sturgeon and could not rise through the slipstream of the tug. The glider became unstable and uncontrollable in pitch, flying into the runway at Aldergrove, Belfast, at 100 mph (161 km/hr). It bounced into a steep nose-up attitude, stalled, rolled to port through 90°, crashed on its side and disintegrated with Brookie lying on soft grass nearby, marvelling that he was still alive. Having no feelings below his waist he suspected that his back was broken as, indeed, it was. After many months in hospital he made an almost complete recovery. After six months convalescence he returned to fly another aero-isoclinic wing, this time in an airframe powered by two 353 lb (160 kg) thrust Palas turbojets. This was the rather more successful Sherpa.

When the order for the V/STOL aircraft was placed, the chairman of Shorts phoned Brookie at Boscombe Down to tell him the news. He reflected that this project 'Put me on a collision course with Sir Isaac Newton' but was elated to realise the scope of the experience ahead of him. S/Ldr Ron Gellatly, the C O of 'D' Squadron, concerned with helicopters, taught him to fly a 'chopper' in one day – by sacrificing lunch. He flew the Flying Bedstead and was allocated a helicopter at Belfast.

Tom quickly realised the immense number of unknowns in the project:

> 'How do you start four engines instantly and simultaneously with one button and one high pressure fuel cock and then control them with one hand, there being plenty of work for the other? What happens when four jets suddenly blast off between one's legs, would the vital compressor-stall boundaries remain secure? Would thrust remain constant in all the lift engines throughout the speed range? Under what circumstances could a compressor surge prove catastrophic? What about control in rearward and sideways flight?'

Even air temperature was important, every degree rise in ambient above standard caused a loss in vertical thrust of 251 lb (11.3 kg) per engine. Brookie had a good appetite and his weight was rudely commented on by the weight control department, he was quite unrepentant and refused to diet!

The SC–1, as the aircraft was known, was tested at Boscombe Down first in wing-borne flight. It lifted off at 170-180 mph (274-290 km/hr) after using most of the two and a half mile (4 km) runway. Initially the propulsion engine had no governor so its speed was affected by both airspeed and incidence on the runway, so, in addition to the normal problems of a first flight Brookie had to keep a close watch on the creep of engine revs at take-off and on landing, the first of which was 'dead-stick' as the turbine flamed-out on final approach. The date of this momentous event was 2 April 1957.

The second prototype, XG905, was being completed with all five engines, the four lift units being mounted in two transverse pairs so that they could be swivelled fore and aft through a range of 35°. In May 1958 it flew within a gantry attached to tethers with counterweights. Brookie was surprised to find that crosswinds as high as 45 mph (72 km/hr) had little effect upon the controls which, in hovering flight were similar to the 'Bedstead' with reaction nozzles at nose and tail and under each wing tip; their air supply was bled from the compressor and distributed through a ring main.

The transition tests were approached very stealthily, the flow pattern of high speed air would be altered when the lift engines were lit and it was felt that the flame-out of the propulsion engine might result. It was also possible that one or more of the lift engines might not start. A visit to the spinning tunnel at Farnborough to see a scale model of the SC–1 on test did nothing for Brookie's morale when he realised that a height loss of 20,000 ft (6,096 m) was likely in the spin whilst his transition tests were to take place at 8,000 ft (2,438 m), so he had rather less than 29 seconds before hitting the ground if the SC–1 entered a spin.

On 6 April 1960, with a chase aircraft in attendance, he fired the four lift engines which lit, as he put it, 'Like a gas cooker'. He carried out a re-light, shut down and then flew back to base to refuel. On the next flight he opened up the lift engines at a forward speed of 190 mph (306 km/hr) and then found that as speed was decreased, necessitating more vertical thrust, a nose-up pitch developed; ultimately he found the control column up against the instrument panel as he ran out of trim. He tried drooping the ailerons and then the elevons but these were of no avail, he had to land much too fast and it became clear that modifications to the control linkages were necessary. When tests were resumed the transition programme was in three stages; the first, at altitude to check stability, control and propulsion at various speeds, the second, at 100 ft (30.5 m) after a vertical take-off from the

Short SC–1 showing the four lift engines. Note the stabilising 'puff-pipes' in fairings at nose and tail and under the wings. (via Aeroplane Monthly)

Tom Brooke-Smith with the Short SC–1, 1956. (Short Brothers, via Mrs J. Brooke-Smith)

long runway at RAE Bedford, decelerating at the end of each run to land vertically. In the event of trouble it would, with luck, have been possible to drop on to the runway with only superficial damage. The records made during each 10 kt (18.5 mph) increment run in both these stages were to be scrutinised and interpreted before proceeding to stage three, which involved the whole test programme in one flight. By the time he was ready for stage three 18 flights had been made but Brookie had no idea how close he had been to the engine compressor stall boundaries.

The gap was closed in less than ideal weather conditions during an eight minute flight. This was achieved on 6 April 1960 at Bedford. So, after five years hard and dangerous work which, in the later stages, he shared with Jock Eassie, a Short Bros test pilot and S/Ldr S.J. Hubbard of RAE, a British V/STOL aircraft had proved itself. Brookie demonstrated the SC–1 at the 1960 Farnborough Show after which he intended to retire as he had informed Short's chairman at the beginning of the test programme. It was intended that Jock Eassie should fly the aircraft back to RAE Bedford, refuelling at Boscombe Down so that the long runway could be used for a normal take-off. Eassie was indisposed so Tom agreed to do the flight. Accelerating down the runway at 180 mph (290 km/hr):

> 'There was a hell of a bang and everything went mad, two tyres on the port undercarriage and one on the nose oleo had burst simultaneously. I thought, my God, this thing's only got to yaw and it'll roll over and that's the end, it's full of fuel. So I called over the R/T for the arrester net at the end of the runway to be triggered and fought the aircraft to keep it straight in spite of the burst tyres.'

The SC–1 came to rest on the grass overshoot at the end of the runway. As a postscript to

Tom Brooke-Smith's distinguished career as a test pilot he was guest of honour at the Air League Ball at Grosvenor House Hotel, London when he received from the Duke of Hamilton the Founders Medal of the League for 'The most meritorious achievement in the whole field of British Aviation during 1960'. He also received from the Duke, with an injunction that it be opened publicly, a parcel. In it was a pair of car number plates – 1 VTO, which His Grace thought he might like to have! He 'wore them' on his car until his death in 1991.

Many engineers were extremely sceptical of the viability of a design which transported through the sky a number of lift engines which were only used at take-off and on landing. Nevertheless the success of the SC–1 and the American X–13 had proved that VTOL was a feasible concept. Another researcher in this field was the famous French designer, Michel Wibault whose name had been borne on airliners and fighters since the early 1930s. He was a protegé of Winthrop Rockefeller who was interested in his projects and financed a number of them from his vast wealth. His VTOL design was known as 'Le Gyroptère'. It was a plump jet fighter with a Bristol Orion prop-jet engine, without the propeller gearbox, installed in the fuselage. In place of the gearbox was one designed to drive through shafts four large centifugal blowers arranged like wheels at the sides of the fuselage. The casings could be rotated so that the jets of air could all blow downwards to provide lift or to descend vertically. To translate to forward flight the pilot merely rotated the casings to direct the jets rearwards; as speed was gained lift was transferred to the wings.

A talented German, Theodor von Karman, moved from America where he held citizenship, to represent US interests in Europe. He was acquainted with Dr Stanley Hooker who had moved to the Bristol Engine Company from Rolls-Royce after a disagreement with the Chairman, Lord Hives. von Karman saw the French design and immediately described the technique of the compressors as 'vectored thrust' – the name is now part of the argot of aviation technology. From these various activities and discussions Hooker and his design team worked on a number of arrangements to replace the individual compressors with their gearing and shafts with a single large engine with air tapped from the compressor into two elbows, one on each side and combustion gases tapped from the turbine into elbows aft. These were to be capable of being rotated by the pilot.

Sir Sydney Camm, the brilliant but conservative chief designer at Hawkers saw the new engine proposals at the 1957 Paris Air Show. He was heavily involved in the completion of the P 1121, a supersonic successor of the Hunter, to be cancelled as a result of the notorious Sandys White Paper of 1957. He sent to Stanley Hooker a note 'Dear Hooker, what are you doing about vertical take-off engines? Yours, Sydney'. Hooker sent him a brochure for his new BE53 engine which became the Pegasus around which the Hawker design team prepared drawings for the P 1127 vertical take-off aircraft which became the Harrier.

Considered by many to be the creative genius behind the P 1127, a young engineer named Ralph Hooper was briefed by Camm to take charge of the design. Two of his major contributions were the recommendation that the twin spools of the engine should rotate in opposite directions to eliminate gyroscopic coupling and that the bifurcated jet pipe of the Sea Hawk should be used rather than the single hot nozzle to provide a four-nozzle thrust-vectoring engine and provide space for an equipment bay to the rear of the exhaust. The basic objective of both Hawker and Bristol Engines was extreme simplicity. Jet reaction nozzles were connected to the stick for pitch and lateral control at low speed and in the hover whilst the yaw controls were connected to the rudder pedals.

The only extra control in the cockpit was the nozzle selector lever controlling thrust vectoring to meet the various demands of vertical or short take-offs and landings, hovering and conventional flight. Height control was via the throttle lever. The engineering and

P1127 prototype XP831 showing extended pitot head, yaw and pitch vanes.
(Bristol Siddeley Engines)

handling problems were awesome in achieving correct control powers, sensitivity and control feel, integrating the V/STOL aspects with conventional flight, providing efficient engine air intakes to cope with extremes of hovering through the range to supersonic diving speed. They extended to the limit the ingenuity of engineers and pilots.

As a prelude to the P 1127 flight test programme Hawkers chief test pilot, S/Ldr A.W. 'Bill' Bedford and his number two, Hugh Merewether, took a helicopter conversion course on a Hiller EH2E. An invitation was received to visit NASA at Moffatt Field, California to acquire some on-the-job V/STOL training. Back at Kingston three prototypes of the P 1127 were under construction, one for test in Hawkers structural test rig. The two pilots used the V/STOL simulator and flew a valuable research aircraft, the variable stability helicopter. At Langley Field, John Stack, director of NASA, became so enthusiastic about the P 1127 design that he arranged for a one sixth scale model to be built and tested in their unique wind tunnel. Looking at the model through windows in the tunnel wall four pilots sat in cubicles with controls, one for pitch, one for yaw, the third, roll and the fourth was responsible for height. It was flown through the whole of the flight envelope from hover to wing-borne flight and back again. It was a fascinating experience for the Hawker pilots to see a film of this operation which revealed encouraging results by comparison with earlier V/STOL devices tested. The V/S helicopter was a great V/STOL educator and enabled Bill and Hugh to have a seat-of-the-pants feeling for Chinese hieroglyphics such as radians per second squared per inch of stick deflection!

The X–14 gave Hugh Merewether a deeply embarrassing experience at Ames Research Center. This aircraft had no autostabilisation system. After a thorough briefing he took off; as he rose the X–14 began an uncontrollable pilot-induced lateral oscillation before it slid sideways into the runway, breaking off the undercarriage. He proved that without autostabilisation the sensitivity (gearing from the stick to the puffer control) was far too low. This was of paramount importance to the P 1127 so urgent information was passed to the Hawker Design Office so that provision could be made for an increase in the P 1127's roll sensitivity. The generous American hosts tried to assuage Hugh's great embarrassment by saying that the X–14 had to be grounded anyway for new engines to be fitted.

Contrary to the Short SC–1 test programme the P 1127 was not flown in wing-borne flight before vertical tests began. Camm, proud of the wonderful flying qualities of all his aeroplanes, assumed that the new one would be equally good and decreed that the first flights would be in vertical lift-off mode. He was prepared, however, to concede that restraint by tethers should be made for the first few lift-offs.

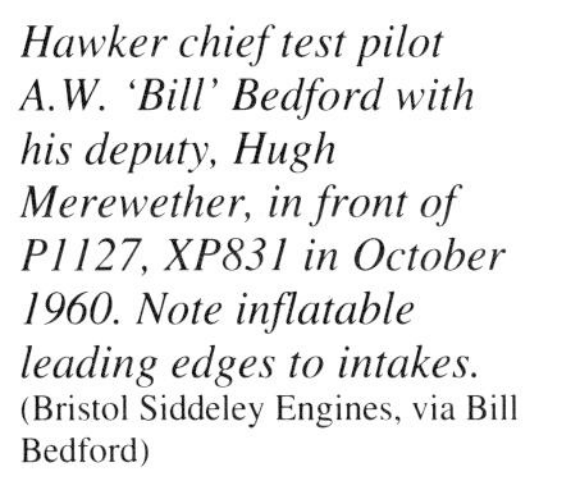

Hawker chief test pilot A.W. 'Bill' Bedford with his deputy, Hugh Merewether, in front of P1127, XP831 in October 1960. Note inflatable leading edges to intakes. (Bristol Siddeley Engines, via Bill Bedford)

The object lesson of the X–14 was that the key to hovering without autostabilisation was high sensitivity. If that was right a simple single-channel autostabilisation system would be acceptable as, if it failed, the pilot could simply fly without it. Nevertheless it was clear that control with jet reaction nozzles would require some clever development work. The pilots were somewhat apprehensive when the Project Office reported that 'when hovering un-autostabilised the plan position over the ground was the fourth integral of stick deflection'. They were relieved to learn that this most erudite advice merely meant that they had to waggle the stick about a bit more than normal!

The service life in the hover mode of the first 11,000 lb (4,990 kg) thrust engine was 20 minutes, later extended to 30, so test sorties had to be carefully planned. The four engine exhaust nozzles were mechanically linked together and actuated by a duplicated air motor system. Later in the life of the aircraft provision was made for the nozzles to remain in the last selected position in the event of drive failure. High pressure air was bled from the engine to the jet reaction control valves at the wing tips, nose and tail, they were linked to the normal flying controls.

Three weeks before the planned date of the first flight Bedford was in a car which was driven into a tree; his ankle was broken but he contrived a medical category unique in aviation –'Fit civil test pilot hovering only!' On Trafalgar Day, 21 October 1960, Bedford lifted XP831 off a gridded platform at Dunsfold Airfield. He proved that he had a measure of control and that the thrust did, indeed, exceed the weight. Lengthening the tethers to give more scope led to serious problems, the aircraft cavorting about the nose-wheel 'like a drunken cow' as Bill described the event. A few minor adjustments allowed a satisfactory hover to be affected with modest control in roll and pitch but yaw control was hopelessly inadequate. Twenty-eight one minute hovers in the first month was a creditable achievement. By the time the tethers were eliminated Bill's medical category had been extended to 'free hovering not above four feet (1.2 m)'. To hover freely felt like a bird being released from its cage but, as there was no radio aboard he had to be content with a red flag operator to warn him if he went too high with the risk of running out of fuel.

In the five months between hovering trials and the first wing-borne flight, ground resonance and systems testing was carried out. For the conventional flight trials the P 1127 was taken to RAE Bedford, by which time Bill's ankle had healed. There was sage advice from an unlikely source; looking at the wing tip outrigger castoring wheels the pundit said 'You'll have trouble with them wheels, I've 'ad it meself!' It transpired that this helpful fellow pushed the tea trolley round the experimental hangar. During the first run all hell was let loose at 150 kt (227 km/hr), with a noise like a cannon going off in the cockpit terminating in an explosion as the tyre burst proving the value of the expert advice received. The manufacturer of the undercarriage said that it had been checked for shimmy up to 180 kts (333 km/hr) without trouble but, on the rig, the tyre was always in contact with the 'ground', providing a damping force. The P 1127 was laterally unstable on the ground with its bicycle undercarriage so, until wing-borne, the outrigger wheels were alternately damped and un-damped. The wheels were modified so that they only castored inwards, this solved the problem.

The first flight was meticulously planned and the Public Relations Department, without reference to Bill Bedford, issued a hand-out intimating that the chief test pilot said 'she handled beautifully and had great potential'. The first part was not quite true, it gave a rough, noisy, vibratory ride, it had no stability in pitch, tightened up in turns, pitched up at high Mach numbers, had a severe transonic wing drop, was short of directional stability with the undercarriage down, it had excessive nose-down pitch with flaps down so the landing had to be flap-less, it leaned like a lame duck in a crosswind and in addition a whole series of engine limitations had to be observed whevever possible. Finally the engine flamed-out on landing and an engine oil fire usually occurred on shut-down. It handled beautifully in roll and, apart from the catalogue of pain and grief there was nothing likely to inhibit slowing down below the stalling speed.

The second prototype, XP836, joined the programme on 7 July 1961 and was engaged in flutter clearance to maximum speed and Mach number, engine vibration testing and the elimination of minor bugs. There was difficulty in devising air intakes for the Pegasus which gave adequate efficiency at hover and at high speed, the first case required a well rounded lip and the second, a sharp lip. To achieve these conflicting needs an inflatable

Hawker P1127 prototype XP831 with metal leading edges to the air intakes.
(Bristol Siddeley Engines)

rubber front edge was applied to the intakes, inflated for hover and deflated for high speed. Bill Bedford said that they 'Were clever but full of problems since, on deflation, they flapped like spaniel's ears and disintegrated!' So a fixed metal compromise design was eventually developed to be refined as thrust increased to 23,800 lb (10,796 kg). To eliminate a pitch-up problem and to make longitudinal stability acceptable the tailplane area was increased and it was given anhedral. Eleven months after the first lift-off, in September 1961, Bill carried out the first accelerating and decelerating transitions with and without the autostabiliser in operation; they were smoothly executed, the only problems being a strong nose-down pitch which developed when the nozzles were moved through the last 30° with flaps down. This was resolved by fitting an 'attention getting' ramp on the nozzle selector quadrant which reminded the pilot to retract the flaps before moving the nozzle lever further.

A major advance during the complex development phase was the substitution of an 'on demand' system for the very extravagant 'constant bleed' system feeding air to the jet reaction controls. Unless a demand for control air was made the valves remained closed. There was a serious lack of roll control power so this was progressively increased by a factor of four. This summary of the dedicated work of engineers and test pilots throughout the stages of development of the Harrier indicates why the Harrier is the V/STOL aircraft against which all others are judged.

Bill Bedford had an alarming experience during flutter tests. He was approaching 550 kt (1,020 km/hr) at low level and hit the stick with the metal 'bonker' used to induce an input of vibration. Suddenly, at 1,000 ft (305 m) there was an abrupt lateral rock, rapid deceleration and marked vibration. He decided to make an emergency landing at near-by Yeovilton Royal Naval Air Station. Hugh Merewether, flying the chase Hunter, could see nothing wrong with the P 1127; as Bill began his final approach at 170 kt (315 km/hr) and at 200 ft (61 m) he realised that he could no longer correct the roll even with full stick

The Commander (Flying) welcomes Bill Bedford and P1127, XP831, aboard HMS Ark Royal IV *on 8 February 1963.* (Bill Bedford)

deflection. The desperate urgency of the situation reminded him of Jimmy Martin's advice, 'If you are short of time, Bill, don't bother with the ejection blind above your head, just grab the lever between your legs!' This saved his life, he made a perfect ejection in the non-rocket seat and, almost as soon as the parachute had deployed, he hit a soft ploughed field. A two or three second delay could have been fatal. There was little left of the P 1127 to indicate the nature of the malfunction but, a day or so later, a farmer appeared with the port forward engine nozzle which had broken away. It had been made of glass reinforced plastic to save weight. The specification was immediately changed to steel.

S/Ldr Jack Henderson was the first RAF officer to join the P 1127 programme and only the third pilot to fly it. John Farley, who later became chief test pilot, converted to the P 1127 at Dunsfold and carried out much of the flying at RAE Bedford where he was a Service test pilot. John recalled that at that time the engine had a one hour life in the vertical flight mode or 25 hours in wing-borne flight. It was then returned to Rolls-Royce for a £60,000 refit. Conversion, therefore, had to be carried out expeditiously. As John said:

> 'People became excited if you sat in the hover for 30 seconds as you had spent £500, the price of a good car in those days. You were permitted a quarter of the engine life – 15 minutes, to convert; at the end of that period you must have carried out satisfactorily all the V/STOL manoeuvres of which the aircraft was capable'.

The development of this remarkable aircraft required a sustained test programme probably unequalled in risk since the 1930s. Bill Bedford and John Farley have talked in matter-of-fact terms about many of the sorties but, unquestionably one of the most dangerous phenomena investigated was known as intake momentum yaw drag. Until the aircraft was flying at around 100 kts (185 km/hr) the fin gave little directional stability; if a sideslip developed in an aircraft with the P 1127 intake system the momentum of 400 lb (182 kg) of air per second was largely dissipated, the aircraft tending to yaw down-wind and become directionally unstable at 20–30 kt (37–55 km/hr). This was not serious but above that speed and with increased incidence a strong rolling moment developed. If this went out of control the pilot was in dire trouble. This first became clear when the C-in-C of Fighter Command, Air Marshal Hector McGregor, visited Dunsfold to see some of the development flying. Bill was flying at 40 kt (74 km/hr) when the aircraft just pirouetted out of control and, even with full opposite rudder, it was very difficult to stop it. The Top Brass was very impressed by the manoeuvrability of the P 1127 and this particular aberration was called the McGregor turn!

The test pilots were alerted to a most serious problem which, later, was to cause the death of Major Chuck Rosburg of the USAF. He was flying a Harrier at Dunsfold in 1969 when he lost control part way through a translation, he ejected when the aeroplane was in a vertical bank at about 50 ft (15 m), sadly he hit the ground still in his ejector seat.

John Farley, whose aeronautical engineering training and analytical mind well suited him for the task, spent many months in low-speed and hover manoeuvres at 50 ft (15.2 m) to analyse the problem and evaluate possible methods of overcoming it. Much of the time he was right on the edge of instability and was, therefore, at high risk. He was able to develop a scheme of buzzers on the rudder pedals to indicate which pedal should be used to recover, the final solution was an autostabiliser connected to the yaw control nozzles.

John's professionalism and courage played a vital role in providing an antidote to this most damaging phenomenon.

On 8 February 1963 Bill Bedford made the first ever fixed wing aircraft V/STOL landing on an aircraft carrier when he gave a series of demonstrations aboard HMS *Ark Royal*. The Flag Officer, Carriers, Admiral Sir Donald Gibson, said to him,

> 'Bill, the thing that impresses me is the complete absence of fright on the part of the spectators; new aircraft usually arrive aboard bigger, heavier and faster, this is a complete reversal of the trend'.

Never in his wildest dreams could Bill imagine the outstanding combat success of the Harrier operated by the Navy and the RAF in the Falklands campaign.

At an early development stage Bill had an embarrassing experience in the P 1127 prototype at Le Bourget during a brilliant demonstration before 150,000 spectators and millions of television viewers watching the 1963 Paris Air Show. On the last Sunday he planned to do a vertical landing and then a take-off from the grass to show the flexibility of operations and independence of special operating surfaces.

As he decelerated prior to landing the nozzles of the Pegasus engine suddenly rotated, uncommanded, from the lift to the thrust position and the P 1127 crashed ignominiously on the special concrete platform so essential for the French Dassault Balzac, his rival! A shower of wheels, undercarriage components and aviation scrap metal was distributed around the site as Bill miraculously emerged from the wreck, uninjured. A fragment of dirt in an air reducing valve to the air drive motors for the nozzles had jammed the valve allowing the nozzles to move of their own accord. Nine months later Bill flew this P 1127 again to test the modifications that ensured that nozzles always remained in the position last selected.

Other Hawker pilots had serious problems on test sorties. In the early sixties Hugh Merewether successfully crash landed two P 1127s following engine failure, one at Tangmere, the other at Thorney Island. These were examples of exceptional flying skill combined with sheer guts. The evidence he recovered was worth its weight in gold and enabled Bristol to solve the problem quickly.

Duncan Simpson was testing the two-seat trainer prototype for low level flutter clearance at 3,000 ft (914 m) at an indicated air speed of 450 kts (832 km/hr). En route from Dunsfold to Boscombe Down the engine slowed to sub-idling speed and no response to the throttle could be obtained. Re-light procedures were ineffective so he was forced to attempt a landing in a field near Stonehenge; he finally decided to abandon the aircraft at 100 ft (30.5 m), the powerful new Martin Baker rocket seat saving his life. He suffered severe back and neck injuries from sections of the canopy, as he descended he realised that he was approaching the fireball which was his aeroplane below him, fortunately the wind drifted him away from it. This accident, too, was caused by a blockage in the fuel control unit, a fault which a year later left Barrie Tonkinson with no engine. He made a brilliant and courageous forced landing at Boscombe Down at 170 kts (314 km/hr), arriving on the grass alongside the runway. Part of the undercarriage failed so he had a very rough ride, the aircraft catching fire.

The next major development phase was the formation of the tri-partite evaluation Squadron at West Raynham RAF base to allow officers from the RAF, the USAF and the Luftwaffe to experience the design under operational conditions. The Unit was formed on 15 October 1964 and was equipped with the militarised P 1127 known as the Kestrel. 938 take-offs were carried out in eleven months, producing a mass of data on the operational value of V/STOL in general and the Kestrel aircraft in particular. The outcome of nine years project development and evaluation was the first flight, by Bill Bedford on 31 August 1966, of the first pre-production Hawker Harrier ZV276, V/STOL battlefield support fighter, the first such fixed wing vertical take-off aircraft to achieve squadron service status.

The first operational Harrier Squadron in the RAF was formed in 1969. In the previous year the United States was operating the A–4 Skyhawk in the Vietnam war flown by the Marine Corps. Quite early in the programme the Corps senior officers had shown interest in the P 1127 but thought that its potential was too limited. In 1968 the Marines Top Brass saw a Hawker Siddeley promotional film of the Harrier, which, by this time, was a very different aeroplane. They were astonished to realise that its bomb load could match that of the Skyhawk with the additional benefit of vertical take-off and landing. With a short 500 yard (457 m) take-off run from, even, a length of road it could also offer the same range and bomb load.

Col. Thomas H. Miller (now Lt-Gen. Rtd) was the Deputy Chief of Staff (Air); with Col. Clarence 'Bud' Baker he attended the Farnborough Air Show later in the year and stayed in the UK to evaluate this remarkable aeroplane which seemed to be tailor-made for the Marines. Later, the two officers, both test pilots, flew it at Dunsfold under the guidance of John Farley.

Col. Miller returned to USA and with Gen. McCutcheon, USMC Chief of Staff, put forward a powerful argument in favour of the Marines buying Harrier; even the Vice-President of Ryan who had worked so hard on the X–13 and other VTOL projects wrote in support saying that for his Company to match the Harrier would involve inordinate expense and development time. The Colonel, being a Phantom pilot, was aware that purchase of the Harrier would cut into the F–4 Procurement Programme but argued that, in the long term,

McDonnell Douglas would benefit from the new work which would ensue. The day was won. The US Government conceded on condition that Hawker collaborated with McDonnell Douglas.

The Colonel's judgement was fully vindicated and, at the time of writing, a co-operative programme between British Aerospace is producing the AV–8B, Harrier II which is virtually a new design built largely of composite materials to save weight. Its performance is greatly enhanced.

From the sparkle in the eyes of the engine and airframe designers in 1957 to the present UK/US partnership has emerged a co-operative venture of the utmost importance and value. During the course of the programme well-merited awards of the OBE were made to Bill Bedford, Hugh Merewether, John Farley and Duncan Simpson.

Chief test pilot, John Farley, and chief designer, Harrier, Dr John Fozard christening the first Sea Harrier. (British Aerospace, Kingston)

Vickers Valiant prototype.
(British Aerospace, Weybridge)

CHAPTER 15
The 'V' Bombers

With hindsight it may be said that Britain's V bomber programme was probably the most extravagant aircraft procurement programme ever launched with two primary designs of considerable technical sophistication, the Avro Vulcan and the even less orthodox Handley Page Victor. Two other jet bombers in the programme as a safeguard against failure were the Vickers Valiant and the Short Sperrin, these both followed well-proven constructional techniques.

It must be appreciated that in 1947 when the Specifications were issued for a new high performance strategic bomber, a category in which Britain had led the world for a number of years, the international situation was fraught with extreme peril and Royal Air Force was still operating the Lancaster, Halifax and the obsolescent Lincoln, a derivative of the Lancaster.

Space precludes a detailed study of all of the test programmes of all of these aircraft so the Victor has been selected as the subject for an in-depth study in this chapter. The Sperrin was a good design, two prototypes being flown by Tom Brooke-Smith and later used as research aircraft. The Valiant was first flown by 'Mutt' Summers from Vickers' Wisley airfield on 18 May 1951. 'Mutt' soon retired, being succeeded by G.R. 'Jock' Bryce. Testing proceeded fairly uneventfully until 12 January 1952 when Jock took off with S/Ldr Brian Foster as co-pilot and a crew of three to carry out engine re-light tests with various combinations of engines.

There had been some problems with the large bomb doors and a sudden bang was attributed to one of these breaking away until the engineer reported that he had lost all instrument readings on the starboard engines. Jock decided to abort the sortie and return to Hurn. He then realised that he no longer had any aileron control as the co-pilot reported flames emerging from the leading edge of the starboard wing. Jock quickly realised that the wing was twisting in the heat and an immediate exit was essential. He gave the order to abandon aircraft, hoping to be able, solo, to attempt a landing on the long runway at Boscombe Down; his co-pilot ejected with the aircraft in a 60° bank and was killed when he hit the fin. Jock, losing control, ejected and landed outside a derelict hut on the old Holmesley South RAF Station which had been his war-time quarters when serving there with Transport Command. It was found that fuel from a previous unsuccessful engine start had leaked into the wing structure and ignited there. A simple modification prevented a recurrence and the Valiant proved itself as a fine bomber, serving in the RAF from 1955 to 1965 when a serious metal fatigue problem led to its withdrawal from service as the cost of rectification was uneconomic.

The Avro Vulcan was the world's first large bomber with a delta wing. Roy Chadwick began work on it to meet Spec B35/46 in 1946 with some knowledge of the work carried out in Germany by Dr Alexander Lippisch and the Horten brothers who had built tail-less

W/Cdr Roly Falk in the cockpit of an Avro 707.
(British Aerospace, Manchester)

gliders and powered aircraft. Data on the Me 163 and the DH 108 was also available. Tragically, Chadwick lost his life in 1947 when the prototype of the Tudor II airliner crashed at Woodford due to crossed aileron controls.

Because of the radical nature of the design it was decided to make a number of scale models of the new bomber, so emerged the Avro 707, single-seat jet powered deltas, the first of which was flown by Eric Esler on 6 September 1949. He was later killed in it when he appeared to lose control near Blackbush airfield. It appeared to be due to a defect in the control circuit for the air brakes so confidence in the delta wing was restored and the first flight of the prototype bomber, Type 698, VX770 was made by Avro's new Superintendent of Flying, W/Cdr Roly J. Falk on 30 August 1952. A second prototype VX777, joined the programme in September 1953 and development testing accelerated with the two versions fitted with 6,500 lb (2,948 kg) thrust Rolls-Royce Avon engines. It was planned to use 9,750 lb (4,423 kg) thrust Olympus 100s but it soon became clear that with these engines the increased performance would bring the aircraft dangerously close to the buffet boundaries. Many 'fixes' were tried on the 707s with no real improvement, so the straight plan delta wing changed to what became known as the Phase 2 wing. The 52° leading edge sweep-back was changed to one with a sharper sweep-back to mid-span when the original angle continued to the tip. In this form the Vulcan went into production, the first aircraft, XA889, flying on 1 February 1955, a year before its rival, the Victor.

The test flying programme for this advanced and unusual bomber was carried out with such thoroughness and efficiency that its introduction to RAF service on 22 February 1957 was entirely straightforward and its performance exceptional. The type remained in service until 31 March 1984.

The prototype, VX770 came to a tragic end during a low-level flypast at an air show at Syerston, Leics. It suddenly reared up, both engines flew out of the airframe which came down tail-first, crashing on top of the airfield control van. This well-used aircraft was flying with a limiting speed as a precaution against fatigue. It was concluded that the pilot slightly exceeded the limit resulting in the leading edge of the wing opening up to rip the structure apart. Some of the production aircraft checked afterwards had cracked wing ribs.

It is appropriate that one of the oldest firms in the aircraft industry, Handley Page, formed as a limited company in 1909 should produce one of the last and best truly British aircraft, the Victor.

Avro Vulcan prototypes in formation with Avro 707s. (British Aerospace, Woodford)

LEFT:
Vulcan prototype disintegrating at Syerston Air Display.
(British Aerospace, Woodford)

By 1945 Sir Frederick Handley Page was convinced that a jet propelled heavy bomber was needed to replace the ageing Avro Lincoln in RAF service. A visit to Germany by Godfrey Lee, the chief engineer and data obtained from an experimental aircraft designed by Dr Gustav Lachmann, the talented HP engineer, in 1936 convinced him that a swept wing design was essential to take full advantage of the new gas turbine power plant. The experimental aircraft was the HP 75, known as the Manx. It was a tail-less aircraft, built in 1940 but delayed by war priorities so that its first flight did not occur until May 1943 with Jimmy Talbot, Major Cordes successor, at the controls. Talbot, with his co-pilot E.A. 'Ginger' Wright was killed in December 1945 when the prototype Hermes I airliner crashed on its maiden flight after major instability in pitch developed. (*See* Chapter 8)

Many discussions with Air Ministry and Bomber Command led to wind tunnel testing of a model in 1947. It had swept crescent wings the tips being turned up to form rudders. There was no vertical stabiliser at the tail. Many hours of tunnel testing led to the elimination of the tip rudders which were replaced with one in the normal location, the swept tailplane being mounted upon the top of it. To prove the aerodynamics of this radical design it was decided to build a scale model based upon a Supermarine 510 fuselage – this was an Attacker fuselage ready to receive swept wings. The crescent-shape wing was fitted to it with an appropriate empennage. It was known as the HP 88, built by Blackburn and first flown by G.R.I. 'Sailor' Parker from the long runway at Carnaby, Yorkshire on 21 June 1951. He reported a high degree of control sensitivity in pitch with extreme instability at 255 kt (472.5 km/hr). Various modifications were made until, after 17 sorties there was no porpoising at speeds up to 450 kt (834 km/hr).

Rear view of Handley Page HP 75 Manx research aircraft. It was powered by two de Havilland 140 hp Gipsy Major engines driving DH variable pitch propellers.
(Aeroplane Monthly)

Handley Page HP 75 Manx research aircraft underneath a Halifax III. (Aeroplane Monthly)

Douglas Broomfield, an HP test pilot, took delivery of the HP 88 and flew it to Stansted for airspeed calibration trials. On 26 August he took off; ten minutes later, flying fast along the runway at 300 ft (91 m) the aircraft broke up, the flight recorder showing a violent pitching oscillation of ± 12 G. It was decided that, ironically, the cause of the accident which killed Duggie Broomfield was the inclusion of a safety device in the form of a bob weight in the elevator circuit to act as a G restrictor. It appeared that the combination of this with a powered elevator control with its phase lag had induced the fatal condition.

Delays in its construction and the progress made with the two prototype bombers led to little data of any value to the bomber being recorded from the 14 hours flying of the aircraft. It had, however, broadly proved the configuration of the aircraft and gave encouragement to the design staff and RAE.

With the Avro 698 six months in advance of the Victor and due to fly in 1952 there was a spirit of great urgency at Radlett. The prototype, WB771, was taken to Boscombe Down with the tail of the fuselage section mounted on a lorry axle, the nose being mounted upon a tractor. On assembly it was found that the centre of gravity was too far aft so steel plates were bolted under the flight deck floor until the production design could be altered; it was also necessary to move transformer rectifier units forward. Further delay was caused by a fire in the rear fuselage during a hydraulic test. Three engineers were injured, one of them, Eddie Eyles, tragically dying from his injuries.

Chief test pilot S/Ldr H.G. 'Hazel' Hazelden had spent many hours since the end of 1950 preparing himself to fly the new aircraft. He had, of course, been closely associated with the design and production departments so that he was familiar with every detail of it. A Hastings prototype had been fitted with two Sapphires in place of the outboard Hercules piston engines and he flew this machine for many hours to familiarise himself with the engines; for high speed experience he flew a Canberra 2 with Sapphires. Just before Christmas when he taxied WB771 from the Boscombe Down hangar to the compass base in a gale, he was pleased with the way it handled. Two days later he commenced taxying trials with fast runs along the runway. Heavy rain prevented a short flight. This had cleared on Christmas Eve and the wind blew directly along the runway so, with his flight observer, Ian Bennett, later to lose his life in this aircraft, he took off for a 17 minute flight making a trial approach and overshoot before a landing which confirmed Godfrey Lee's prediction that the aeroplane would have the ability to land itself as it entered its ground cushion which would initiate the flare-out. All that was needed was an accurate alignment with the runway centre line. The runway at Radlett was being extended northwards so, for two months, tests continued at Boscombe Down. On 25 February WB771 returned to base.

On 9 February 1953, on the seventh flight, the undercarriage was raised for the first time. It had been a design requirement that the brakes must be applied to stop the wheels rotating before retraction commenced since gyroscopic forces might cause the gear to foul the interior of the undercarriage bay with serious results. To ensure that this condition was met a small flap was attached to the parking brake lever so that it covered the 'UP' selector button until the lever was moved to the brake 'ON' position. The small flap then covered the 'DOWN' selector button until the lever was moved to the brakes 'OFF' position as required for landing – it seemed a reasonable solution to the problem requiring no complex hydraulic sequencing.

Handley Page 88. This photograph was carefully posed to avoid revealing the shape of the crescent wing.
(Handley Page Association)

However, apart from handling reports the design department called for retraction and lowering times so, for this purpose, several 'up' and 'down' cycles were made. When, on this flight, the undercarriage was about to be raised, the parking brake was applied but, before the 'UP' button was pressed a red warning light came on to indicate high temperature in the hydraulic system. The undercarriage was then retracted. Hazel checked the cockpit indicators for landing – three greens on the undercarriage – dive brakes and half flaps at take-off position – there was no need for further use of the hydraulic system so he proceeded to land. The landing seemed to be a very smooth one until the toe brakes were recognised as inoperative. Hazel realised that the parking brake was still 'ON', he instantly moved it to 'OFF' but it was too late – all sixteen tyres on the main legs burst and the wheels, too, were damaged beyond repair.

As Hazel said, in a letter to the author 'A mistake – yes – but a lesson had been learned so modifications ensured that it was not repeated'. In April a further undercarriage problem arose when, on landing, the port bogie bounced and stayed in the vertical position. Hazelden made a very smooth 'tip-toe' landing with no damage to the aircraft.

On a later flight, as Hazel brought it in to land, he selected flaps down and immediately a roll began to develop; thinking that he had a flap actuation malfunction he landed without them. To his astonishment he found that the whole of the flap assembly on one side had disappeared. Appropriate modifications to the fixings were made. A very intensive test programme checked out the function of the Mach trimmer fitted to compensate for centre of pressure changes due to compressibility effects. It was found necessary to fit a yaw damper to control the tendency, common to swept-wing aircraft to develop a dutch roll instability at high altitudes. In a dutch roll the aeroplane yaws and swings in the rolling plane giving an unpleasant wallowing motion.

The pilots were intrigued by the Victor's ability to land with no flare-out action by them. The later fin height reduction was welcomed as it eliminated the capability which was seen by them, and by RAF pilots, as an invitation to exercise less care on the approach. The unusual effect was due to the high tailplane being out of the downwash created by the flaps when in the landing attitude. As soon as the machine arrived at the point where the ground cushion effect became apparent and the throttles were closed, the Victor levelled out and touched down.

By the middle of October 1953 Hazel had flown to 50,000 ft (15,240 m) without experiencing buffet and had reached M 0.80 at 47,000 ft (14,326 m) with power in hand. His assistant, Ken Dalton-Golding, achieved M 0.88 at 47,500 ft (14,478 m) at which height he extended the dive brakes which were in the form of 'petals' at the tail cone. Deceleration was smooth. He was critical of damping in the yaw plane at altitude with the aircraft continuing to 'snake' slightly after the rudder was centralised.

It appeared that drag rise due to compressibility had not yet materialised, a good augury for the high speed end of the range. Hazel reached M 0.91 at 47,500 ft (14,478 m) and reported a slight nose down trim change. In February 1954 he flew at M 0.925 at 45,000 ft (13,716 m) again reporting the slight nose down trim change between M 0.90 and 0.91. Steep turns were made at M 0.88 and these were buffet free. By the end of the year problems with the braking parachute system had been overcome and another flap problem emerged when one of the inboard ones broke away. The crew were not aware of the loss until after they had landed.

By the end of February 1954 the prototype had logged 60 hours and was ready for a major check-out and various modifications to improve aileron effectiveness and some minor changes to extend the flight envelope. Back in service in June 1954 Hazelden prepared for a series of airspeed indicator calibration trials. This work required steady runs

Handley Page Victor prototype WB771.
(Handley Page Association)

at a height of about 150 ft (46 m) past a special ground based camera, at different speeds from just above the stall up to maximum permissible. The low level circuits necessary for this test cause considerable annoyance in populated areas such as that surrounding the Radlett airfield so the trials were planned to take place at the airfield of the College of Aeronautics at Cranfield, Bedfordshire, which is in fairly open country. The trials were planned for 14 July and the ground crew, with camera, set off for Cranfield by road with instructions to telephone Radlett when everything was ready. Hazel would then take-off in the Victor to carry out the test runs and return to base without landing at Cranfield. Since all the flying would be at very low level the endurance of the aircraft would be restricted to little more than two hours.

The all-clear call came from Cranfield and, almost immediately came another call, this one was from Handley Page's Woodley plant asking Hazel to come to Woodley immediately to fly a Marathon, a small four-engined airliner, on an acceptance flight for the Japanese customer. This had been planned for the afternoon to follow the Victor trials at Cranfield, but the admiral had to alter his plans so the flight had to take place before lunch. Hazel's deputy, Ken Dalton-Golding had been killed tragically when the controls of his Canberra jammed on his approach to Radlett over the railway embankment; his new assistant, Ronald 'Taffy' Ecclestone had joined him a few weeks earlier and could see the problem of being in two places at the same time. He immediately asked if he could do the Victor job. After some thought Hazel agreed and gave Taffy a thorough briefing on the trials going into detail on the circuit and its landmarks. He was quite confident in Ecclestone's competence to carry out the trials and so set off by road for Woodley.

Tail assembly of Victor prototype WB771.
(Handley Page Association)

The Marathon flight was carried out and afterwards the customer was taken to a local restaurant to be entertained to lunch. As the party arrived Hazelden was asked by the manager to telephone Radlett most urgently. He was shocked to receive the news that the Victor had crashed. Taffy, with his observer, Ian Bennett, Bruce Heithersay and Albert Cook were flying above the runway at high speed; after several such runs ground observers saw the leading edge of the tailplane rise fractionally from the fin and suddenly detach, the Victor immediately nosing down and disintegrating as it hit the runway at high speed. This tragic accident to a prototype, which had shown such great promise and killed a highly skilled and dedicated crew, was a fearful shock to all who had an interest in it and a 24 hour a day test programme was instituted to resolve the problem which had caused it. Two weeks later it was announced that the metal around the three tailplane fixing bolts showed fatigue cracks which had allowed the bolts to loosen and shear one after the other. Modifications to the fin included an alteration to its construction, the fixing of the tailplane by four bolts to reduce the stress concentration and the reduction of the fin and rudder height to decrease even further the stress levels at the fin/tailplane joint.

In the meantime flight test was at a standstill as the second prototype was not yet ready. It was, of course, modified to include the lessons learned from the crash. Finished in the same black and silver grey finish as WB771, the new machine, WB775 made a flight over the Farnborough Show on 11 September prior to continuing the test programme which began to concentrate upon flutter characteristics whilst, in parallel, investigations were carried on at the Radlett Research Department into flutter at high subsonic and transonic speeds using models built to reproduce as far as possible the aero-elastic characteristics of the actual aircraft.

In August 1954 Flt Lt John Allam, a Boscombe Down test pilot, joined Handley Page as second in command to Hazel. He was soon checked out on the Victor so that Hazel could concentrate upon the new Herald airliner, whilst still overseeing the Victor programme. Allam commenced work on the stalling programme at the end of 1954, this had previously been explored to a limited extent. It was found that, despite all predictions based upon other high-tail swept wing aeroplanes, the Victor had an abundance of natural stall warning. The machine had a leading edge section which could be drooped in the first tests with the flaps set at the maximum lift position. At around 152 kt (277.5 km/hr) a mild buffet developed and continued to 135 kt (250 km/hr) where it doubled in amplitude; this continued to about 120 kt (222 km/hr) where it doubled in amplitude again. These elements of stall warning were quite distinct and recognisable. They became known as first stage, second stage and third stage buffet and they were fairly constant regardless of the configuration of the aircraft. From this point it was necessary to see what happened at speeds below 120 knots. At about 105 knots the third stage buffet persisted but the aircraft began an unpleasant 'roller coaster' bucking motion with the nose high; this was obviously most undesirable as it would have a serious effect upon the fatigue life of the airframe and could, indeed, cause structural failure; the lowest speed which John Allam can remember on that sortie was 98 kt (181 km/hr). On the return to Radlett the whole inner section of the starboard flap assembly had disappeared.

Tailplane of WB771 on Cranfield aerodrome after detachment in flight. (Handley Page Association)

At the test pilots conference following this flight the conclusion was that the Victor was not likely to have stalling characteristics similar to most other aeroplanes and that any attempt to stall it would probably result in a structural failure. It was agreed that the Pilots Notes would prohibit stalling and that the RAF squadrons could take it to the second stage buffet which was so clearly defined. Each production aircraft would be cleared by the test pilot to third stage buffet to ensure that the point of buffet was in the right place; thereafter, this stage would not, again, be experienced.

This highly satisfactory development ensured that the Victor did not have to be fitted with stick pushers or any other form of stall warning; the aeroplane has been entirely without stalling problems throughout its Service career.

An immense amount of work was carried out to ensure vice-free characteristics under all conditions of manoeuvre; even in turns at high speed the buffet stages were easily identifiable if a little harsher.

The second Victor prototype, WB775, showing the Kreuger leading edge flaps originally fitted. The aircraft is approaching the Radlett runway after the loss of part of the starboard inner flap system. Note the position of the ailerons necessary to keep the starboard wing up.
(Handley Page Association)

Jock Still joined Handley Page as a test pilot with some trepidation. He was aware of the deaths of Duggie Broomfield, Ken Dalton-Golding and Taffy Ecclestone and wondered if the Victor programme was a fairly dodgy one, however, he had total faith in Hazel Hazelden as an extremely competent test pilot with long experience in 'B' Squadron at Boscombe Down. He also had equal regard for John Allam so agreed to join the Company. He was allotted the flutter programme which had already commenced with the second prototype, WB775, which had been equipped with eccentric excitation devices in the rear fuselage; these were weights which were rotated by electric motors to give differing vibrational frequencies at different motor RPM. (*See* Figure 1)

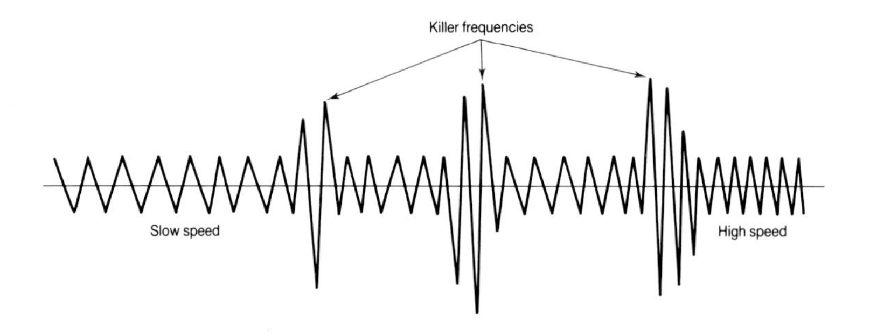

Fig. 1 Method of Operation of out-of-Balance Exciters

J.W. 'Jock' Still.
Jock Still)

To establish the dangerous flutter frequencies the out-of-balance exciters were started and slowly increased in speed by means of a cockpit control to cover the whole range of frequencies. This operation was called a 'sweep' and its objective was the identification of dangerous values, known as the 'Killer modes' in the analysis department. The results were recorded on a cathode ray oscilloscope and produced a trace similar to that shown in Figure 1.

If, at a speed of 250 kt (462.5 km/hr) and the dangerous frequencies were identified at, say, 3.8 cycles per sec, 4.9 cps and 8.1 cps the flight would be made at 260 kt (481 km/hr) and the exciters tuned, respectively, to 3.8, 4.9 and 8.1 cps. Hopefully, a good damping effect would be recorded at those frequencies. If this was not so, further investigation would follow. When the flight analysis proved satisfactory, results the tests would continue progressively at 10 kt (18.5 km/hr) increments. (*See* Figure 2)

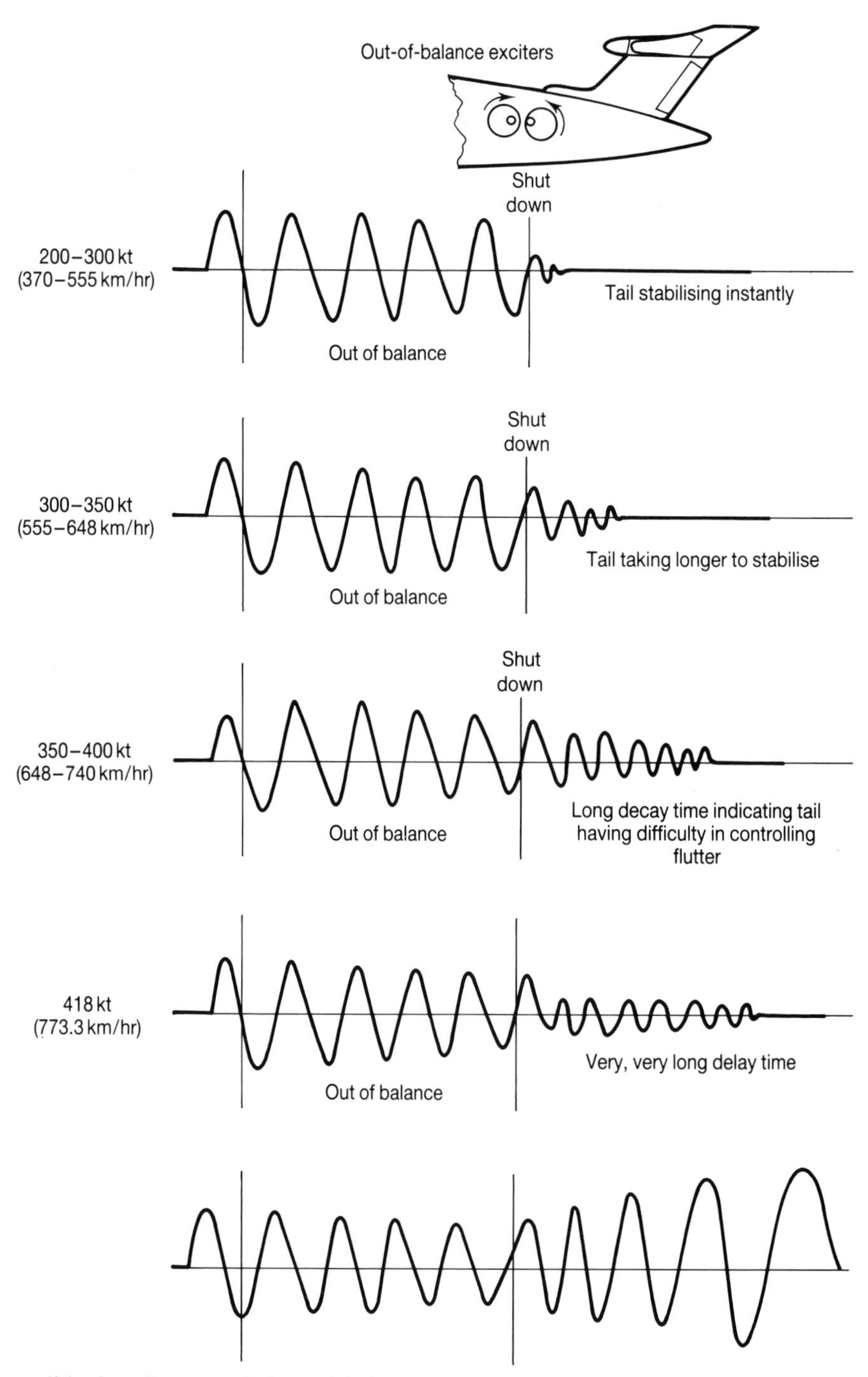

Fig. 2 Victor Bomber – Flutter Investigation Traces. Diagrams by courtesy of Jock Still.

Right from the original design studies for the Victor flutter had been recognised as one of the most crucial and difficult areas. There was concentration upon the swept wing at a Mach number well beyond the critical number and, from that point, the particular special problems associated with the crescent wing; the T tail was a new concept for the Company so it, too, required special consideration. The study was approached on a broad front; calculations, wind tunnel tests, ground resonance testing and, finally, flight tests. Some dropped model tests were also carried out. The work on the wing had been entirely successful but, as has been recounted earlier, the calculations on the tail were not wholly successful for three reasons; the joint between fin and tailplane was less stiff than on the wind tunnel test model, the dihedral on the tailplane was large to give additional lateral area at little structural cost and the forces exerted by the dihedral were much larger than had been anticipated and when the fin twisted in a roll.

The excitation of the weights was inertial during flight and, as the critical frequency was low at around 2-10 cps the amplitude applied at the important frequencies was also low. To avoid turbulent air affecting the recorded readings the sorties were carried out in calm air early in the morning.

To identify the flutter speed the tailplane of WB775 was deliberately weakened so that when the instrumentation indicated proximity to the disintegration speed, strengthening of the tailplane would take the maximum flight speed into the 'safety zone'. When the exciters had been used to initiate the vibration they were immediately braked so that the rate of decay could be recorded, (Figures 1 and 2 show the principles involved). If the decay did not occur satisfactorily as soon as the exciters were braked, the flutter could become divergent to end in structural failure. Jock approached all these flights with a high degree of prudence but, on one of the last ones, at around 415 knots the exciters were started at 20,000 ft (6,096 m), somewhere over Lincolnshire the problems arose. In Jock's own words:

> 'There was a BANG and the aircraft started to buck and weave, pretty well out of control; many emergency "dolls-eye" indicators started flashing on the instrument panel and an enormous degree of vibration developed. I warned Jock Ogilvy, my observer, to stand by to eject and then pulled the machine into a fairly steep climb, at the same time I closed the throttles of all four engines. As speed dropped the vibration diminished but did not vanish entirely, although, by the time I had reached 25-30,000 ft (7620–9144 m) speed had fallen to about 250 knots (463 km/hr). The aircraft appeared to be controllable so I turned South giving quick resumés on the RT to Radlett control, at the same time I called out "MAYDAY" on the radio. As I flew south, by deduction from the evidence on the dolls-eyes of the emergency panel, I concluded that something had happened to the starboard wing. I was also losing fuel rapidly from the tanks in that wing. Quick calculations indicated that fuel might suffice to reach Radlett, however, some of the gauges were entirely blank and I did not know if the tanks were empty or the gauges unserviceable. A bonus was a radio message from Peter Bugge, a de Havilland test pilot flying a Comet out of Hatfield, in the vicinity of the Victor, he offered assistance. I gratefully acknowledged and asked him to fly alongside to investigate the condition of the starboard wing. Within two minutes he was formatting with me and reported that I had lost a large part of the wing and fuel was pouring out of the hole.
>
> By this time Radlett control had everything on emergency stand-by – ambulance, fire wagons and British Rail whose London to the North line passed alongside the airfield and had to be crossed to land. I decided upon a "straight-in" approach, as speed

reduced I experienced more and more difficulty in holding up the right wing until all the trim facility was used up. As I lowered the flaps on the final approach, we experienced even greater vibration – this was caused by the aircraft shedding even more of the damaged wing plus some of the landing flaps. At 150 knots I found that I could only just hold the wing up, although the control column was fully over so I decided to land at this speed even though the normal was 125-130 knots (231-241 km/hr) so, at the higher speed I managed to place the wheels firmly on the runway and deployed the tail braking parachute.

I was very, very thankful when I felt the "slow-down" jolt as the 'chute opened and, with full foot brakes on, we came to a halt 200 yards (183 m) from the end of the runway.

It transpired that I had lost a substantial section of the wing area at the trailing edge between the aileron and the landing flap – but, as each piece tore away with the vibration, it also took additional pieces with it. The RAF did a great job in recovering virtually all of the wing debris spread over miles of countryside between Lincoln and Huntingdon with another large amount on the run-in to Radlett when the flaps were lowered. Thankfully, all the bits, about 200 in all, fell in open country.

The design office was able to establish that the cause of this near-disaster was the trailing edge box of the wing which was not supposed to be taking any strain during flutter tests. This area was suitably strengthened and we went on to clear its maximum flutter "envelope."'

This extraordinary occurrence showed the Victor to be an aeroplane of remarkable aerodynamic and structural quality in that it could continue to fly after such a major structural aberration and was capable of being landed safely back at base by a pilot of great courage and dedication. The incident led to Handley Page being recognised at the time as the leader in flutter investigation and they advised many other aircraft builders at home and overseas. Boeing were experiencing some wing flutter with the B-707 due to uneven consumption of fuel in the wing tanks. Jock Still had a number of discussions and flights with their test pilots including Boeing's chief test pilot the renowned Tex Johnston who, at the Seattle Power Boat Races in 1954 was due to carry out a fly-past in the prototype Dash 80, as it was known. Not content with just a sedate pass over the crowd of 200,000 people he carried out two rolls at altitude and then came down to a very low level and repeated the manoeuvre! – with a full test crew on board! John Allam and Spud Murphy demonstrated barrel rolls and half loops at the 1958 SBAC Show.

In concluding the account of the flutter programme it is appropriate to quote Godfrey Lee who, in an *Aerospace* article on Victor development commented:

> 'In my opinion these flight tests were outstandingly and courageously done and I consider that the crew, Jock Still, the pilot, with Frank Haye and Jock Ogilvy, the observers, deserve great credit for this work'.

John Allam, Geoff Wass and other pilots were also involved in this part of the programme.

Having satisfactorily concluded the Contractor's Trials WB775 was flown to Boscombe Down on 14 March 1955. Three service pilots flew it for eight hours in the first week and it was soon pronounced satisfactory for night flying. Bombing trials at Orfordness in June proved it to be a good bombing platform with the autostabiliser engaged but tiring to fly without it. Flying characteristics were highly praised with adequate manoeuvrability stall margin at M 0.873 and an altitude of 47,000 ft (14,325 m).

Very limited bomb release trials were undertaken by Handley Page pilots, the prototype Victor, WB775, was fitted with doors to a flash bomb bay at the rear of the main bomb bay; these were declared unnecessary and did not appear on production aircraft. Two huge bomb bay doors extended the full length of the bay which was almost twice as large as the Vulcan bomb bay. It was designed to carry the projected 10,000 lb (4,540 kg) nuclear store or 35 conventional 1,000 lb (454 kg) bombs. The doors retracted into the fuselage. When they were first opened at high altitude on 3 February 1955 the crew was delighted to find that the amplitude and frequency of the inevitable buffet was much lower than expected with such an immense aperture under the fuselage and longitudinal trim change was insignificant. The amplitude of the buffet was affected primarily by high indicated airspeed and very little by high Mach number. This was very fortunate as the aircraft was designed to bomb from high altitude where IAS was low and Mach No high, so the buffet did not affect the Victor as a bombing platform.

Even at high IAS at low altitude the buffet, although more severe, would not prevent the aircraft bombing at high speed low down. Bombing trials commenced in July 1957 using a production Victor, XA921. Initially 1,000 lb (454 kg) bombs were loaded at Farnborough where the official bomb loading assessments were made. Although the Victor sits very close to the ground, special arrangements had been designed to facilitate loading. The technique was entirely satisfactory and loading proved to be an easy task. The bombs were dropped over the range at Orfordness on the East Coast. This proved to be difficult as, although the range was a designated danger area, coastal shipping skippers did not seem to recognise this and navigated their vessels straight through the range with gay abandon! Range Control at Orfordness would, therefore, only clear aircraft to make bombing runs when the area could be seen to be clear of shipping. Not until this notification had been received at Farnborough could the aircraft take-off. On occasions a ship would enter the range just as the bomber began its run so the pilot had to hold clear until the offending vessel departed the range boundary.

Eventually some 1,000 lb (454 kg) bombs were dropped. They fell in steady trajectories after faultless releases. The simultaneous drop of 35 of these bombs was an impressive exercise and was made by A&AEE pilots. Photographs taken over the Song Song range in the Far East in 1964 showed Victor XH648 with all 35 bombs just below it.

Next came the carriage and dropping of the 10,000 lb (4,540 kg) store, the main weapon for which the Victor was designed. Again XA921 was used, the bomb being loaded at Farnborough in a remote area surrounded by high security screens. The rules were so strict that John Allam, as captain of the aircraft, was to be prevented from entering the area until the bomb was loaded and the bay doors closed. He objected to this and said he would not fly any aircraft with something inside it that he had not actually seen. With considerable reluctance on the part of the security authority the whole crew was cleared to witness the loading of what turned out to be a dummy. The first flight was to be made with the store in place to assess the handling qualities of the Victor fully loaded. The sortie was made from Farnborough and it showed no handling problems whatever. After landing the bomb was removed in the special security area. Three days later it was loaded again with the intention of dropping it over the Orfordness range. However, shipping in the range area was persistent and it was not possible to even obtain a start-up signal from Range Control via Farnborough Air Traffic Control. Eventually it was reported that a 'window' was unlikely on that day. Completion of the trials had become urgent so, after some high level discussions, the crew was cleared to make a free drop from 10,000 ft (3,048 m) into the English Channel east of the Isle of Wight. It was, however, to be their responsibility to clear the area of shipping themselves! On that assumption they were given clearance to take-off and they headed south for the Channel. The weather was fine and clear giving good visibility, they carefully studied the sea and found an area clear of shipping. Bomb doors were opened and the bomb released. As one 1000 pounder represented only 0.6% of the weight of the Victor the release of one of them was almost imperceptible to the crew – the 10,000 pounder was a quite different matter! The aircraft still felt entirely normal so Allam banked rapidly to port and was just in time to see the splash as the bomb hit the water – and they did not hit any ships!

As all the bomb dropping trials were considered fully acceptable, apart from the future trials with the Blue Steel weapon on the Victor B2 no further bomb releases were carried out by Handley Page pilots. All further work was completed by A&AEE and by RAF squadron pilots.

The Ministry of Supply was fully satisfied with the Victor B1 in meeting all the requirements so the aircraft went into service with No. 232 Operational Conversion Unit at Gaydon at the beginning of 1957 whilst the design office considered many variants to meet RAF future needs. All of these, if accepted, would require intensive test flying.

In June 1957 John Allam caused a sensation when he became the first pilot to achieve Mach One in a four-engined bomber. He was carrying out trim investigation tests reaching speeds of M 0.98 in a modest 19° dive; the aircraft was behaving so well that he decided to let it accelerate to M 1.015 at 40,000 ft (12,192 m) – there was no change of trim but a robust sonic bang was heard by Charles Joy, the chief designer as he shopped in Watford. Not until the sortie data was being studied after the flight did he realise that the Victor was responsible. The inevitable publicity created a little irritation at A.V. Roe; Roly Falk, in charge of test flying, let it be known that the Vulcan regularly exceeded M 1.0, indeed, VIPs had been taken on flights and had seen the meter reading exceeding unity. Unfortunately he could not produce anyone who had heard a Vulcan generate a sonic bang so the inevitable conclusion was that the meter was reading high due to position error.

John Allam, with a considerable number of types in his logbook, considers that the Victor was, unquestionably, the one which gave him most pleasure although he did not fly the tanker Mk 2 version on a test flight. In 1991, however, he was invited by 55 Squadron at Marham to fly one of those in service. He took the right hand seat and had control for most of a refuelling sortie and was very pleased to have an invitation to do three ILS approaches on return to base. He expressed considerable disappointment that modifications to the elevator gearing since Handley Page ceased to be responsible for the Victor had spoiled its very agreeable flying characteristics.

Philip 'Spud' Murphy joined Handley Page in February 1958 from Vickers at Wisley where he had tested the Valiant in the flight refuelling role and with the use of Rocket Assisted Take-off Gear (RATO). This experience was of particular value to the Victor programme as the aircraft was envisaged with both of these facilities when fatigue problems led to the withdrawal of the Valiant from service. A Victor B1 was fitted with various lengths of probe for the trials which were delayed by considerable obstruction on the part of the Ministry of Technology who were reluctant to allocate Lightnings which were to be used as the receiving aircraft. Spud was acquainted with the Commander-in-Chief, Fighter Command who soon made arrangements for senior officers of 17 Squadron, operating Lightnings, to visit Radlett. Refuelling probes were fitted overnight to some of their fighters by RAF ground crew (the Ministry required a week to do the same work if and when a Lightning could be identified from Ministry of Technology resources). The first exercise with 17 Squadron was the simulation of a refuelled flight to Malta. It was completely successful.

Inevitably the RAF demanded higher performance from the Victor so the development of

The first and only rocket-assisted take-off from the de Havilland runway at Hatfield.
(Handley Page Association)

the Mk 2 was initiated. This was to have Rolls-Royce Conway by-pass engines with a thrust of 17,350 lb (7,870 kg) replacing the 11,000 lb (4,990 kg) Armstrong Siddeley Sapphires. The Conway was ultimately up-dated to give 20,500 lb (9,300 kg) of thrust. This substantial increase in power necessitated a major re-design of the airframe; whilst this was in progress the test programme continued with the B1 in the flight refuelling role and with various flap and equipment variants. The RATO capability was required as the Air Staff had ordered that the V bomber force should be dispersed for security reasons to airfields where the runways might be short. Spud Murphy was the only test pilot at Radlett with RATO experience so it, and the tanker project, became his personal responsibility. There were two thrust augmentor units under the wings, just outboard of the fuselage under the engine bays. The de Havilland Spectre rocket motors developed 6,500 lb (2,948 kg) thrust each.

During his work on the Valiant, Spud encountered serious vibration problems which were not experienced on the Victor. The main difficulty was the recovery of the RATO units by parachute after take-off; at this point they were jettisoned and automatically inflated airbags were intended to cushion the impact when the heavy and expensive units hit the ground. In practice a bounce to 40–50 ft (12–15 m) occurred at the top of which the bags turned them over to land upside down. Practice drops were made at Radlett but the problem was not solved. Forty per cent of these costly fireworks were written off. Just as the first live take-off was to be made from the de Havilland Hatfield runway the programme was cancelled by the Ministry.

Naturally the cancellation caused considerable media interest and a show was laid on for the press. Spud told of one particular pushy journalist who was 'a pain in the butt!' He continually enquired what was going to happen and asked where he should stand to take a good photograph. It was suggested that he should take up his position at the dummy firing pit, just behind the Victor. When the rockets fired a large volume of water from the pit was blown all over him. Profuse apologies were, of course, made and, to add insult to injury, it was suggested that the water may have been contaminated with dangerous high test peroxide fuel so it was important that, as a precaution, he should be hosed down! As a final indignity, having made the one and only live firing take-off, Spud carried out a low, fast flypast over the press men – the pushy one measured his length on the grass!

The B 2 version had problems; the wing root had been altered to accept the larger Conway engines and it was necessary to modify the wing leading edge to improve the airflow characteristics and reduce drag to achieve the higher operational ceiling made possible by the more powerful engines. John Allam flew the first one, XH668, on 20 February 1959. This was flown, initially, to investigate the engine performance up to 30,000 ft (9,144 m), by June it had logged 46 hours. The Victor had shown the remarkable ability to carry fuel weighing more than the empty weight of the aircraft so this presented problems with the fuel usage affecting the centre of gravity. To overcome this difficulty all aircraft had been fitted with a mechanical device to draw fuel proportionately from the tanks without affecting the CG. This too had to be checked out on the B 2.

The prototype B 2 was delivered to Boscombe Down for a preview appraisal by the test pilots there. By 20 August it had flown 100 hours, mostly by HP pilots with John Allam in command. On this day it took off to climb to 52,000 ft (15,850 m) with two A&AEE pilots, S/Ldr R.J. Morgan and S/Ldr G.B. Stockman of B Squadron at the controls and a crew of three including a Handley Page test observer, Bob Williams, to check the performance of the Conway engines. A ground radar operator in Kent occasionally checked the progress of the aircraft as it flew towards the Irish Sea. An hour into the sortie he picked up the trace at 40,000 ft (12,192 m), suddenly it disappeared. At approximately the same time the crew of a small coasting vessel off the Pembrokeshire coast heard what appeared to be two sonic bangs and saw a large splash about 8 miles (12.9 km) away, in the direction of the Smalls lighthouse. The Victor had maintained radio silence since leaving Boscombe Down; it was never seen again.

When it became overdue it was presumed that the radar plot and the reported splash indicated without doubt that the aircraft had dived into the sea so an immediate search was initiated in the area by four trawlers and a salvage vessel under the direction of the Accidents Investigation Branch of RAE. After six months searching in appalling weather conditions the main wreckage was found at a depth of 400 ft (122 m). Nine months later, by November 1960, using special trawls designed for the job and HMS *Reclaim*, the salvage vessel, with underwater TV and a diving bell, 75% of the aircraft weight had been recovered; altogether about 600,000 items were brought up from the sea bed, the largest weighing 570 lb (259 kg). The magnetic wire recorder was not found but the pilot's watch, stopped on impact, confirmed the evidence of the Kent radar operator's log. The integrity of the electrical system was proved by a voltmeter reading 200 volts when it was smashed on impact. There was a suspicion that a violent decompression at altitude may have resulted from loss of the canopy escape hatch, the fixings of which had given slight trouble; this may have rendered the crew unconscious immediately. However the hatch was found and it had been jettisoned. Neither ejection seat had been fired. What appeared to be a significant discovery was a pair of wing tips; on the port tip the pitot static head was still in place but the starboard one was missing, the condition of the mounting indicating that it disappeared before impact with the sea. Vibration tests proved that it was possible for it to come adrift in buffet conditions. This particular head was especially significant as it operated, in addition to the instruments for the pilot and co-pilot, the Mach trimmer and Q detector associated with synthetic feed-back to the pilots indicating aerodynamic loads on the control surfaces. If the head had departed from its mounting a spurious loss of airspeed would be registered and the Mach trimmer activated to depress the elevators to initiate a dive to recover the speed. At the same time the stall detector would have operated the nose flaps which, with the head in position, could not move because a high speed over-ride switch would prevent actuation at that speed. It was concluded by the Board of Enquiry that the pitot head had detached at above 23,000 ft (7,010 m) with the aircraft being forced instantly into a catastrophic dive from which the pilots were unable to recover.

This certainly offered an acceptable explanation but several of the HP test pilots, among others, are convinced that the conclusion was erroneous. John Allam had flown every sortie in that aircraft, XH668, always as captain but with other HP pilots including Spud Murphy and Peter Baker who had just joined the Company, sometimes in the left hand seat. He had experienced Mach trimmer runaway on several occasions as part of the test programme to investigate the outcome of such a defect. The trimmer was disconnected, the pilot counted to ten and then considered the attitude of the aeroplane which resulted from the runaway. This test was done on one occasion when a test engineer in the back seat operated the switch which switched off the trimmer system so the pilot was not expecting the runaway. In each case there was no problem whatsoever in controlling the aircraft to overcome the effect. The actuating motor for the elevator control operated very slowly indeed so a swift disaster situation was not an acceptable hypothesis to the test pilots.

Among other factors emerging from the enquiry was the Rolls-Royce statement that the engines were developing full power right to the time of impact, the airbrakes were closed and the dive was calculated to be supersonic down to about 8,000 ft (2,438 m). The question then has to be asked 'What was the crew doing?', obviously nothing. Were they incapacitated? There must be a strong assumption that they were; no 'Mayday' signal was received, no attempt had been made to eject, although there was some indication that the co-pilot had taken some action at the last second. John Allam expressed his doubts at the Enquiry but no notice was taken of his views. He put the point that if the crew was not incapacitated the first action in a dive resulting from a trimmer runaway would be to cut the power and deploy the airbrakes, but this would only be necessary if the runaway had not been noticed at an early stage. Absence of any action to do these things must imply incapacitation of the crew. If this is accepted, how could it have happened? The only possible explanation must lie in a malfunction of the oxygen system – could the bottles have been filled with air instead of oxygen? It will never be known so the official report, highly unsatisfactory to a number of competent people, is left to posterity. At least it reflects no discredit upon the unfortunate crew. The salvage operation remains one of the most remarkable such events in the history of aviation.

With Victors now on the production line there was concern in high places lest there should be a fundamental weakness in the design, so a special investigation was launched at Radlett called the Special RAE Trial under the control of RAE – XH670 was allocated for the task. Allam was certain that the Ministry and RAE were convinced that they were about to lose another Victor because they insisted that only a pilot and co-pilot should fly the machine; at least their ejector seats would give them a good chance of survival if the worst happened. This decision left the essential air electronics officer's panel in the rear compartment un-manned. Consequently, the panel was moved to a position in front of the co-pilot, the co-pilot's panel being removed. This was a major task and delayed the commencement of the tests. A curiously illogical stipulation was that two separate pilots would carry out identical tests to ensure an un-biassed judgement but the same co-pilot was used throughout the series. The co-pilot was Harry Rayner whilst John Allam and Peter Baker flew as No 1 on alternate flights. Most of the flights were to 55,000 ft (16,764 m) and were mainly concerned with manoeuvre margins.

A slightly ludicrous situation developed during the run-up to the trials when a man from the Ministry telephoned John Allam and made the eminently sensible demand that a chase aircraft should accompany the Victor on all of these sorties; he asked which aeroplane could be used for this task. John said that the only one which could follow a Victor to the height and speed required was another Victor. The man was not amused and he clearly envisaged the loss of two Victors. Ultimately the Gloster Javelin was chosen. This aircraft would only reach 48,000 ft (14,630 m). As the trials would be carried out in periods of two and a half hours, the Javelin endurance was quite inadequate so a ludicruous situation developed with three Javelins in relays staggering along at 48,000 ft – up to 50,000 (15,240 m) when light on fuel, whilst the Victor carried out its manoeuvres about a mile above them with no possibility of any useful observation being made. If, for any reason, the Javelin relieving the previous incumbent was delayed the Victor tests had to be suspended, the machine cruising until the next Javelin radioed that the Victor was in sight!

The only information which was learned from the trials was that there was nothing whatsoever wrong with the Victor, as, of course, had been clear from the original test sorties on the prototype. It was, however, feasible to explore the outermost regions of the flight envelope which had not been required on earlier sorties. It was found possible to perform a 2G turn at M 0.95 at 55,000 ft (16,764 m), a truly remarkable performance for a heavy bomber. On one occasion John Allam, making the turn, tried to roll out of it by applying aileron, the Victor continued in the turn. John said to his co-pilot, Harry Rayner, 'Crikey, you'll have to help me, we need more aileron power'. As he made the remark the thought occurred that the ailerons had stalled and that more power would be ineffective as Harry quickly proved. Many ideas went through John's mind, from throttling back and deploying the air brakes to another phenomenon which he recalled discussing with other pilots, the reversal of roll with yaw. When an aeroplane is flying straight and level at high speed the application of rudder will initiate yaw in which the outside wing over which the airflow becomes faster than that over the inside wing will generate more lift and, consequently apply bank. This seemed a possible explanation particularly as he was holding a boot-full of top rudder. It followed that, in theory, he was trying to make an aileron turn to recover to straight flight whilst the top rudder was attempting to continue the turn, so the forces were neatly in balance. He took off the top rudder and the Victor smoothly rolled out of the turn.

When this circumstance was investigated further it was found that its simulation required a Mach number of about 0.925; application of rudder to right or left in straight flight had no effect whatsoever, the aircraft flew straight on. At M 0.90 application of right rudder would, as may be expected, raise the left wing. Right rudder applied at M 0.93 would raise the right wing. The pilots were astounded at the critical nature of the phenomenon which was easily reproducible. It was, however, of purely academic significance as the manoeuvre was outside the normal Service pilot's flight envelope.

During the trials of the B 2 Victor Spud Murphy was involved at a catastrophic accident to XL162, the thirteenth B 2 which had spent a period at Rolls-Royce, Hucknall for an investigation of engine surge problems. It was then flown to Boscombe Down for armament and radar trials. On 23 March 1962 Spud took off with S/Ldr J. Waterton as co-pilot, an Air Electronics Officer, John Tank and two HP test observers, P. Elwood and M.P. Evans in the rear compartment. During the flight the aircraft entered a super stall. Waterton was in the left hand seat and had made an approach to the stall, the normal warning buffets were observed until speed dropped to about 130 knots. Murphy noticed that the control column was being pushed forward to control speed reduction at one knot per second. He ordered 'I have control' and took over. With the column hard against the instrument panel, which should have achieved a positive response and a need to back off rapidly, there was no change in the attitude of the Victor. By this time speed had fallen to 115 knots, lower than had been planned. Spud tried everything to recover from the stall, pulling hard back, rocking, using the rudder to swing the nose, nothing worked and it became clear that it was locked in the stall. The undercarriage and flaps were down and the vertical descent was extremely rapid with a G force of less than one and a slightly floating sensation in the seat. At 12,000 ft (3,658 m) he gave the order 'abandon aircraft' and continued with his attempts to recover. The crew door opened immediately the order was given and Murphy looked aft to see what was happening in the crew area behind the bulkhead. From his limited viewpoint it was apparent that the middle and the right seats were empty so he concluded that the occupants were already descending on their parachutes. John Waterton was attempting to send Mayday calls with the Victor descending at a frightening rate. Murphy considered deploying the braking parachute at 6,000 ft (1,830 m) but realised that departing crew members would probably be netted into it. He continued to apply full power and raised the flaps but nothing made any difference to their hideous dilemma.

He hit John Waterton's shoulder to indicate that he should 'bang out' and warned the rest of the crew to 'abandon aircraft'. Waterton pulled his seat blind and there was a long pause before the canopy above him lifted ready to be torn away thus pulling the lanyard attached to it to fire the seat gun. Four or five seconds later he was on his way. Spud realised that his options had run out so made a final check on as much of the crew compartment as he could see from his seat. He left the aircraft at about 300 ft (91 m), blacking out momentarily, under acceleration. As he came to he was falling towards the tailplane, almost touching it he separated from his seat. As the parachute deployed he bounced one or twice and found, from the considerable discomfort, that his crutch harness was too loose. At that moment he landed on a massive run of telephone wires which, miraculously, arrested his fall. As they broke underneath him he quickly took a turn with his parachute lines around the wires and descended slowly to the ground, with the last of the wires catching under his chin, lifting his mask which injured his forehead.

He realised that he may have sustained internal injuries so lay flat on the ground; within two or three minutes a farm worker on a bicycle arrived. He said that he had seen the aeroplane crash on a farmhouse so Spud told him to go there and give whatever help he could. Two minutes later a little Austin Ruby car appeared, from which a retired district nurse stepped out to assist. By this time he was aware that his back was probably broken so she rolled up the parachute and put it under his head. Her husband then left the car and took one look at the pilot who was covered in blood, the husband was obviously unwell and showed signs of acute distress. His wife said that he had heart trouble so Spud sent them away too whilst he awaited the ambulance which arrived ten minutes later from the damaged farmhouse with the farmer's wife, who had been having lunch with her husband when the Victor crashed on the back of the house killing two women working in the kitchen. The front of the house collapsed on the owners, resulting in the farmer having a broken pelvis and leg and his wife being knocked over and winded and slightly burned by fuel splashes. They were both taken to the RAF Sick Quarters at Cranwell where Spud was recognised by the Station Medical Officer, an ex-member of the Institute of Aviation Medicine. The back injury was beginning to give him considerable pain so, as the Sick Quarters could do little for him, he was taken to the nearby RAF Hospital, Nockton Hall, which had the appropriate facilities. Six months later he was fit again. The story of the crew was especially tragic. John Waterton sustained back injuries in landing; those in the rear compartment, not visible to the pilot, were wearing a new type of personal equipment connector, which were being used, preparatory to a trial with full pressure suits in which they would be mounted integrally with the suit. For this flight they were mounted upon an adaptor which necessitated groping down the side of the seat to release them instead of moving a simple level as in earlier designs. When the exit door on the port side was opened, the AEO managed to get out by tearing away the connectors; he ended up in an apple tree which he split from fork right to ground level. The others, finding themselves anchored by the connectors, went back to their seats to try to release the connections, which they were unable to do in time, so they died in the wreck.

It was considered that the rate of descent of the Victor from 10,000 ft (3,048 m) to the ground was about 136 mph (220 km/hr) arriving in about fifty seconds. Coincidentally, on 22 October 1963 two Vickers test pilots, Mike Lithgow and Dickie Rymer with a test crew of five took off from Wisley in a BAC III airliner to measure stability at approaches to the stall with the CG in its aft position. Forty-two such approaches were made in different configurations. On the forty-third the aircraft entered a super stall from which recovery proved to be impossible. All of the crew died as the aircraft descended with little forward speed at a rate of 15,000 ft (4,572 m) per minute. This occurrence emphasised the good fortune which allowed some of the crew of the Victor to survive.

During the Victor B 2 development programme it was decided to replace the leading edge nose flaps with a 'hard' cambered leading edge designed to achieve the same objective of the retention of the attached airflow over the nose flap but without a significant cruise performance penalty, at the same time saving weight. The nose flaps had to be lowered very rapidly and heavy hydraulic accumulators in the wings were needed to ensure this. Spud Murphy's accident occurred during investigations into the effect of the modifications upon stalling characteristics. It became clear that those of the B 1 were different to those of the B 2 with the modified leading edge and that this disparity was a contributory cause of the accident. Spud believes that both the Company and the Ministry were deceived by wind tunnel tests which showed that even up to an incidence of 22° the stability curves of the two wing shapes were nearly coincident. In practice it was found that above 22° they diverged, the nose-down movement of the B 1 wing not being repeated; furthermore, the enlarged wing roots for the Conway engines may have altered the stalling characteristics of the wing roots.

A few weeks later Peter Baker had a similar experience at a much higher altitude, 55,000 ft (16,764 m), when an unintentional spin developed from the recovery procedure. Spinning was an unknown territory for the Victor and strictly prohibited. Simulation of a Mach trimmer runaway was being carried out with the CG aft to clear the design of the new leading edge. A stable stall, à la Spud Murphy, was recognised as a possibility so an anti-spin parachute would have been a prudent precaution. However, for high altitude tests the specification of the cartridge used to deploy the parachute was inadequate due to the very cold conditions at 55,000 ft. Peter Baker had decided that in an emergency, the braking parachute would be deployed. The worst happened and the Victor departed into a spin to port; after three turns the parachute was operated after the failure of normal recovery techniques; recovery occurred at 30,000 ft (9,144 m). It was then realised that three engines had flamed-out; they were quickly re-lit and a landing made at RAE Bedford for inspection to ensure that no structural damage had occurred in the spin. The airspeed had been very low, however, with about 45 knots being recorded on the inner wing pitot head and 70 knots on the outer one.

Peter Baker said that it was an extraordinary experience to be virtually hanging in a perpendicular position from the parachute which had a breaking link in the line designed to fail at 190 knots. His co-pilot, Harry Rayner, was concerned lest an overspeed should develop in the dive-out and leaned across to selection the air brakes out; even so Mach 0.90 was recorded in the dive.

An interesting sequel to this occurred after a Victor B 2, to be used for Blue Steel guided weapons trials at Woomera in Australia, was flown out to Edinburgh Field RAAF Base near Adelaide by two pilots who had visited Radlett, just after the inadvertent spin, for instruction in flying the aircraft. During general discussions with them Peter mentioned that

Victor SR2, XM716 of 543 Sqdn Wyton, minutes before its fatal crash at Warboys, Cambridgeshire, in June 1966.
(Handley Page Association)

in a similar emergency he would deploy the braking parachute. The trials involved a flight at 47,000 ft (14,325 m) with the huge weapon in the bomb bay; at this height and still climbing, the pilots saw that the Machmeter in one position was leading 1.02 and the other a very much lower figure. They elected to believe the unbelievable, that the high figure was correct. The speed brakes were put out and the engines throttled back, a mistake which was brought to their notice by the Victor stalling and departing into a spin. The specially instrumented Blue Steel round was over its normal 15,000 lb (6804 kg) weight and weighed 18,000 lb (8156 kg). The crutch supporting the round was stressed to 3 G. To recover from the spin the parachute was deployed, fortunately with no problems and recovery was achieved. The round had moved upon its crutch so they decided to jettison this extremely expensive and one-off test vehicle upon a site allocated for this purpose.

The pilot, for some curious reason, encouraged publicity for what was a serious error of judgement and adverse press publicity resulted. He was withdrawn from the programme so Peter Baker went out to complete the trials, dropping Blue Steel successfully.

The RAF required that both the Victor Mk 2 and the Vulcan Mk 2 should be capable of auto-landing. Systems to achieve this were in development at RAE Bedford and trials were in progress with a de Havilland Comet so both V bombers were fitted with an integrated auto-pilot/auto-throttle flight system which could interpret signals from a ground Instrument Landing System/leader cable installation to enable the aircraft to be landed entirely by the auto-pilot. Victor B 2 XH672 was designated as the auto-land trials aircraft, testing commencing in mid-March 1964. By this time Alf Camp had joined the HP team as a test pilot. He had previously been a member of the Bedford auto-land team and his experience soon became invaluable. Camp and John Allam handled the whole of the work on auto-land. The first flights at Bedford were to assess the acquisition and lock-on to the ILS, the accuracy of this ILS approach to the runway and the touch-down. In those days it was still a case of 'over to the pilot' after touch-down.

ILS acquisition and lock-on presented no problems, at glide-slope intercept the aircraft began its descent and maintained the glide-slope accurately. The pilot dialled in the required speed in accordance with the phase of the approach, the auto-throttle maintaining this speed accurately even in turbulent conditions. Two problems arose, the first resulting from the ILS localizer and glide-slope aerials being mounted outboard on the starboard wing whilst the leader cable aerial was mounted on the nose of the aeroplane – on its centre-line.

The sequence of events was for the approach to land to be made on the ILS and, at 300 ft (91 m) above touch-down height directional control was taken over by the leader cable system to provide greater accuracy in arriving spot-on the runway centre-line. What actually happened was that the aircraft tracked down the ILS offset to the left of the runway centre-line by precisely the distance of the ILS aerial to the right of the aircraft centre-line. This was because the flight director/auto-pilot combination flew the localizer aerial along the localizer centre-line. At 300 ft (91 m) above touch-down height the system automatically changed from localizer to leader cable for directional control. At this point the leader cable aerial was situated to the left of the runway extended centre-line so, as soon as control was transferred to the leader cable aerial the offset was sensed and a correction made which resulted in a right/left jink to align the aircraft correctly with the runway centre line. Up to this point the approach was stable, smooth and accurate but the directional upset caused at 300 ft (91 m), so close to touch-down, gave the system no time to sort out the signals and re-establish a stable approach. The obvious answer was to mount the ILS aerial on the centre-line of the Victor so that the transition from localizer to leader cable was smooth and uninterrupted. Thereafter the Victor made a smooth approach all the way from ILS interception to landing.

The other problem was, paradoxically, that the landing was light and very smooth. This caused the aircraft to skip into the air slightly, a circumstance which could not be tolerated as the auto-land system disengaged at touch-down so the pilot would have to take over immediately and re-establish a touch-down in, probably, low visibility conditions. It was essential that the aircraft remained firmly on the ground after the wheels touched, the pilot would then be responsible for decelerating it to a stop on the runway. To overcome the problem the landing height datum in the flight director was adjusted to sense the runway surface as being two feet lower than its actual height. Although the aircraft would still flare normally the outcome was a very positive landing by 'flying on'. Landings were, perhaps a little heavier than was desirable but they were positive and the machine always remained on the ground. The pilot was able to take over immediately and either roll and overshoot or bring the aircraft to rest.

Some fifteen flights were made to resolve these problems and 'fine-tune' the combined systems to enable the Victor to be considered suitable to enter service with an auto-land clearance. Before A&AEE would grant this clearance the HP test pilots had to demonstrate 200 auto-landings without any upsets. John Allam made 102 successful auto-landings in 11 sorties without a single failure. Alf Camp also completed at least 100 landings in a similar number of sorties. So the Victor was ready for A&AEE to carry out their own assessment to confirm the HP results. Before the check trials could commence the requirement for auto-land was cancelled and, so far as John Allam is aware, no further auto-landings were made.

During the whole of the 200 sorties only two were aborted, one because the ground installations became unserviceable after departure from Radlett. The other resulted from a failure of the flight recorder system in the aircraft. Not once did the Victor itself give any trouble and none was experienced with the auto-land system. The whole of the trials programme was 100% successful, the aircraft meeting in its entirety the specification for the auto-land requirement.

During the period demonstrations were made at four different airfields with landings being made into wind, in cross-winds from both sides of the runway and, on at least one occasion, with a slight tail-wind.

John Allam and Godfrey Lee visit No 55 Sqdn at Marham in 1984. Behind them is a Victor K2 tanker.
(Handley Page Association)

John Allam said that from the pilot's point of view the success of the trials was infuriating, because, regardless of the wind, the Victor was capable of making precisely the same firm landing every time at exactly the same point on the runway! He points out that, after all, that is what it was designed to do and that is exactly what it did! One tends to take auto-land for granted in these high-tech days but it cannot be denied that the remarkable success of the Victor system, wasted effort though it proved to be, nearly forty years ago, was a great tribute to all those concerned in its development and test flying.

It will be apparent that the test programme of this magnificent British bomber was beset with difficulty and a measure of tragedy and it is appropriate that the man who, by common consent, was the presiding genius responsible for its design shall have the last word. Godfrey Lee, in his *Aerospace* article said

> 'The concept of the Victor and the design techniques could stand comparison with anything in hand elsewhere in the British aircraft industry; in my view we led the way in some aspects ... when one reflects upon the size of the firm involved with only 3,500 employees and compare it with current aerospace teams the achievement seems even more remarkable ... when we started the Victor in 1946 no-one had built a long-range high speed jet aeroplane.'

On 11 June 1993 three Victors of 55 Squadron proudly led the fly-past of the Queen's Birthday Celebrations, and the Squadron was disbanded on 15 October 1993 with appropriate ceremony and valedictions at RAF Marham. It is relevant to note that the Valiant remained in service for only 9 years, the Vulcan 27 years and the Victor 35 years, surely a great tribute to the Company and to its great pioneering founder, the late Sir Frederick Handley Page and to the dedicated work of the design, production and test flying personnel.

John Allam had the honour of being aboard the last flight of a Victor from RAF Marham on 30 November 1993 to RAF Shawbury where B Mk 2 XH2672 will be dismantled and transported by road to the Aerospace Museum at Cosford. As the pilot of the first B Mk 1 to fly into Marham on 19 July 1956 he was involved in the first in and the last out of that famous RAF Station.

The author is indebted to 'Hazel' Hazelden, John Allam, 'Spud' Murphy, Jock Still and Peter Baker for their co-operation in preparing this account of the Victor Test Programme and for the loan of photographs. Harry Fraser-Mitchell of the Handley Page Association has also generously loaned photographs. Thanks are also due to Godfrey Lee for permission to quote from his article in *Aerospace* and to Roger Brooks, Chairman of the Handley Page Association, for his advice.

A gathering of veterans at the home of the author, 1984. Left to right, Gp Capt S. Wroath, W/Cdr Ralph Havercroft, A.E. 'Ben' Gunn, W/Cdr Charles McClure, Ron E. Clear, W/Cdr R.W. Martin, Gp Capt L. S. Snaith, S/Ldr Pingo Lester, Jeffrey Quill and Michael Daunt.
(Don Middleton)

Epilogue

Largely for reasons of space these accounts of epic test flying programmes end in the 1960s – what of the future? The text ends at what is probably an appropriate watershed in the art of experimental flying as so much of the preliminary work can now be carried out on computers and simulators, work which once had to be done in the air. This has certainly not made the task of the test pilot any easier but it has reduced some of the risk although the complexity of the modern aeroplane increases dramatically the test flight time and cost expended. Ten thousand hours of test flying time is not unreasonable for a modern high technology aeroplane.

The question is sometimes asked, 'Is there any longer a need for test pilots when aircraft can be so comprehensively automated?' The answer must be an emphatic *yes* as no computer can replace the trained human brain in command of an aeroplane applying high standards of airmanship to achieve an objective and subjective appraisal of that aeroplane. It is quite inconceivable that a new and immensely costly prototype could ever be entrusted to remote control on its initial flights. Fly-by-wire, brilliant concept though it is, has already presented major problems in the case of some prototypes although a pilot sat in the cockpit.

Bibliography

Andrews, C.F. & Morgan, E.B., *Supermarine Aircraft since 1914*, Putnam, 1981
Barnes, C.H., *Handley Page Aircraft since 1907*, Putnam 1976
Beamont, W/Cdr Roland P., *Testing Years*, Ian Allan, 1980
Bridgeman, W., *The Lonely Sky*, Cassell, 1956
Brooks, A, *V Force*, Janes 1982
Brown, Capt Eric M., *Wings of the Navy*, Pilot, 1980
Wings of the Weird and Wonderful, Airlife 1983
Bullen, A. & Rivas, B., *John Derry*, Kimber 1982
Burnet, Charles, *Three Centuries to Concorde*, Mechanical Engineering Publications 1979
Cobham, Sir Alan, *A Time to Fly*, Shepheard-Walwyn, 1978
Cooksley, P.G., *Skystreak*, Hale, 1980
Courtney, Capt. Frank, *Flight Path*, Kimber 1973
Donne, M., *Leaders of the Sky (Rolls-Royce)*, Muller 1981
Duke, S/Ldr Neville F. & Mitchell, H.W., *Test Pilot*, Allen Wingate, 1953
Gibson, T.M. & Harrison, M.H. *Into the Air; A History of Aviation Medicine in the R.A.F.*, Hale, 1984
Gillman, Capt. R.E., *Croydon to Concorde*, Murray 1980
Grierson, John *Jet Flight*, Sampson Low, 1946
Gunston, Bill, *Early Supersonic Fighters of the West*, Ian Allan, 1976
Jewell, John, *Engineering for Life*, Martin Baker Aircraft Co. Ltd., 1979
Johnson, Brian & Heffernan, Terry *Boscombe Down: A Most Secret Place*, Janes, 1982
Hallion, Richard P, *On the Frontier, Flight Research at Dryden*, Smithsonian, 1984
Hallion, Richard P, *Test Pilots, the Frontiersmen of Flight*, Smithsonian, 1988
Henshaw, Alex, *Sigh for a Merlin*, Murray, 1980
Kinsey, Gordon, *Martlesham Heath*, Terence Dalton 1975
Lanchbery, Edward, *Against the Sun* (Roland Beamont), Cassell, 1955
Lithgow, Mike, *Mach One*, Allen Wingate, 1954
Mason, Francis K., *Hawker Hunter*, Patrick Stephens, 1981
Middleton, D.H., *Airspeed, the Company and its Aeroplanes*, T. Dalton 1982
Test Pilots, the Story of British Test Flying, Collins, 1985
Composite Materials in Aircraft Structures, (Gen Ed). Longman, 1990
Myles, Bruce, *Jump Jet*, Brassey, 1978
Pegg, A.J. 'Bill', *Sent Flying*, Macdonald, 1959
Penrose, Harald J., *British Aviation; Ominous Skies*, 1935-39. RAF Museum, 1980
Adventure with Fate, (Autobiography), Airlife, 1984
No Echo in the Sky, Cassell 1958
Powell, W/Cdr H.P. 'Sandy', *Men with Wings*, Allen Wingate, 1957
Quill, Jeffrey K., *Spitfire: A Test Pilot's Story*, Murray, 1983
Reed, Arthur, *B.A.C. Lightning*, Ian Allan, 1980
Sharp, C. Martin, *D.H.: A History of de Havilland*, Faber & Faber/Airlife, 1960 & 1982
Sharp, C. Martin & Bowyer, M.J.F., *Mosquito*, Faber & Faber, 1967
Shute, Nevil, *Slide Rule*, Heinemann, 1954
Taylor, H.A., *Airspeed Aircraft since 1931*, Putnam 1970 & 1991
Taylor, J.W.R. & Allward, M., *Westland 50*, Ian Allan, 1965
Thetford, Owen, *Aircraft of the Royal Air Force since 1918*. Putnam, 1957 *et seq*
Thompson, Milton O., *At the Edge of Space. The X–15 Flight Program*, Smithsonian Institution Press 1992
Wheeler, Air Commodore Allen H., *That Nothing Failed Them*, Foulis, 1963
Wolfe, T., *The Right Stuff*, Jonathan Cape 1979.

Index

Numbers in italics refer to illustrations

Adam, F/Lt M.J. 70
Adams, Major Michael *155*, 157
Aird, George 82, 126-7, *128*
Airspeed
  Ambassador 29, 90-1, *90*, *91*
  Courier 19, 37
  Horsa 82-3, *83*
  Oxford 31-2, *31*
  Queen Bee 33
  Queen Wasp 32-4, *33*, 118
Alington, Geoffrey 45
Allam, Flt/Lt John 9, 60, 199, 204, 206, 208, 209, 210, 214, 215, *215*, 216
Allen, Eddie 24, 59, 60
Alston, Gwen 56
Alston, Peter 56
Apt, Mel 145-6
Armstrong Whitworth
Albemarle 55
AW 52 111-12, *112*
Armstrong, Neil 158
Auty, Godfrey L. 138, 161
Avro
  707 115, 190, *190*, *191*
  Anson 31
  Ashton 87, *87*
  Canada 87
  Lancaster 49, *49*
  Lancastrian *73*, 85
  Manchester 47-8, 49
  Tudor 85, 86
  Vulcan 189-91, *191*, *192*, 206
  York *84*, 85

BAC 221 136, *136*
TSR2 9, *10*
BAC/Aérospatiale Concorde 121, 157-66, *163*, *165*
Bailey, Harry 38
Baker, Capt Valentine 80
Baker, S/Ldr Peter 209, 212-13
Balfour, Paul 77
Barr, Julius 25
Beamont, W/Cdr Roland ('Bee') 9, *10*, 119, 120, 121, 122, 143, 147
Bedford, S/Ldr A.W. (Bill) 82, 133, 180, *181*, 182, 183-4, *184*, 185-6, 187
Bell
  P-59 Airacomet 73, *74*
  X-1 104, 139, 140-3, *141*, 144, 151
  X-1A 145
  X-2 140, 145-6, *148*
  X-3 153
  X-5 140, 153
  X-14 175, 181
Bell Boeing SV-22 Osprey 168
Bennett, Capt D.C.T. 22
Bennett, Ian 195
Birch, Peter 38
Blackburn Firebrand 83
Boeing
  B-17 Flying Fortress 16, 18, 25
  B-29 Superfortress 59-60, *60*, *114*, *149*, 151
  B-52 Stratofortress *114*
  Model 299 16, *17*, 18
  Model 307 Stratoliner 24-6, *25*, 26
  Model 707 26, 95
  Washington 60
  Y1B-17A 18
Bonar, E.W. (Jock) 35, 36, 38, 101
Boulton Paul P 111 114, 115
Brabham, Lowery L. 79
Breese, Vance 14, 58, 77
Bridgeman, William 146-8, 149-50, 151, 152
Bristol
  Belvedere 88-9
  Blenheim 31
  Brabazon 87, *88*
  Britannia 93-4, *94*
  Scout 22
  Type 133 20
  Type 138A *71*
  Type 170 Freighter/Wayfarer 85
  Type 173 88, *89*
  Type 188 137-8, *137*
British Joint Services Commission (BJSC) 16
Brooke-Smith, Tom 44, 121, 176, 177-9, *178*, 189
Broomfield, Douglas 194
Brown, Capt Eric 56, 67-8, 84, 104, 108, 109-110, 134
Brown, Capt H.A. 47
Brown, S/Ldr C.B. 89
Bruce, Robert 13
Bryce, G.R. (Jock) 92, 93, 189
Bulman, Gp/Capt P.W.S. (George) 37, 58, 101
Burcham, Mich 74
Burrell, George 79

Cable, S/Ldr F.J. 90
Camm, Sydney 37, 119, 131, 179, 181
Camp, Alf 214, 215
Campbell-Orde, W/Cdr Ian 77-8
Campbell, T.W. 20
carrier-borne aircraft 83-4
Carr, S/Ldr W.J. 50
Carter, George 68
Carter, Nick 58, 82
Cazalet, S/Ldr Robert 56
Cessna, UC-78 Bobcat *113*
Chadwick, Roy 86, 189, 190
Chaplin, Roy 37
Child, Lloyd 15
Cierva
  Air Horse 89-90, *89*
  C30 Rota 26
Clear, Ron 83, 90, 91, *216*
Clousing, Larry 74

Clouston, Arthur E. 26-7, 28, 52
Cobham, Sir Alan 19, 21
Cochrane, John *165*
Coleman, James 170
Collins, James 14
Colman, Flt/Lt Cyril 31
Comsrock, Lt 79-80
Consolidated Liberator 48
Convair
  B-36 113, 114, *114*
  B-58 Hustler 157
  F-102 Delta Dagger 138, 157
  F-106 Delta Dart 157
  XF-92A 140
  XFY-1 170
Cordes, Major James *10*, 11, 24, *25*, 50
Corps, Gordon 166
Cotton, Doug 45, 46
Cotton, George 44
Courtney, Frank 9
Crosby-Warren, John 74-5
Crosby, Harry 112-13
Cross, Carl 153
Crossfield, Scott 145, *149*, 155, 156, 157
Crossley, W/Cdr Mike 58
Cunningham, Gp/Capt John 95, 106, *106*, 107
Curtiss Hawk 15

Dalton-Golding, Ken 196, 197
Dalwood, Harry 9
Dansfield, Bob 60
D'Arcy Grieg, Flt/Lt 26
Dassault, Mirage 136, 157
Daunt, Michael 53, 54-5, 70, 71-2, 73, 74, 75, *216*
Davie, S/Ldr W.D.B.S. (Douglas) 70, 75, 104-5
Davies, David 87
Davis, Frank 59
de Havilland
  DH1 *8*
  DH Comet 1A 127, *127*
  DH 88 Comet 29
  DH 91 Albatross 29-31, *30*
  DH 98 Mosquito 24, 31, 56-8, *57*, 84
  DH 100 Vampire 73, 84, *103*, 104, *106*, 107, *124*, 126
  DH 106 Comet 95, *95*, 105, 112
  DH 108 Swallow 105-6, *105*, 108-10, 139
  DH 110 Sea Vixen 108, *109*, 127, *128*
  Hornet 102
  Sea Vampire 84
  Tiger Moth 32
  Trident 118
de Havilland, Geoffrey 29
de Havilland, Geoffrey, Jr 29, 30, 56, 57, 58, 105, *105*
de Havilland, John 58
de Villiers, Desmond 121-2
Defence Research Agency 101-2
Defer, Gilbert 162
Dell, Jimmy 121, 126
Derry, John 106, 107-8, 110, 147
Dittmar, Heini 65, 66
Donaldson, Gp/Capt E.M. 76, 105, 130
Dornier Do 335 102
Douglas
  D-558-1 Skystreak 139, 140, 144, *144*, 146
  D-558-2 Skyrocket 139-40, 146-50, *147*, *149*, 151, 152
  Dauntless 14, *14*
  DC-2 29
  DC-3/C-47 85
  DC-3 Dakota 85
  DC-4/C-54 26, 59, 85
  DC-4E 59
  X-3 140, 152, *154*
Duke, S/Ldr Neville 130-1, 132-3, *133*
Dyar, Lt 79-80

Eassie, Jock 178
Ecclestone, Ronald 197, 198
Edwards, Capt Glen W. 114, 139
ejection seats 80-2
Else, W.H. 111
Empire Test Pilots School (ETPS) 15-16, 80
English Electric
  Canberra 80, 96, 119-20, *119*
  Lightning 80, 101, 122, *122*, 123, 125-6
  P1 121-2, *121*
Errington, George 31-2, 34, 82, 90, 91, 118
Esler, Eric 115, 190
Everest, Pete 145, 147, 148, 151
Everitt, W.L. 175

Fairchild, AT-14A *113*
Fairey
  Barracuda 56
  Battle 35, *45*
  FD 1 134
  FD 2 134-5, *135*, 136, 138
  Gannet *129*
  Hendon 11
  P-4 27, 28
Falk, W/Cdr Roly 190, *190*, 206
Farley, John 184, 185, 187, *187*
Fifield, S/Ldr 82
Folland F4/37 54
Folland, Henry 54
Foster, S/Ldr Brian 189
Francke, *Dipl Ing* 61
Franklin, Eric 111
Fraser, Pat 26
freelance test pilots 9

Garner, S/Ldr Peter 97-8
Gellatly, S/Ldr Ron 176
Genders, Flt/Lt George 110
General Aircraft, GAL 65 108
Gibbins, George 58
Gibb, W.F. 94
Girard, Peter F. 167, 172, 173, 174-5
gliders 82-3
Gloster
  E28/39 68-70, *69*, 104-5
  Javelin *104*, 108, 114-19, 210
  Meteor 69, 70-3, 74-6, 102
Goodden, Major Frank 7
Goodlin, Chalmers 140
Graves, S/Ldr Mike 98, 99
Greensted, Bryan 81
Griffith, A.A. 167
Griffiths, Eddie 99
Grumman
  Avenger 84
  XF3F-1 14
Guingard, Jacques 157

Hagg, Arthur E. 90
Hamson, Lt 99
Handley Page
  Halifax 49-51, *51*, 85
  Hampden 24, *25*, 28, 52
  Hastings 85
  Hermes 85-6, *86*
  Heyford *8*, 11-12
  HP 75 Manx 193, *193*, *194*
  HP 88 193-4
  Type 115 160, *161*
  Victor 9, 118, 189, 191, 199-216, *207*, *213*, *215*
  WB 771 194, 195-8, *197*, *198*, *199*

WB 775 198-9, 200, *200*, 203-5
Hare, Flt/Lt Maurice 23
Harker, Ronald W. 38, 77, 78
Harvey, S/Ldr Jock *130*, 169
Hawker
Demon 12
Harrier 186-7, *187*
Henley 36
Hurricane 37, 38-9, 40, 53
P 1067 Hunter 119, 131-3, *133*
P 1072 131
P 1082 130
P 1127 179-80, *180*, 181-6, *181*, *183*, *184*
Sea Hawk 119
Tempest 101
Typhoon 53-4, *54*, 101
Hawker, Harry 9
Hawkins, S/Ldr C.R.J. 26, 28
Hay, W.T. 82
Hazelden, S/Ldr H.G. 85-6, 195, 196, 197, 198, 200
Heinemann, Ed 14, 152
Heinkel
He 70 35-6, *35*
He 111 15
He 177 61-2, *61*
He 178 62
Henderson, S/Ldr Jack 160, 184
Henshaw, Alex 40-1
Heyworth, Harvey 38
Heyworth, S/Ldr Jim 38, 72, 98, 169
Hill, Captain G.T.R. 12, 13
Hives, Ernest W. 34, 78
Hooper, Ralph 179
Hoover, Herb 142-3
Hosegood, C.T.D. 87-8
Hubbard, S/Ldr S.J. 178
Humble, Bill 54, 130

inflatable delta-wing aircraft *130*

Jodlbauer, Dr 16
Johnston, Tex 204

Kapruski, Lt-Cmdr 99
Keep, Capt A.S. 9
Kincheloe, Iven 145
Kirlew, Reg 48-9
Kronfield, Robert 108

Lankester Parker, John 20, 21, 22, 44, 45, 111
Lawrence, Peter 83, 118
Le Gyroptère 179
Le Vier, Tony 153
Learoyd, S/Ldr R.A.B. 28
Lee, Godfrey 204, *215*, 216
Lilly, Howard 143, 146
Lithgow, Lt-Cdr Mike 118, 133, 134, 212
Lockheed
C69 Constellation 26, 59, 85
F-104 Starfighter 138, 152-3, 155
Hudson 31
P-38 Lightning 13, 16
P-80 Shooting Star 74, *75*
SR-71A Blackbird 157, *159*
XFV-1 Salmon 170
XP-38 16, *17*
YP-38 16
Lowdell, George 92
Lucas, Philip 38, 39, 53
Lumley, A/Cdre E.A. 81
Lynch, Bernard 81, 82

Macmillan, Capt. Norman 9, 34
Marsh, Alan 89, 90
Martin
B-57 120
MB 2 80
MB 3 80
MB 5 80, *81*
Martindale, S/Ldr A.F. 15, 38, 102
Martin, Sir James 28, 80, 81, 82
Martin, W/Cdr R.F. 118
Masters, S/Ldr David 128-9, *130*
May, Gene 146, 147, 148, 149
McClure, W/Cdr Charles 69-70, *216*
McDougall, Flt/Lt 33-4
McGuire, S/Ldr Jack 47-8
McKay, John 156
Merewether, Hugh 180, 181, *181*, 183, 186, 187
Messerschmitt
Bf109 16
Me 262 63, *64*, 65, 68, 71, 72, 104
Me 163 *64*, 65-8, 104
Miles
Hawk 26-7
Kestrel 34, 35, 36
M52 102-3
Master 36
Miller, Col. Thomas H. 186-7
Mitchell, R.J. 37, 39
Morgan, S/Ldr R.J. 208
Morton, S/Ldr Eric 44
Muller-Rowland, Flt/Lt Stewart 110
Murphy, Frank 132
Murphy, Philip ('Spud') 118, 204, 206, 207, 209, 210-11, 212
Myers, John 112

NACA (National Advisory Committee for Aeronautics) 15, 139
NASA (National Aeronautics and Space Administration) 155
Nord Griffon 157
North American
F-86 Sabre 143-4, *149*
F-100 Super Sabre 157
P-47 Thunderbolt 101
P-51 Mustang *76*, 77-8, 101
X-15 153, 155-7, *155*, *156*
XB-70A Valkyrie 152-3, *153*
XP-86 143
Northrop
Type N-9M 113
Vengeance 58-9
XB-35 113-14, *115*
XBT-1 14
XP-79B 112-13, *113*
XS-4 140
YB-49 114
Northrop, John 112, 113
Norway, Nevil Shute 19

O'Gorman, Mervyn 7
Ohain, Hans von 62
Opitz, Rudolf 66-7
Orrell, Capt. H.J. 86, 87
Orr, Lt S. 134

Paget, Louis 12
Parker, G.R.I. 193
Parker, Joe 79
Pegg, A.J. (Bill) 18, 87, 88, *88*, 93, 94
Penrose, Harald 12, 13, *13*, 43, 96, 97, 98, 99
Petter, W.E.W. (Teddy) 13, 43, 80, 96, 119, 120
Pöhs, Joschi 67
Popsen, Major Ray 153
Porte Baby 22
Porte, Cmdr John 22
Project Mercury (manned space flight) 155

Quill, Jeffrey K. 22-3, 40, 41, 133, *216*

R100 airship 22
RAF Central Flying School 9
Rayner, Harry 209, 210, 212
Raynham, Fred 9, 11
Reiss, Flt/Lt S. 50
Reitsch, Hanna 67
Republic, P-47 Thunderbolt 16, 78-80, *79*
Rickert, *Flugkapitän* 61
Ridley, Jack 144
Rogers, S/Ldr Cliff 99-100
Rolls-Royce Thrust Measuring Rig 168-70, *168*
Rosburg, Major Chuck 185
Ross, F/Lt R.J. 118-19
Royal Aircraft Establishment, Bedford 9
Royal Aircraft Establishment, Farnborough 19, 26
Royal Aircraft Factory
  FE8 7
  RE8 7
Ryan
  VZ-3RY 167, 174-5, *175*
  X-13 Vertijet 167-8, 170, *170*, *171*, 172-4
Rymer, Dickie 212

Saab Gripen 9
Salmon, Flt/Lt 23
SATC (Supersonic Aircraft Technical Committee) 157
Sayer, Flt/Lt P.E.G. 54, 68, 69, *69*, 70
Schafer, Fritz 62
Scrope, John 58
Shepherd, Capt R.T. 34, 35, 36, 38, 78, 169
Short
  Gurnard II 20-1
  Maia 21, 22
  Mercury 21, 22
  R24/31 20, *21*
  SB-1 176
  SB-5 120-1, *120*
  SC-1 176-9, *177*, *178*
  Sherpa 176
  Sperrin 176, 189
  Stirling *42*, 44-7, *46*
Short-Mayo Composite 21, *21*
Simpson, Duncan 186, 187
Slade, Gordon 134
Slee, S/Ldr Charles 57-8
Smith-Barry, Capt R.R. 7, 9
Smith, Joe 40
Spate, *Hauptmann* Wolfgang 66
spinning research tunnel 15, 19, 20
Squier, John W.C. 121, 123-5, 126
Stack, T. Neville 45
Stanbury, F/Lt Philip 75-6
Staniland, Chris 56
Stanley, Max 113
Stewart, W/Cdr W.K. 81
Still, Jock 200, *201*, 203-4
Stockman, S/Ldr G.B. 208
Stokes, Rendell 38
Summers, 'Mutt' 22, 23, 39, 189
Super-Mystere B-2 157
Supermarine
  Spitfire 15, 37, 38, 39-41, *39*, *41*, 102
  Swift 131, 133-4
survival equipment 125
Swain, S/Ldr F.D.R. 70

Talbot, Jimmy 85, 193
terminal velocity vertical dive 13, 15
Thompson, Flt/Lt Arthur 83
Thorne, Flt/Lt S.A. (Bill) 47, 86
Tiltman, Hessell 19, 32, 33, 34
Tobin, S/Ldr J.R. 15, 102
Tonkinson, Barrie 186
Tower, Les 16, 18
Trubshaw, Brian 161-2, 164-5, *165*
Tupolev Tu-144 162
Turcat, André 157, 162
Turner-Hughes, Charles 55
Twiss, Peter *130*, 134-5

Ursinus, *Flugkapitän* 61
Uwins, Capt. Cyril 12, 18, 20, 70

V bomber programme 189-216
V/STOL 167-87
Vickers
  B9/32 23, *24*
  Jockey 19-20
  Valiant *188*, 189
  Vespa 70
  Viking 85, 128-9
  Viscount 90, 92-3, *92*, 112
  Warwick 48-9
  Wellesley 22-3, *23*
  Wellington 23, 28, 48, *72*
Virden, Ralph 16
Von Karman, Theodor 179
Vultee V-72 58

Wade, S/Ldr T.S. 130
Waight, Bob 29
Walker, Joe 152-3, 156
Wallis, Barnes 22
Warsitz, *Flugkapitän* Erich 62, 65
Waterton, John 211
Waterton, S/Ldr W.A. (Bill) 108, 115-18, 130
Welch, George 143
Westland
  Pterodactyl Mk IV 12
  Pterodactyl Mk V 12-13, *13*
  Walrus 9
  Whirlwind *42*, 43-4
  Widgeon 12
  Wyvern 95-100, *96*
Wheeler, Gp/Capt Allen 57
White, Capt Bob 156
Whittle, Frank 62, 68, 69, 71
Wibault, Michel 179
Wilson, Gp/Capt H.J. (Willie) 26, 47, 70, 73, 105
Woolams, Jack 140
Wörndl, Alois 67
Wright, E.A. 193
Wroath, Gp/Capt S. 15, 16, 38, *216*

Yeager, Capt. Charles 141-2, 143, 144, 145, 147, 149, 150, 151

Zeigler, 'Skip' 145, 153
Zurakowski, Jan 80